All-Breed
Dog Grooming

Revised Edition

164 Breeds & Varieties

Bathing

Trimming

Scissoring

tfh

All-Breed Dog Grooming Revised Edition

Project Team
Editor: Mary E. Grangeia, Heather Russell-Revesz
Design: Mary Ann Kahn

TFH Publications
President/CEO: Glen S. Axelrod
Executive Vice President: Mark E. Johnson
Publisher: Christopher T. Reggio
Production Manager: Kathy Bontz

TFH Publications, Inc.
One TFH Plaza
Third and Union Avenues
Neptune City, NJ 07753

Printed and bound in China

10 11 12 13 14   1 3 5 7 9 8 6 4 2

Library of Congress Cataloging-in-Publication Data

All-breed dog grooming / contributors, Denise Dobish ... [et al.].

    p. cm.

 Includes index.

 ISBN 978-0-7938-0647-8 (alk. paper)

 1. Dogs--Grooming. I. Dobish, Denise.

 SF427.5.A55 2010

 636.7'0833--dc22

           2010019128

The Leader In Responsible Animal Care for Over 50 Years!®

www.tfh.com

Contents

General Information

EXTERNAL PARTS OF A DOG

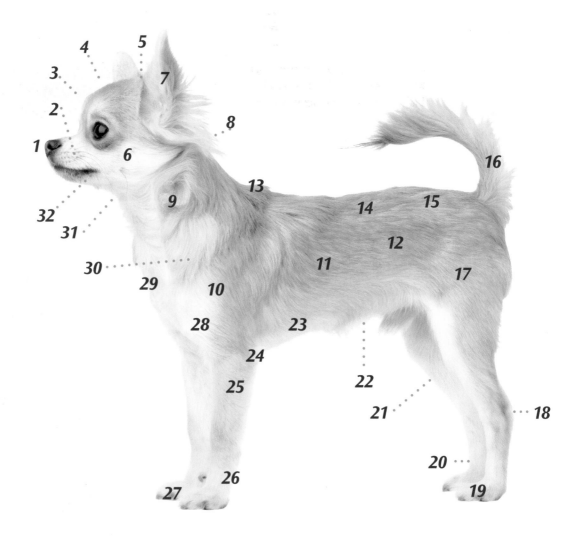

1. Nose	9. Neck	17. Thigh	25. Foreleg
2. Muzzle	10. Shoulder	18. Hock joint	26. Pastern
3. Stop	11. Ribs	19. Rear feet	27. Front feet
4. Skull	12. Loin	20. Metatarsus	28. Upper arm
5. Occiput	13. Withers	21. Stifle	29. Forechest
6. Cheek	14. Back	22. Abdomen	30. Shoulder blade
7. Ear	15. Croup	23. Chest	31. Throat latch
8. Crest of neck	16. Tail or stern	24. Elbow	32. Lip corner

Getting a dog accustomed to grooming at an early age will—in the long run—make it an easier job for you. Firmness and patience on your part, along with a calm environment, are important requirements. Establish that you are in control at the very start of the grooming procedure. Give the dog commands in a kind yet firm manner. During the grooming session, praise him when he obeys your commands. Never try to rush through a grooming routine.

DEMATTING

Spray the coat with a detangling lotion, ensuring that you saturate all tangled areas. Let the dog sit for 5 or 10 minutes before you start working on his coat. Using a slicker brush and a matting comb, start at the bottom of his legs and work in very small sections at a time, taking the coat in layers. Brush the coat up and then down to loosen the mats, alternating with the matting comb. It is important that all mats be combed out before the bath because shampoo gets caught in them and is hard to rinse out. Also, water tends to tighten a mat, and drying shrinks it into a tighter knot. So you can see what a mess you'll have if you fail to comb out mats prior to bathing.

Some breeds of dog will need less grooming than others.

Brush the dog's coat before bathing him.

Dematting should never be torturous for the dog. Dogs have different degrees of tolerance. Some dogs do not seem to mind the tugging and pulling involved, while others get extremely upset with just the slightest degree of pulling. Dematting should never cause a dog severe stress. If the dog does not accept dematting, or if it is impossible to remove the mats, the groomer should get permission from the owner to shave the coat down with a #10 or #7 blade. When the new coat comes in, the dog should be groomed on a regular basis so it does not get severely matted again. Dogs who do not tolerate combing easily should be groomed on a 3 to 4 week schedule or sooner.

Brush Burns

Brush burns, the result of excessive force when brushing during dematting, are a sign of carelessness on the part of the groomer. Brush burns result when the wire bristles of the slicker brush abrade the dog's skin. For brush burn treatment, your veterinarian can prescribe an unguent that will soothe and heal the injured areas.

BATHING

A good bath is all important to a good grooming. You cannot finish a dog well if he is not clean. In order to thoroughly clean the dog, you must be sure to lather well to remove all dirt and rinse well to remove all soap. Shampoos available today do not strip oil from a dog's coat, rather they add to the coat. A good bath makes a dog feel better, look better, and definitely smell better.

Be sure to brush the dog's coat before the bath. Brushing removes dead hair and debris, separates the hair, and stimulates circulation. All mats and tangles should be combed out (see "Dematting" section) prior to bathing a dog.

It is recommended that you use a nylon leash and nylon collar to secure the dog in the tub. Properly securing the dog will keep him safe

It is important that all mats be combed out before the bath because shampoo gets caught in them and is hard to rinse out.

and prevent you from getting soaked. The use of a nylon leash and collar also helps keep a dog still while you bathe him. If a dog should ever become upset or start thrashing around and you need to get him loose quickly, you can always cut him loose if you use nylon instead of metal chains.

If the dog is cooperative, you'll need only one hook in the wall, about middle of the tub, to tie him to. For dogs that are more active, or for large breeds, it's good to have three hooks on the back wall behind the tub—one at the front for his head, one in the middle, and one at the back end of the dog. The dog's head can be hooked to the front and middle hooks if necessary, and a belly band can be put on the dog and hooked to the back. To prevent yourself from getting soaked, be sure the dog's head does not extend over the edge of the tub. Hooking the dog in this way makes him feel secure, and it prevents him from turning around or sitting down during the bath. Be sure to use a rubber mat in the tub to prevent slipping.

Getting a small dog into the tub is no problem. A 90 pound (41 kg) bruiser is another story! The

You cannot properly groom a dog without first bathing him.

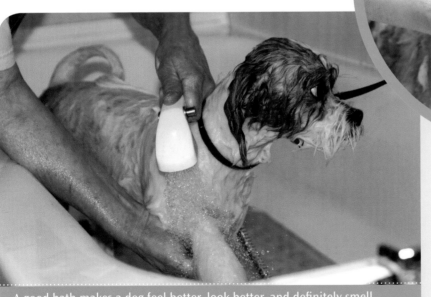

A good bath makes a dog feel better, look better, and definitely smell better.

Rinse thoroughly to remove all the soap from the dog's coat.

most comfortable tubs for dog groomers are waist high, so you need to work at training large dogs to be cooperative. Most dogs can be trained to walk up a ramp, especially if the ramp is against a wall. If you do not have a ramp, place the dog's front paws on the edge of the tub and boost him from the rear. If the dog balks at going into the tub, put your grooming table in front of the tub, place his paws on the table, and boost from the rear. He should then walk into the tub.

After the dog is well secured in the tub, wet the coat thoroughly with warm water, using a hose with a spray attachment. Water should run freely down the tub drain so that the dog does not have to stand in a tub full of water. Dispense shampoo into the coat with a plastic squeeze bottle or a lather machine. Work the shampoo through the hair with your hands, adding water as necessary to make a good lather. Do not just wash the top hair! Work the shampoo through the hair to the skin. Be sure to do the entire dog—under the stomach, under the tail, under and between the foot pads, inside the ear leather, etc. Do not get shampoo in the dog's eyes; tearless shampoos may not sting, but any type of shampoo (and dirt) can cause eye infection. If certain areas are extremely dirty, such as the legs or feet, use a small bristle brush to gently scrub these areas.

When the dog's coat is well lathered, rinse with warm water, using a spray with a good force of water. Rinse the head back from the eyes so soap does not run into them, and protect the ear canal with your thumb, being careful not to direct spray into it. Rinse around one ear first, then do the other. If a dog is extremely dirty, lather the entire coat again. Rinse until all traces of soap are removed from the coat.

Squeeze the water out of the coat with your hands, or use a high-velocity dryer to blow water off the dog while he is still in the tub. Wrap the dog in a large towel and take him out of the tub, placing him on a grooming table covered with a heavy bath mat. Towel drying the dog on the mat helps absorb water from the feet and speeds up drying time.

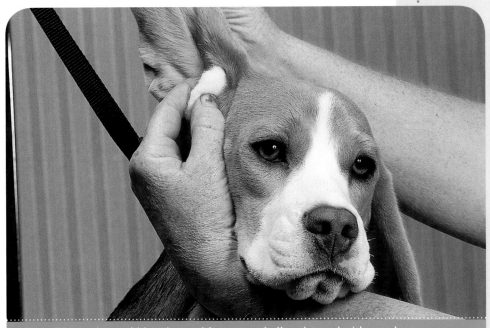
Clean the ears by swabbing them with a cotton ball moistened with ear cleaner.

CLEANING THE EARS

Remove ear dirt and wax by swabbing the ears with a cotton ball moistened with ear cleaner. Then dry out each ear with a dry cotton ball, and dust the ear with a medicated ear powder. The ear powder makes it easier to pull hair out of the ear and also helps prevent ear infection.

With some breeds, there is more accumulation of hair at the entrance to the ear canal than with other breeds, so it must be removed. Ear hair may be pulled out with the fingers or with ear forceps. If you use your fingers, be sure to wash your hands well between dogs because ear mites can be transmitted under the fingernails. When you pull ear hair, take hold of the dog's ear, lift it up, and lay it flat on his head. This allows you to pull hair from the external ear but closes off the inner ear and protects it. Pull small bits of hair at a time in order to make it more comfortable for the dog.

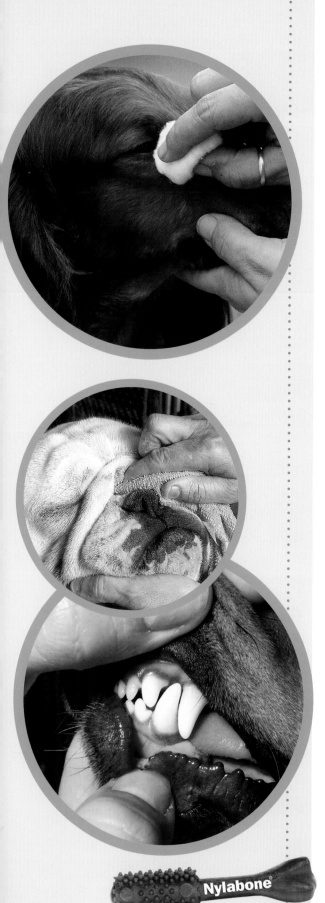

CLEANING THE EYES

Eye cleaning should not be overlooked as a part of grooming. The frequency of eye cleaning care varies according to the breed of dog. A dog with protuberant eyes, such as the Bulldog, should have his eyes cleaned regularly. A veterinarian should be consulted if the eyes are red or tender. He or she can also recommend preparations that can be used to clean stains caused by normal eye secretions.

CLEANING FACIAL WRINKLES

In a dog such as the Shar-Pei, and others, special attention must be given to facial wrinkles. Keeping the wrinkles dirt-free and dry will ward off irritation and infection.

Facial wrinkles should first be cleansed with warm water and then gently dried. If signs of redness are present, apply a light dusting of corn starch, baby powder, or talcum powder. Facial wrinkles should be cleaned weekly.

CLEANING THE TEETH

Part of the grooming job is examining the teeth. Large accumulations can be removed simply with a scaler or probe, but this is not considered part of a groomer's job and should be deferred to a veterinarian. But you should examine the dog's teeth and report to the owner about their condition. Good teeth are clean and white, and you should not be able to see any residue on them.

Suggest to the owner using any number of dental chews, like the ones Nylabone makes, that help to remove plaque. These products come in edible and nonedible varieties, and help clean teeth and freshen breath. Toys and chews should not replace brushing, but they will help to remove some of the plaque, exercise a dog's jaw, and satisfy his need to chew.

Toys and chews are important for another reason—they will satisfy a dog's need to gnaw on something, while diverting him from chewing on inappropriate items. Chews are available in a wide variety of shapes and sizes. Specially designed nylon and rubber bones, like the ones Nylabone makes, are excellent for satisfying a dog's need to chew. Some interactive rubber toys are hollow inside, and treats can be placed inside for a dog to find. Plush toys vary in their durability. Some are easily shredded, so opt for the durable models if a dog is likely to shred, disembowel, and then attempt to consume the innards.

NAIL CLIPPING

Dogs that regularly exercise or play outdoors on abrasive surfaces will generally require less frequent nail clipping than those kept mainly in the house or on soft ground.

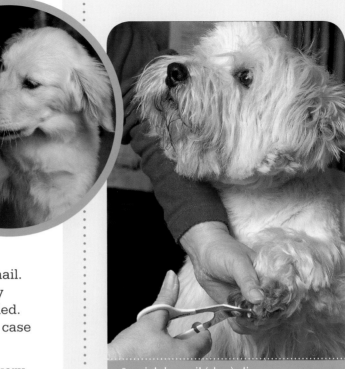

When clipping a dog's nails, one must be careful not to cut the quick, a blood vessel in the nail. Cutting the quick will cause the dog pain and may result in future "battles" when a manicure is needed. Keep styptic powder (or a styptic pencil) handy in case of an emergency.

Holding the dog's paw carefully, snip off just the very tip of each nail. Ragged nail surfaces may be smoothed away by using a file.

[Note: Although the correct terminology for nail, as applied to dogs, is claw, nail is used throughout the text as it is the favored word in the grooming trade.]

Special dog nail (claw) clippers are available to make nail clipping a fast and painless procedure.

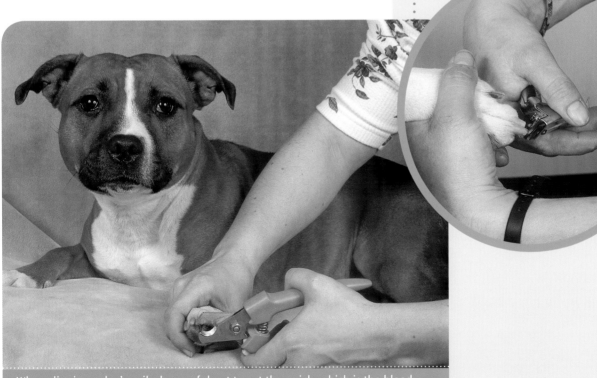

When clipping a dog's nails, be careful not to cut the quick, which is the blood vessel in the nail.

In almost all cases, simple brushing will keep a dog's coat in excellent condition.

CONDITIONING THE COAT

Keeping a dog's coat in condition may be compared with keeping your own hair in condition. Just as human hair care specialists offer special oil treatments, massages, and chemicals, so are there similar products available for conditioning the coat of a dog.

In almost all cases, simple brushing will keep a dog's coat in excellent condition. Dogs need oil in their coats to maintain their essential waterproofing. If a dog's coat is dry, it means that his diet is probably lacking in fats.

There are many products on the market that can be called coat conditioners. Try a few to see which ones work best because each may be good for certain types of coats and poor for others.

DRY CLEANING THE COAT

A dog has just been groomed and runs under a parked car and gets oil or grease on his back. A puppy is too young to be bathed and gets himself dirty. What to do? The answer is simple. Use a dry cleaning agent.

Basically, a "dry cleaner" may or may not be "dry." There are foams and sprays, but these products should be considered "spot removers." You can use these foams and sprays on the entire dog if you wish, but it's a lot of work. There are dry cleaning powders, too. No product works as well as a good bath, though, if you must clean an entire dog. All, however, work pretty well for removing small dirty areas, especially on white dogs.

Experience will dictate which type of dry cleaner to use in a given situation. One word of caution: All dry cleaners have a chemical basis to them. They may cause skin problems for sensitive dogs, and they may cause serious matting in longhaired breeds. Use care.

FORCED DRYING

In your own case, you can choose to air dry your hair, use a series of dry towels and rub vigorously, or use an electric hair dryer that blasts your hair with hot air. The same techniques are available for dogs.

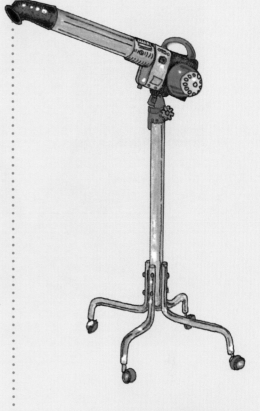

All professionals must have their own forced hot air dryers. In this manner, a dog's hair, like a human's hair, can be blown dry, making it fluffier and more professional looking. Blow drying as a technique requires using a brush to fluff the coat as you dry it. The brush entangles the hair, twisting and lifting it to expose the roots. The hot air is then directed against the brush (it would be too hot to direct against the dog's skin). As soon as the hair on the brush is dried, the blower is moved away and the hair is brushed to fluffiness. This is repeated over and over again until the entire dog is dried. Obviously this technique cannot be used on shorthaired breeds! Success in using it with certain breeds like Poodles requires greater skill than with other breeds because the fluffed shape of the head and body is important to the general appearance of the dog.

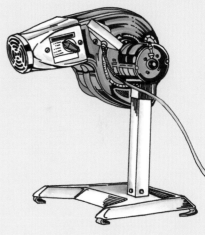

Hot-air drying is standard for professional grooming. A floor model dryer can be used as you blow dry and brush, or it can be located in front of a cage. A table model dryer can be hand-held and directed more exactly than a floor model.

With some breeds, air drying and towel drying are acceptable in the summer.

Cage drying is another option in which a dryer is attached to a cage so that the heated dry air constantly bathes the dog thus drying his wet coat. This is a technique used mainly with shorthaired breeds or breeds whose coats do not need fluffing, like Irish Setters. Special drying cages are available; they offer lots of ventilation.

Towel or air drying merely allows the dog to shake himself free of excess water in his coat. After the dog shakes out, briskly rub him all over using dry towels. Although the dog is still damp, he is released. The hair dries normally or, more usually, the dog rolls around on the grass or on your carpet to hasten the drying process. Air drying and towel drying are acceptable in the summer. But when it is cold outside, the dog should not be allowed freedom until his coat is thoroughly dried.

All-Breed Dog Grooming

GROOMING THE FEET

Longhaired breeds are highly inbred strains. They are abnormal when compared to the wild dogs, wolves, and dog-like descendants from which we assume dogs have originated. Thus the long hair on the body includes abnormally long hair on the feet. The hair growing between the pads of the feet must be removed in all longhaired breeds, except the Poodle and certain longhaired breeds that spend a lot of time walking on ice or snow. A clue to a dog's need to have his feet groomed is that he constantly chews on them.

Using small scissors or a clipper with a suitable fine blade (#10 or #15), clip the hair on the feet between the pads but leave stubble as this protects the delicate skin between the pads, especially in the winter. Many dogs want to jump into their master's arms when they have to walk on ice because their feet are so cold!

GROOMING THE UNDERSIDE

When grooming the dog's feet, you also can groom his stomach and anal areas. The same tools are required: scissors and/or a clipper with a #10 blade. The stomach on most dogs should be shaved close but not absolutely clean. Male dogs should have the hair on their penis

After grooming the dog's feet, you also can groom his stomach and anal areas.

cropped closely, too, so it doesn't pick up dirt. The anal pore should be clipped clean, and the hair on longhaired breeds should be cropped in the anal area so the hair doesn't pick up debris as the dog excretes. Never use a clipper on the anal muscle, upon which no hair grows. This is a sensitive area and grooming it will make your dog uncomfortable, perhaps even causing an infection. Scissors are, perhaps, the best tool for the job of removing hair around the anal pore because they don't have actual contact with the skin and will remove enough of the longer hairs to do the job.

Doggy Odors and Colognes

Every dog has two glands alongside his anal pore; these glands must be emptied. Nature usually takes care of this when the dog defecates. Sometimes, though, the glands become clogged and enlarge, making them uncomfortable for the dog. It is not a dog groomer's responsibility to empty these glands, even though it is relatively easy. This is a job for a veterinarian. There may be serious underlying reasons why the glands are not emptying themselves, and the vet should be consulted. If that area of the dog has a bad odor, have him checked to rule out any health issues.

Using colognes and/or deodorizers is a matter of choice. There are many owners who use expensive perfumes on their dogs because they carry

them and don't want their dog's cologne to conflict with their own. Spray colognes are a service to be sold. They provide no value to a dog's health or well-being, but they may make a dog more huggable!

CARE OF PASTERNS AND LEG JOINTS

Some large breeds, such as the St. Bernard and the German Shorthaired Pointer, require special attention to their pasterns and leg joints (hocks and elbows). Irritation and bald spots, caused by the dog's lying on abrasive surfaces, may occur. For prevention or relief, use a preparation recommended by your veterinarian.

REMOVING THE WHISKERS

Show groomers pay special attention to facial hairs. Pet owners, however, have different tastes as far as whiskers are concerned. If these hairs are to be removed, use the same tools as before, namely scissors or a clipper with a #10 or #15 blade. Many dogs, especially Poodles, have the shape of their faces determined by grooming. Thus it is up to the individual owners as to how they like their dogs to look.

PLUCKING AND STRIPPING

In days long gone by, plucking wire-haired breeds was considered the way to go. This painful technique should be used only when the dog is shedding

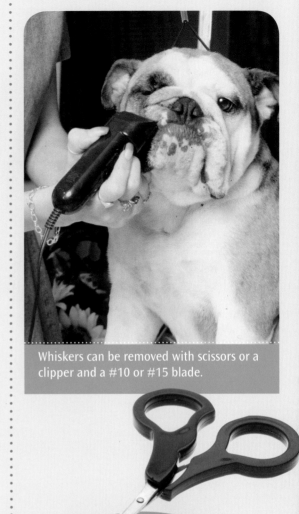
Whiskers can be removed with scissors or a clipper and a #10 or #15 blade.

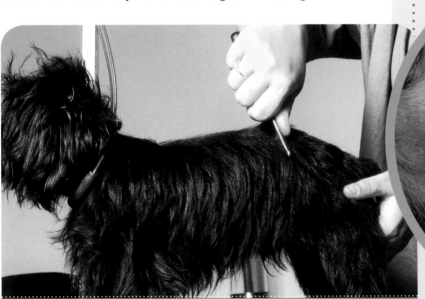
Stripping is like plucking, but you use your thumb against a stripping knife blade and cut as you tear.

normally. Using your thumb and index finger, you grasp a small group of hairs and quickly jerk it out. It hurts just to think about it, but that's all that plucking is. It's very similar to the way you pluck your own eyebrows (if you do!). It hurts. Show ring groomers use plucking with certain wire-haired breeds such as Schnauzers and terriers. It is not recommended.

Stripping is like plucking, but you use your thumb against a stripping knife blade and cut as you tear. This is a technique that was considered more humane than a plucking job, but it is far too trying for the groomer—to say nothing about the dog! Thinning shears serve the purpose almost as well, as does normal clipping.

CARE OF CORDED COATS

The coat of a breed that has distinctive mop-like cording, such as a corded Puli, is not necessarily a challenge to maintain if the right grooming guidelines are followed. The coat must be groomed so that the natural cords hang properly and are well defined.

SHEDDING

Most dogs shed naturally. With longhaired breeds, such as the Old English Sheepdog, a thorough brushing about three times a week will prevent matting and help maintain the overall appearance of the coat.

CLIPPING

The basis of modern dog grooming is the clipper, which has different blades. Just as human hair was once cut only with scissors, it is now often cut (especially for men's short hair) with a clipper. The idea in using a clipper is to gently cut away excess hair, leaving hair in a desired, predetermined length. The clipper is not an electric razor, which removes all of the hair.

Flexibility of the wrist is important whenever you are clipping a dog. By following this simple guideline, you will avoid clipper nicks as well as mistakes in coat styling.

Work carefully. Keep the blade flat against the section being clipped, and always move the clipper in the direction of the grain of the hair, unless grooming instructions specify another method.

Never dig into the skin with a clipper. It produces burns and cuts. Learning how to use a clipper is easy, but it is an art that must be mastered.

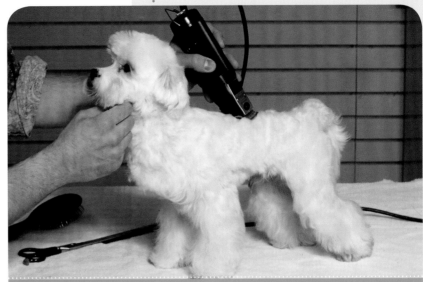

The idea in using a clipper is to gently cut away excess hair, leaving the coat in a desired, predetermined length.

The same is true of scissoring. After the clipping, scissors are used to put on the finishing touches. How you use a pair of scissors is a measure of your skill. In any case, the scissors must be very sharp at all times or they'll pull the hair and perhaps earn you a dog bite!

Clipping and scissoring are what dog grooming is all about. If you can't handle these two techniques, let someone else do the grooming.

Clipping and scissoring techniques are what dog grooming is all about.

Grooming the Mixed Breed Dog

Every dog has his day, or so the saying goes, and that surely has to be true about man's best friend, the "mutt" or mixed breed. Although mixed breeds are not purebred dogs, they have many of the desirable traits one looks for in a companion dog. As a result, they often make fine pets and household guardians. Mixed breeds come in every shape and size, with the larger shepherd-mix types maintained and groomed as their namesakes or the husky-mix type dogs groomed according to the thickness of their coat. Owners of the small- to medium-sized mixed breeds (i.e., terrier or Poodle mixes) realize it is just as important to have these dogs groomed on a regular basis as it for purebreds. The terrier mixes tend to have hairy-textured coats, and these dogs can look good with a Wire Fox Terrier clip, for example. Many of the Poodle mixes have wooly-textured coats and the owners of these dogs often prefer them in one of the Poodle clips (i.e., Lamb or Kennel clip). However, if a different style is desired for either the terrier or Poodle mix, the groomer can

appropriately clip the dog in what is known as a "Teddy Bear," or puppy, clip. Groomers should be encouraged to use their own discretion on the smaller mixed breed dogs, for example, Lhasapoos, Maltesepoos, Yorkiepoos, to name just a few. Generally, owners prefer a short, cuddly look that is easy to maintain.

When working on a dog, a groomer, sensing individuality, can decide on a round, cute face or a longer, more distinguished-looking face and adapt a "Teddy Bear" clip accordingly. A similar idea works for the Schnoodle (i.e., Schnauzer/Poodle), with some owners wanting a Schnauzer clip if the dog has a tendency to look more like this breed. If the dog has Schnauzer coloring, but has a wooly-textured coat, like that of a Poodle, again the groomer can always resort to the round, cuddly look of a teddy bear. The thick-coated Cockapoos are hard to maintain in a Poodle Lamb clip—surely many groomers have had experience with this sort of coat, that of the American Cocker Spaniel/Poodle type. Cockapoos are generally more comfortable in a short style, and, depending on the owner's preferences, either a Kennel clip for a Poodle look or a suitable Teddy Bear clip (with the head and face scissored shorter) works well. Another alternative for the mixed breed dog is a terrier head, either with eyebrows or a "visor" covering both eyes.

Grooming mixed breed dogs is the true test of a groomer. The whole idea is to make the dog appealing and, at the same time, sanitary.

The Teddy Bear Clip, aka the Puppy Clip

The Teddy Bear clip, sometimes referred to as the puppy clip, is a type of clip that can be used on certain breeds, such as Lhasa Apsos, Shih Tzus, Yorkshire Terriers, and mixed breeds, where a cute, round, cuddly look is desired. After grooming, bathing, and fluff drying the dog, continue with the following steps. [Note: The #15 blade is used for Yorkshire Terriers only (to shave the tips of the ears).]

GROOMING PROCEDURE

1. Using a #1, #1½, or #2 blade attachment comb (depending on the length of the coat desired), clip the entire coat, starting at the base of the skull, from the base of the ears and from under the jaw line (thus omitting the head, face, beard, and ears).

2. Fluff all ends evenly with a medium metal comb and scissors, except the tail.

3. Comb forward the front ½ inch (1 cm) of hair on the head over the eyes and scissor evenly across the eyes. Scissor the head to blend into this line and continue to blend into the ears and the side of the face. [Note: The head, face, and beard should be scissored according to coat length on the body.]

4. Comb face and beard downward, and scissor around from the base of each ear across the beard, thus forming a round "U" shape from the front.

5. Blend the sides of the face into the beard and around the "U" shape.

6. Comb through with a fine metal comb and scissor evenly all loose ends.

7. Finish the dog by scissoring the feet as instructed earlier in the general grooming instructions.

TOOLS AND EQUIPMENT

- Cotton balls
- Matting comb
- Metal combs (medium/fine)
- Medicated ear powder
- Nail clipper
- Oster A-5 clipper/#10, #15 blades, and #1, #1½ , #2 blade attachment combs (use with a #30 blade)
- Rubber bands
- Scissors
- Slicker brush

The Teddy Bear clip is used when a round, cuddly look is desired.

Equipment

BRUSHES

Pin brush: Comes in many sizes and shapes from small, used on toy dogs, to large, used on Collies, etc. Excellent for breaking up the coat and removing loose hair. Pins must be good quality and retain their shape.

Pure boar bristle brush: Excellent for regular brushing. Removes loose hair and distributes the dog's natural oils from the skin down the hair shaft. Promotes a healthy, shiny coat.

Rubber brush: One of the finest brushes for removing dust and loose hair on shorthaired breeds. Also works well on cats.

Rubber curry brush: Takes dust and dirt out of coats on shorthaired breeds.

Slicker brush: Wire pin brush with a hook pin that helps break up mats.

Slicker brush, curved: Contoured slicker brush with heavier pins. Removes loose hair, mats, and debris. Works extremely well on heavily long-coated dogs, such as the Old English Sheepdog.

Slicker brush, ever gentle: Fine wire pin brush, lighter in weight, for use on Poodles and matted toy dogs such as Yorkshire Terriers.

Brush types include pin, slicker, and curry.

COMBS AND RAKES

Combs: Combs come in many shapes and styles. The most commonly used comb is the fine/medium combination. It is important that the comb is comfortable in your hand and that the teeth are properly spaced for the particular coat you are working on.

Mat comb: Mat combs are designed to cut through mats without destroying the coat. They have a heavier tooth, are sharp on one side, and can be resharpened. Left-handed groomers can use these combs with ease as they are reversible. Some mat combs have one tooth only and have replaceable razor blades in them. Mat combs must be kept in good condition.

Molting comb: These come in two styles, one for shorthaired breeds and one for longhaired breeds. They do an excellent job of removing loose undercoat.

Wood utility comb: Excellent for getting through really long coats, like that of the Collie. Easy on the hand, they are excellent for combing deep into a heavy coat and pulling out loose undercoats.

Undercoat rake: Excellent to loosen up the coat and remove dead undercoat. Especially good on breeds like the German Shepherd Dog.

Combs come in many shapes and styles.

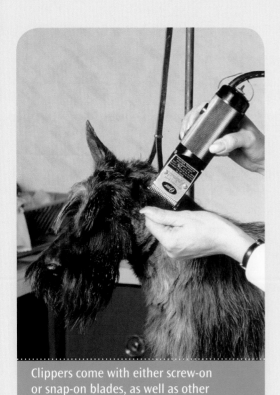

Clippers come with either screw-on or snap-on blades, as well as other attachments.

CLIPPERS AND ATTACHMENTS

Nail clippers (guillotine style): Come in a regular size for most medium-sized dogs and an extra-large size for larger breeds. The scissors-style clipper is recommended for small dogs and cats. The extra-large scissors-style clipper is excellent for dewclaws that grow excessively long.

Oster A-2 clipper: Blades on this clipper must be removed with a screw driver or you must have interchangeable heads. This clipper will accommodate a nail grinder.

Oster A-5 clipper: Clipper with snap-on blades. Very serviceable, easy to maintain, and cuts through any coat.

Oster blades: Made for both the A-2 and A-5 clipper. The higher the number, the closer it cuts. Blades include #30, #15, #10, #9, #8 ½ , #7, #7F, #5, #5F, #4, #4F, #5/8, #7/8, and #8/8.

Oster spray lube: Used to cool and lubricate blades. Helps prevent blades from getting dull quickly.

Snap-on combs: Comb-like attachments that fit over the clipper head; available in various sizes. As the coat is clipped, the hair is uniformly cut to a predetermined, desired length.

Curved shears: Used to achieve curved lines on a dog's coat, especially in the shoulder, flank, and chest areas.

CUTTING AND STRIPPING TOOLS

Duplex dresser: Stripping knife with a removable razor blade.

Ear forceps: Come in various sizes and weights. Some are curved; others are straight. A groomer's preference determines which is most comfortable to use.

Shed'n blade: Removes loose hair only. Pulls out loose topcoat and undercoat.

Small shed'n blade: Takes out loose topcoat and undercoat. Good for small dogs, like Chihuahuas, and shorthaired cats.

Stripping knife: Comes in fine, medium, and coarse styles. Generally, fine is used on the head, ears, and areas where hair is fine and delicate. Medium and coarse blades are usually used on the body.

Scissors: Scissors come in various sizes, from tiny ear and nose scissors to long, straight grooming shears. Scissors must be well balanced and comfortable to use, and they should hold an edge well. Select ones that can be resharpened. Because everyone has a personal preference for a particular style of scissor, select yours with care.

Thinning shears: The type of thinning shears you use depends on the type of coat you are working on. Styles include those with a double or single edge, 30 to 46 teeth.

Polishing gloves shine the coat.

POLISHING GLOVES AND CLOTHS

Chamois cloth: Used to polish and shine the coats of shorthaired dogs.

Hound glove: Polishes and shines short coats, such as those of Doberman Pinschers and Basset Hounds.

Silk handkerchief: Used on shorthaired white dogs to shine the coat.

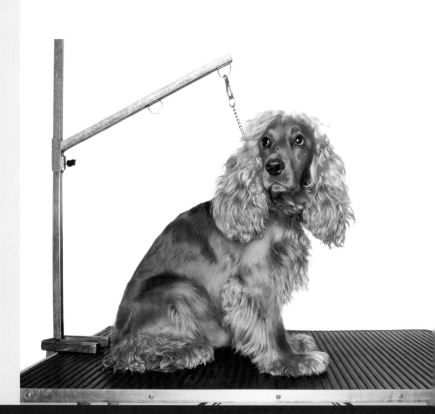

GROOMING TABLES AND POSTS

Grooming posts: Come in various styles and sizes. If you wish to groom large dogs, the post should be at least 48 in (122 cm) high in order to give stability when raised to accommodate their height and size. Posts that go through the table (as opposed to those that fasten to the table edge) are most convenient because you can move freely around the table without bumping into them or catching clipper cords on them. A second post can be fastened to the back of the table in order to attach a "belly band" loop. This band prevents the dog from sitting down. Grooming loops should always be nylon and should have a secure lock; they are easy to open but secure enough so that the dog cannot slip out.

Grooming table: Standard grooming tables are 24 in x 36 in (61 cm x 91 cm); however, there are smaller tables that measure 18 in x 24 in (46 cm x 61 cm). If you are not grooming large dogs, use the smaller table. Some dogs behave better if they do not have a lot of room to dance around on. All tables should have a top made of rubber or some other nonskid material that is easy to disinfect.

Hydraulic table: These tables come in various sizes and shapes. They can be raised, lowered, and turned in a full circle. Although hydraulic tables are more costly than standard models, the ease of control and the comfort they give a groomer's neck and back more than make up for the initial investment. These efficient tables are useful for all dogs, particularly for large breeds.

DRYERS

Cage dryer: Attaches to the cage so that a dog may be dried in the cage.

Floor stand dryer: Works well for blow drying on the table, as well as cage drying. A good-quality dryer should swivel and have a post that can be raised and lowered.

High-velocity dryer: This dryer can be used while a dog is still in the tub. It blows the water down the hair shaft and off the hair with tremendous force. Because it has no heating element, it uses very little electricity and cuts down tremendously on drying time.

OTHER GROOMING AIDS

Lather machine: A machine that dispenses shampoo. Very economical to use because it dispenses lather instead of liquid shampoo and it eliminates shampoo waste.

Ramp: A great aid for getting big dogs in the tub or on the table. Collapsible models fold up and can be stored when not in use.

A floor stand dryer works well for blow drying on a table or in a cage.

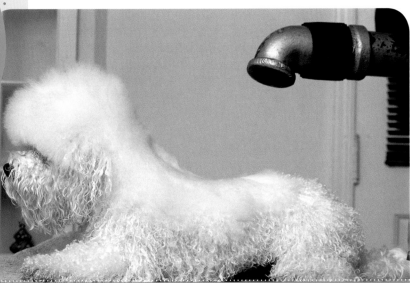

A good-quality dryer should have a post that can be raised and lowered.

Various Blades Available for the Oster

BODY CLIPPING

Size 4	**Size 4F**	**Size 5**	**Size 5F**	**Size 7**	**Size 7F**
Skip Tooth	Full Tooth	Skip Tooth	Skip Tooth	Full Tooth	Full Tooth
$3/8$ inch	$3/8$ inch	$1/4$ inch	$1/4$ inch	$1/8$ inch	$1/8$ inch
(0.95 cm)	(0.95 cm)	(0.6 cm)	(0.6 cm)	(0.3 cm)	(0.3 cm)

ALL-PURPOSE

Size 8 ½	**Size 9**	**Size 10**	**Size 15**	**Size 30**
All-purpose— ideal for terriers	Medium—smooth finish	Medium—general and underbody	Medium close— best all-around Poodle blade	Close—preferred by professionals for show clips
$5/64$ inch	$1/16$ inch	$1/16$ inch	$3/64$ inch	$1/100$ inch
(0.2 cm)	(0.16 cm)	(0.16 cm)	(0.12 cm)	(0.03 cm)

SPECIAL

Size 40	**Blocking Blade (Rug Blade)**	**Size $5/8$**	**Size $7/8$**	**Size $8/8$**	**Extra-Wide "Regular" Groomer Blade**
For clipping surgical area	This specially designed blade is perfect for "skimming"	$5/8$ inch (1.6 cm) wide—close cutting for trim and finish	$7/8$ inch (2.2 cm) wide— close cutting for trim and finish	1 inch (2.5 cm) wide—close cutting for trim and finish	For maximum length cut; allows fast and easy grooming because of added blade width
$1/125$ inch	$1/32$ inch	$1/32$ inch	$1/32$ inch	$1/32$ inch	$1/16$ inch
(0.02 cm)	(0.08 cm)	(0.08 cm)	(0.08 cm)	(0.08 cm)	(0.16 cm)

The Illustrated Breeds

Affenpinscher

TOOLS AND EQUIPMENT

- Blending shears
- Comb
- Cotton balls
- Ear cleaner
- Nail clipper (guillotine or scissor)
- Shampoo (all-purpose or texturizing)
- Slicker brush
- Straight shears
- Stripping knife
- Styptic powder

GROOMING PROCEDURE

1. Nails should be cut by removing only the tips; avoid cutting into the quick. If the nail bleeds, apply styptic powder to stop the bleeding. Any rough edges may be smoothed with a file.

2. Using your fingers, pull out any hair that grows in the ear canal. Clean the ears with a liquid cleaner. Apply the cleaner to a cotton ball and wipe all accumulated dirt and wax out of the crevices of both ears.

3. Brush out the entire dog with a slicker brush to remove dead coat and any mats.

4. With a stripping knife, pluck out the dead and loose hair that grows on the back until the hairs that are left are all a uniform length and lie flat. The hair on the neck, from the base of the skull down over the shoulders, to the elbows, across the rib cage, and down over the thighs should be plucked out as well.

5. Bathe the dog in a shampoo of your choice, and rinse thoroughly.

6. Towel dry the dog, and finish drying him in a cage dryer.

7. With straight shears, cut the hair that grows in between the foot pads. Slightly round the paws.

8. With blending shears, remove the hair that grows on the outside of the ear leather from the base of the ear to the tip of the ear. With the straight shears, cut the hair that sticks out beyond the edge of the ear even with the outer edge of the leather.

9. With blending shears, give the face a round appearance when viewed from the front. Excess hair growing from the corner of the eye may be removed as well.

10. The legs may be shaped with blending shears by removing any hair that is sticking out. This keeps them looking natural rather than scissored.

11. The hair growing down from the chest should be shaped with blending shears, starting from the elbow and tapering slightly to the loin.

12. Hair around the anus may be scissored. The tail may be neatened up with blending shears.

The Affenpinscher should appear neat without looking overly scissored. The natural look is in order for this breed, which should be groomed every 6 to 8 weeks.

GROOMING PROCEDURE

1. The Afghan Hound is shown in his natural state. The coat is not clipped or trimmed. A thick, silky, fine-textured coat with close, short hair that forms a saddle along the back is the groomer's goal.

2. Prior to bathing, the coat must be thoroughly brushed. This procedure removes all dead hair and eliminates all mats and tangles.

3. Begin by lightly dampening a section of the coat with a good-quality coat dressing or mink oil conditioner. Brush with an upward motion using a large pin brush. Comb down with the teeth of the comb placed directly against the skin.

4. Brushing out is the first and most important step in the grooming of an Afghan Hound. Thorough brushing before bathing requires the correct tools and a great deal of manual labor. The coat that is bathed when tangled or matted will be very difficult to work with. If a dog's coat is so badly matted that the dematting procedure would be injurious to the animal, it is best to strip the coat and allow the new growth to be handled properly. The dog is less likely to become agitated if brushing begins at the hindquarters, doing rear leg and undersides, then the body sections, front legs, and finally the head and tail.

5. The nails are then cut. Doing so prior to bathing eliminates the possibility of too close a cut soiling (with blood or styptic powder) the cleaned foot.

6. The ears should be swabbed out with a cotton ball moistened with a good-quality ear cleaner. At this time, check for signs of infection.

7. The bath follows, using the shampoo considered most appropriate for the animal's skin and coat condition.

8. Fluff drying is the next step. When the coat is dry, it should be checked with a comb for any snags or small tangles.

9. The feet are now scissored around the outer edges to give a round appearance. The inner pad area is scissored to remove excess hair from the underside of the foot.

10. The whiskers and long cheek hairs are removed with a #10 blade. Beards are left alone.

11. The area of the coat above the hocks on the hind feet is parted and brushed forward. Coat dressing is applied to keep it in place.

12. In the puppy styling, a part is formed from the eyes over the forehead and down to the tail. Once the saddle (a smooth strip of hair) grows in, only the head is parted. The neck and back hair lie naturally.

TOOLS AND EQUIPMENT

- Coat dressing
- Cotton balls
- Ear cleaner
- Grooming spray
- Large pin brush
- Matting comb
- Matting rake
- Nail clipper
- Oster A-5 clipper/#10 blade
- Scissors
- Slicker brush
- Steel comb
- Styptic powder

Airedale Terrier

TOOLS AND EQUIPMENT

- Cotton balls
- Eye drops (eye stain remover)
- Large nail clipper
- Mat-splitting comb
- Medicated ear powder
- Metal comb (medium)
- Oster A-5 clipper/#10, #8½, #7, #5 blades
- Scissors
- Slicker brush
- Thinning shears

GROOMING PROCEDURE

1. Brush the entire coat and tail with a slicker brush. Comb through with a metal comb. (The coat texture varies from coarse and hairy to soft and cotton-like, the latter tending to mat.) Remove any mats with a mat-splitting comb.

2. Clean the ears using medicated ear powder, and lightly pluck any stray hair from the insides.

3. Moisten a cotton ball with eye drops and wipe the eyes clean. Some brands of eye drops also help remove any stains around the eyes.

4. Cut the tips of the nails with the large nail clipper, being careful not to cut the quick.

5. With a #10 blade on an Oster A-5 clipper, shave the head, starting at the center of the eyebrows, back to the base of the skull. [Note: When shaving the head, face, and throat, shave with the grain of the hair.] Then shave from the center again to the outer corner of the eyes. This line should be about ¾ inch (2 cm) above the inner corner of the eye, tapering into the outer corner, thus making a triangle. Next shave down from the outer corners of the eyes to within ¾ inch (2 cm) from the corners of the mouth and continue this line across and under the chin.

6. Shave both sides of the ears, and from the back edge of the ears, shave down diagonally to a point at the base of the throat, thus forming a "V" shape.

7. Shave the anal area, being certain not to put the blade in direct contact with the skin (⅛ to ¼ inch [0.3 to 0.6 cm] each side).

8. Shave the abdomen area from groin to navel and down the insides of thighs.

9. With a #8½, #7, or #5 blade on the Oster A-5 clipper (according to the length of the coat desired), start at the base of the skull and clip down the back to the base of the tail.

10. Clip the top half of the tail and blend down either side of the fringe. Comb the fringe downward and scissor the lower edge, thus making a feather shape.

11. With the clipper, clip down the sides of the neck to the shoulder and down to the elbow.

12. Clip down the chest to the breastbone, and slope the pattern down diagonally to the center front of the legs.

13. From the first clip down the back, clip down the sides of the stomach, arching the pattern over the hips. (From the side, the pattern line should slope down diagonally from the breastbone, straight across the tops of the front legs, sloping up across the stomach, arching up over the hips and down to a point in the rear.)

14. Brush through the coat with a slicker brush to remove any excess hair.

15. Place a cotton ball in each ear (this prevents any water from entering the ear canal), and bathe the dog. Cage dry him. [Note: For Airedales that have a cotton-like coat, it is recommended that you fluff dry the dog to prevent matting.]

16. Brush and comb through the coat.

17. Using the same blade on the Oster A-5 clipper as before, repeat the process for the pattern, blending the hair down from the top of the pattern with the blade.

18. Scissor around the edges of the ears.

19. Scissor a "V" shape in the center of the eyebrows.

20. Comb the hair on the face and eyebrows forward and downward. Align your scissors at an angle from the base of the nose to the outer corner of the eye. Scissor the eyebrows from this angle, thus making a deep triangle (being careful not to cut any hair from the top of the muzzle).

21. Lightly scissor stray hairs from around the edge and the sides of the beard. Using thinning shears, shape the beard, which should be long and barrel-shaped.

22. Use thinning shears to trim any stray hairs from the top of the muzzle.

23. Trim hair from between the foot pads, and while the dog is standing, scissor around the edges to give a round effect. [Note: Doing this first will give you a guide for scissoring the legs.]

24. Scissor the front legs into straight, tubular shapes.

25. Scissor evenly the bottom of the chest fringe.

26. Scissor the bottom of the belly fringe following the contour of the dog's body, tapering up from the elbows on the front legs to the flanks at the rear.

27. Scissor the rear legs following the natural contours. (In rear view, the legs should be straight on the outside. On the inside, they should be straight, up to the thighs, and should arch up and into the shave line, thus forming the "Airedale Arch.")

28. Lightly comb through the legs, fringes, and face, removing all excess hair and trimming any stray hairs as necessary.

The Airedale Terrier should be groomed every 6 to 8 weeks. The ears should be checked weekly and cleaned if necessary, and the nails should be checked and cut at the grooming session.

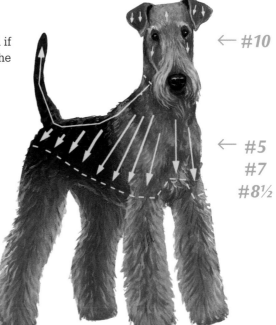

← #10

← #5
#7
#8½

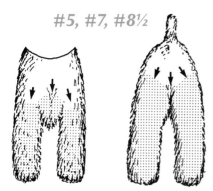

#5, #7, #8½

Akita

TOOLS AND EQUIPMENT

- Cotton balls
- Eye drops (eye stain remover)
- Large nail clipper
- Large pin brush
- Medicated ear powder
- Metal comb (wide-toothed)
- Metal rake (wide-toothed)
- Scissors
- Slicker brush

GROOMING PROCEDURE

1. Starting at the head, brush the entire coat.

2. With a metal rake, gently rake through the coat. During the nonshedding season, do not rake out the undercoat; only untangle it with a rake or metal comb.

3. Clean the ears using medicated ear powder, and lightly pluck any stray hair from the insides.

4. Clean the eyes by wiping them with a cotton ball that has been moistened with eye drops. Certain eye drop products will also help in removing any stains.

5. Clip the tip of each nail with nail clippers, being careful not to cut into the quick.

6. With scissors, clip the whiskers from the muzzle, the chin, the sides of the face, and above the eyes. [Note: Clipping the whiskers is a decision to be left to the owner.]

7. Place a cotton ball in each ear (this prevents any water from entering the ear canal), and bathe the dog. Fluff dry him. You can also cage dry the dog first, drying most of the outer coat, and then fluff dry with a large pin brush.

8. Brush through the coat briskly with a large pin brush, then comb through with a metal comb to remove the loosened hair.

9. With scissors, snip the hair from between the pads and toes on the feet and around the edges of each foot to give a neat appearance.

GROOMING PROCEDURE

1. Spray the entire coat with protein coat conditioner. This adds body to the coat and helps repair split ends. Brush through the entire coat with a slicker brush to remove loose hair. Then, comb with a molting comb to take out loose undercoat.

2. Swab the ears with a cotton ball moistened with ear cleaner. This will remove dirt and control ear odor. Follow this with a dry cotton ball, and dust the ears with medicated ear powder.

3. Cut the nails with a guillotine-type nail clipper. Nails should be cut monthly.

4. Bathe the dog with a tearless protein shampoo that is pH-alkaline. This will add fullness and body to the coat and restructure damaged hair.

5. Use a high-velocity dryer to blow excess water off the dog while he is still in the tub. This will speed up the drying time and help prevent the coat from becoming overly dry. Cage dry the dog until the hair is damp. Then finish drying on the table using a blow dryer and a pin brush to separate all of the hair and remove all of the loose coat. Finish with a steel comb through the entire coat, paying special attention to the fine hair behind the ears. Use the fine side of the comb for this area.

6. Check between the foot pads and under the feet for burrs, tar, etc. Scissor the hair under the feet even with the pads. Trim around the paw and neaten the entire foot. Use thinning shears to trim the hair growing out from between the toes. Be sure to neaten the hair on the backs of the rear pasterns.

Alaskan Malamute

TOOLS AND EQUIPMENT

- Cotton balls
- Ear cleaner
- Eye stain remover
- High-velocity dryer
- Medicated ear powder
- Molting comb (#564) for shorthaired breeds
- Nail clipper
- Protein coat conditioner
- Pure boar bristle brush
- Scissors
- Slicker brush
- Steel comb (medium/fine)
- Tearless protein shampoo

American Staffordshire Terrier

TOOLS AND EQUIPMENT

- Chamois cloth
- Cotton balls
- Eye drops (eye stain remover)
- Lanolin coat conditioner
- Medicated ear powder
- Nail clipper
- Scissors
- Sisal (natural bristle) brush

GROOMING PROCEDURE

1. Brush the entire coat with a sisal brush, using long deep strokes for a thorough massage.

2. Clean the ears using medicated ear powder.

3. Clean the eyes by wiping them with a cotton ball moistened with eye drops; this also helps to remove any stains around the eyes.

4. Cut the tips of the nails with a nail clipper, being careful not to cut the quick.

5. With scissors, snip the whiskers from the muzzle, under the chin, the sides of the face, and above the eyes. [Note: Clipping the whiskers is a decision to be left to the owner.]

6. Place a cotton ball in each ear (this prevents any water from entering the ear canal), and bathe the dog. Cage dry him.

7. Put a few drops of lanolin coat conditioner into the palms of your hands, rub together lightly, and massage this into the coat.

8. Brush the coat with a sisal brush to distribute the conditioner, then lightly rub over the coat with the chamois cloth. This gives it a nice sheen.

The American Staffordshire Terrier should be groomed every 10 to 12 weeks. The ears should be checked weekly and cleaned if necessary, and the nails should be checked monthly and cut if necessary.

GROOMING PROCEDURE

1. Nails should be cut by removing the tips only; avoid cutting the quick. If a nail bleeds, apply styptic powder to stop the bleeding. Any rough edges may be smoothed by filing.

2. Clean the ears with a liquid cleaner. Apply liquid cleaner to a cotton ball and wipe accumulated dirt and wax from all crevices in both ears.

3. Brush out the entire coat with a slicker brush to remove mats and/or dead coat.

4. Comb the hair so that it is standing straight out from the dog's body. With straight shears, scissor the neck and body coat to an even length of about 1 to 2 inches (2.5 to 5 cm).

5. Bathe the dog in a shampoo of your choice and rinse thoroughly.

6. Towel dry the dog and either air dry him if it is warm or place him in a cage with a dryer. Do not brush or comb the dog after he is dry because the objective is to get the coat to curl.

7. Remove excess hair from the underside of each foot (between the foot pads) with straight scissors.

8. With blending shears, remove any excess hair that grows on top of the foot in between the toes. The foot should appear tight and compact.

9. With blending shears, remove excess hair from the back of the hock.

10. Trim hair on the underside of the tail into a sickle shape.

11. With blending shears or straight scissors, remove any stray hairs that may be sticking out and ruining a tidy outline.

12. With blending shears, remove excess hair on the muzzle and on top of the head. The skull should be made to look broad and rather flat.

The entire coat of a properly groomed American Water Spaniel should have a curly appearance in conjunction with a tidy outline. This breed should receive a complete grooming every 6 to 10 weeks.

American Water Spaniel

TOOLS AND EQUIPMENT

- Blending shears
- Comb
- Cotton balls
- Ear cleaner
- Nail clipper (scissor or guillotine)
- Shampoo (all-purpose or dark coat)
- Slicker brush
- Straight shears
- Styptic powder

Anatolian Karabash Dog

TOOLS AND EQUIPMENT

- Cotton balls
- Eye drops (eye stain remover)
- Medicated ear powder
- Metal comb (medium)
- Nail clipper
- Pin brush
- Scissors
- Sisal (natural bristle) brush

GROOMING PROCEDURE

1. Brush the coat vigorously with a sisal brush. Brush through the coat and tail with a pin brush to remove all loosened hair.

2. Clean the ears using medicated ear powder.

3. Clean the eyes by wiping them with a cotton ball that has been moistened with eye drops. This will also help in removing any stains.

4. Cut the tips of the nails with a nail clipper, being careful not to cut the quick.

5. Using a damp cotton ball, clean the insides of the lips, removing any trapped food particles.

6. With scissors, snip the whiskers from the muzzle, under the chin, the sides of the face, and above the eyes. [Note: Clipping the whiskers is optional. Check with the dog's owner.]

7. Place a cotton ball in each ear (this prevents any water from entering the ear canal), and bathe the dog. Cage dry him.

8. Clean the furrows on the face with a cotton ball that has been saturated with eye drops. (Daily use of eye drops or medicated talcum powder on the furrows will keep them clean and help prevent soreness or infection.)

9. Brush the coat thoroughly with a sisal brush to bring up a nice sheen.

The Anatolian Karabash Dog rarely needs bathing if he is brushed by the owner on a regular basis. (Depending on his environment, bathing can be every three months or so.) The ears should be checked weekly and cleaned if necessary, and the nails should be checked monthly and cut if necessary.

GROOMING PROCEDURE

1. Brush the entire coat with a pure boar bristle brush; then comb thoroughly.

2. Swab the ears with a cotton ball moistened with ear cleaner. This will remove dirt and control ear odor. Follow this with a dry cotton ball, and dust the ears with medicated ear powder.

3. Cut the nails with a guillotine-type nail clipper. Nails should be cut monthly.

4. Check between the foot pads and under the feet for burrs, tar, etc. Scissor the hair under the feet to prevent debris from adhering. Trim any hair around the paw that touches the ground or grows out between the paws with thinning shears.

5. Bathe the dog with a tearless protein shampoo that is pH-alkaline. This will add fullness and body to the coat and restructure damaged hair.

6. Use a high-velocity dryer to blow excess water off the dog while he is still in the tub. This will speed up the drying time and help prevent the coat from becoming overly dry. Cage dry the dog until the hair is damp. Then finish drying him on the table using a blow dryer and a pin brush to separate all the hair and remove all of the loose coat.

7. Leave the whiskers intact.

8. Spray a pure bristle brush with protein coat conditioner and top brush the coat to add brilliance and fragrance. For show purposes, there is to be no scissoring of any kind.

Australian Cattle Dog

TOOLS AND EQUIPMENT

- Cotton balls
- Ear cleaner
- High-velocity dryer
- Medicated ear powder
- Nail clipper (extra large)
- Pin brush
- Protein coat conditioner
- Pure boar bristle brush
- Scissors
- Steel comb (medium/fine)
- Tearless protein shampoo
- Thinning shears

Australian Kelpie

TOOLS AND EQUIPMENT

- Cotton balls
- Eye drops (eye stain remover)
- Medicated ear powder
- Nail clipper
- Pin brush
- Scissors
- Sisal (natural bristle) brush

GROOMING PROCEDURE

1. Brush the coat vigorously with a sisal brush. (Use a pin brush during the shedding season.)

2. Clean the ears using medicated ear powder.

3. Clean the eyes by wiping them with a cotton ball that has been moistened with eye drops.

4. Cut the tips of the nails with a nail clipper, being careful not to cut the quick.

5. With scissors, snip the whiskers from the muzzle, under the chin, the sides of the face, and above the eyes. [Note: Clipping the whiskers is a decision to be left to the owner.]

6. Place a cotton ball in each ear (this prevents any water from entering the ear canal), and bathe the dog. Next, cage dry him.

7. Brush the coat with a sisal brush, using firm strokes, to obtain a nice sheen.

The Australian Kelpie should be groomed every 8 to 10 weeks. The ears should be checked weekly and cleaned if necessary, and the nails should be checked monthly and cut if necessary.

GROOMING PROCEDURE

1. Spray the dog with coat gloss to lubricate the coat and prevent hair loss. Brush with a gentle slicker brush, and then comb thoroughly with a molting comb to remove dead undercoat.

2. Swab the ears with a cotton ball moistened with ear cleaner. This will remove dirt and control ear odor. Follow this with a dry cotton ball, and dust the ears with medicated ear powder.

3. Cut the nails with a guillotine-type nail clipper. Nails should be cut monthly.

4. Check between the foot pads and under the feet for burrs, tar, and so forth. Scissor the hair under the feet to prevent debris from adhering. Trim any hair around the paw that touches the ground or grows out between the paws with thinning shears.

5. Trim the hair around the anus with scissors, and remove any long hair under the tail that hangs over the anus and may become soiled.

6. Bathe the dog with a tearless terrier shampoo that adds body and texture to the hair and does not soften the coat.

7. Cage dry until the hair is damp, and finish drying on the table using a blow dryer and a stiff, natural bristle brush. Spray with coat gloss to eliminate flyaway hair and static. Brush the coat straight from neck to tail, with no part. Then brush down over the shoulders and sides. Comb thoroughly with the medium side of a steel comb.

8. Clip the stomach area with a #10 blade, going with the grain.

9. Dead, straggly hair should be removed from the neck, body, and tail with a medium stripping knife or with the thumb and fingers.

10. Tidy the dog's hind parts and rear legs. Blend the coat slightly from stifle to hocks. Trim close from hock to foot with thinning shears.

11. The hair on the underside of the tail should be trimmed short. Remove dead, straggly hair from the tail tip and blend the tail into the back. If the tail is short, leave hair beyond the tip to lengthen; if long, trim close to the tip.

12. From the tail on each side and on the back of the hip, blend the coat down to the cowlick on the back of each leg.

13. Never flatten the topknot. Train up with a brush and a fine-toothed comb (use face comb).

14. Strip long, surplus hair on the face and cheeks. Pluck with the fingers around the ears, between the eyes, and slightly under the eyes to enhance expression. This can be done with thinning shears also.

continued

Australian Terrier

TOOLS AND EQUIPMENT

- Coat gloss
- Cotton balls
- Ear cleaner
- Fine face comb
- Gentle slicker brush
- Medicated ear powder
- Molting comb (for long hair)
- Nail clipper (extra large)
- Oster clipper/#10 blade
- Protein coat conditioner
- Pure boar bristle brush
- Scissors
- Steel comb (medium/fine)
- Stripping knife (medium/fine)
- Tearless protein shampoo
- Thinning shears, double edge

15. Clean the black, leathery space on the bridge of the muzzle in a "V" shape.

16. Whiskers can be removed.

17. Strip or pluck the back of the ears so that they are free of long hair—usually one-third to two-thirds down to the base—and trim very close. Outside edges are to be trimmed neat and sharp. Ears can be clipped with a #10 blade.

18. Use a medium stripping knife to lightly strip the back of the neck—to emphasize length—blending into the shoulders and body.

19. Strip slightly underneath the chin to about the center of the underjaw. Comb the muzzle forward.

20. Brush the ruff out from under the throat to the shoulders to create a bib-like ruff. Chest should be combed down to form an apron.

21. Trim excessive long hair from the front legs with thinning shears. Leave feathering on the back of the legs. Excessive tufts around the elbows should be removed. Trim close from the hock joint down.

22. Trim the feet with scissors to neaten.

23. If showing, bathe the dog at least four days before the show.

24. Spray a pure bristle brush with protein coat conditioner and top brush the coat to add brilliance and fragrance.

GROOMING PROCEDURE

1. Brush the entire coat with a pin brush to loosen up the hair; then brush with a sisal brush.

2. Clean the ears using medicated ear powder.

3. Clean the eyes by wiping them with a cotton ball moistened with eye drops. This will also help remove any stains around the eyes.

4. Clip the nails with a nail clipper, being careful not to cut the quick.

5. Using scissors, clip the whiskers from the muzzle, the chin, the sides of the face, and above the eyes. [Note: Clipping the whiskers is a decision to be left to the owner.]

6. Put a cotton ball in each ear to prevent water from entering the ear canal. Bathe the dog and cage dry him.

7. Put a few drops of lanolin coat conditioner into the palms of your hands, rub your hands together lightly, and gently massage into the coat.

8. Brush the coat with a sisal brush (to distribute the conditioner), and then lightly rub over the coat with a chamois cloth to give it a nice sheen.

The Basenji needs only to be bathed every 3 or 4 months. Regular brushing by the owner with a sisal brush will help maintain a healthy, shiny coat. The ears should be checked monthly, and cleaned if necessary, and the nails should also be checked and clipped if necessary.

Basenji

TOOLS AND EQUIPMENT

- Chamois cloth
- Cotton balls
- Eye drops (eye stain remover)
- Lanolin coat conditioner
- Medicated ear powder
- Nail clipper
- Pin brush
- Scissors
- Sisal (natural bristle) brush

Basset Fauve de Bretagne

TOOLS AND EQUIPMENT

- Cotton balls
- Eye drops (eye stain remover)
- Medicated ear powder
- Metal comb (medium)
- Nail clipper
- Oster A-5 clipper/#10 blade
- Scissors
- Slicker brush
- Thinning shears

GROOMING PROCEDURE

1. Brush the coat thoroughly with a slicker brush.

2. Comb through the coat to remove all loosened hair.

3. Clean the ears using medicated ear powder, and lightly pluck any stray hair from the insides.

4. Clean the eyes by wiping them with a cotton ball that has been moistened with eye drops.

5. Cut the tips of the nails with a nail clipper, being careful not to cut the quick.

6. With a #10 blade on the Oster A-5 clipper, shave the stomach from groin to navel and down the insides of the thighs.

7. Shave the anal area, being certain not to put the blade in direct contact with the skin (½ inch [1 cm] on either side).

8. Put a cotton ball in each ear (this prevents water from entering the ear canal), and bathe the dog. He can then be cage dried.

9. With scissors, snip hair from between the pads and toes of the feet and around the edges for a neat effect.

10. With scissors or thinning shears, trim straggly hairs from around the ankles on the front feet and from the hocks down to the feet on the hind legs.

11. Comb through the entire coat to remove all loosened hair.

The Basset Fauve de Bretagne should be groomed every 8 to 10 weeks. The ears should be checked weekly and cleaned if necessary, and the nails should be checked monthly and cut if necessary.

GROOMING PROCEDURE

1. The Basset Hound is shown in a coat that is short and smooth. The skin should be loose.

2. Prior to bathing, brush the coat thoroughly to remove all dead hair. If heavy shedding is evident, a shedding blade may be stroked lightly over the coat, or a curry brush may be used in a circular motion prior to brushing.

3. Clean the inner ear by swabbing it with a cotton ball that has been moistened with a good-quality ear cleaner. Check the ears for signs of infection. The Basset's long ears might have crusted edges due to dried-on food debris. These edges can be moistened with mineral oil before bathing. The flews and deep haws also should be checked for blistering or food debris.

4. Dip the nails.

5. Bathe the dog with proper shampoo for skin type and coat conditioner. Any discolored white areas of the coat will benefit from an application of a bluing rinse (one cup laundry bluing to three quarts water) before the final rinsing is done.

6. The Basset Hound can be cage dried.

7. After drying, scissor the hair on the underside of the foot pads.

8. Scissor all facial whiskers. The facial wrinkles should be checked to make certain they are thoroughly dry. An application of baby powder in these areas will keep them from becoming irritated.

9. The tail feathering is not removed.

10. Application of a lanolin coat conditioner is the final step. Put a few drops of the conditioner in your hands, rub your hands together, and gently massage into the coat.

Basset Hound

TOOLS AND EQUIPMENT

- Baby powder
- Cotton balls
- Ear cleaner
- Hound glove
- Lanolin coat conditioner
- Mineral oil
- Nail clipper
- Scissors
- Shedding blade
- Short bristle brush (or very gentle slicker)
- Styptic powder

Beagle

TOOLS AND EQUIPMENT

- Cotton balls
- Curry brush
- Ear cleaner
- Lanolin coat conditioner
- Nail clipper
- Scissors
- Short bristle brush
- Styptic powder
- Thinning shears

GROOMING PROCEDURE

1. The Beagle is shown in a coat that is close, hard, and glossy. Prior to bathing, brush the coat thoroughly to remove all dead hair. A curry brush used in a circular motion may precede brushing.

2. Clean the inner ear by swabbing it with a cotton ball that has been moistened with a good-quality ear cleaner. Check for signs of ear infection.

3. Dip the nails.

4. Bathe the dog with proper shampoo for skin type and coat conditioner. Any discolored white areas of the coat will benefit from an application of a bluing rinse (one cup laundry bluing to three quarts water) before the final rinsing is done.

5. The Beagle can be cage dried.

6. The facial whiskers may be scissored. Thinning shears might be necessary on the neck from the bottom of the ear corner to the front of the shoulder.

7. Apply a lanolin coat conditioner.

GROOMING PROCEDURE

1. Spray the entire coat with protein coat conditioner. This adds body to the coat and helps repair split ends. If the coat is matted in areas, spray the matted areas with tangle remover. Let the dog sit 10 to 15 minutes with both products on the coat until they are absorbed and the coat is partially dry.

2. After 15 minutes, spray the entire coat with coat gloss. This lubricates the coat for easier brushing and combing and prevents hair breakage. Brush through the entire coat with a pin brush, using a slicker brush and a utility comb in the matted areas of the coat. Start at the rear of the dog at the bottom of the skirt area. Work in sections, lifting the hair and brushing it layer by layer. Mist each section with coat gloss as you work. Never brush a dry-coated Bearded Collie. Work through the entire coat from the back to the neck area.

3. To get a nice natural part along the spine, comb all of the undercoat out along the spine. The topcoat will then lie flat, naturally parted. The coat should fall naturally to either side. Comb hair down on each side. Never bathe this breed with mats in the coat, as water tends to tighten mats and make them harder to remove.

4. Swab the ears with a cotton ball that has been moistened with ear cleaner. This will remove dirt and control ear odor. Follow this with a dry cotton ball, and dust the ears with medicated ear powder. Pull out any dead hair inside the ears with your fingers or ear forceps.

5. Cut the nails with a guillotine-type nail clipper. Nails should be cut monthly.

6. Check between the foot pads and under the feet for burrs, tar, etc. Scissor the hair under the foot even with the pads to prevent debris from adhering. Trim any hair around the paw that the dog walks on.

7. Scissor any long hair under the tail that hangs over the anus and that may become soiled with feces. Scissor the hair around the anus and be sure the opening is clear. Trim or blend down the area under the tail if it is profuse; otherwise, it may collect feces and become a nidus for infection.

8. Bathe the dog with a tearless protein shampoo that is pH-alkaline. This will add fullness and body to the coat and restructure damaged hair. Use the whitening shampoo on white areas of the coat.

9. Use a high-velocity dryer to blow excess water off the dog while he is still in the tub. This will speed up the drying time and help prevent the coat from becoming overly dry.

continued

Bearded Collie

TOOLS AND EQUIPMENT

- Coat gloss
- Cotton balls
- Ear cleaner
- Ear forceps
- Eye stain remover
- High-velocity dryer
- Large pin brush
- Long-hair molting comb (#565)
- Medicated ear powder
- Nail clipper (extra large)
- Protein coat conditioner
- Pure boar bristle brush
- Scissors
- Slicker brush
- Steel comb (medium/fine)
- Tearless whitening shampoo
- Tearless protein shampoo
- Wood utility comb (matting comb)

10. Allow the dog to sit and air dry for about 30 minutes, but do not use the dryer as it may dry areas and cause curling. Next, dry the dog on the table using a blow dryer set to "warm" and using a pin brush to separate and straighten the entire coat for a smooth, silky look.

11. Be sure to brush down to the skin, and follow this by combing with a long-toothed steel comb.

12. Scissor around the outside edges of the feet to make them oval and neat. Hair is left between the toes, and the feet are to be well covered with hair. Depending on the dog's environment and living conditions, profuse hair between the foot pads and toes can be scissored for cleanliness.

13. The skull should be broad and flat, so straggly hair can be removed to conform with the desired appearance.

14. Pluck hair from the inside corner of the eyes and the stop. Pluck the hair out over the eyes until a nice arch is shaped to add to the inquiring expression this breed is to have. Hair over the eyes is combed up and to the sides to frame the eyes and blend smoothly into the coat on the sides of the head.

15. The bridge of the nose is sparsely covered with hair, which should be combed down on each side of the muzzle to form the typical beard.

16. Ears are to be long and natural.

17. The neck should blend smoothly into the shoulders. Clumps of hair in this area may be thinned with thinning shears. Always use thinning shears in combination with a comb. Hold the thinning shears pointed in the direction the hair grows. Thin out and comb the hair to achieve the desired look. Never cut across the grain.

18. Brush each side of the body hair down to encourage the natural part.

19. The topline should be straight and the tail set low. If the dog's rear is higher than his front and you have profuse hair on the rear, you can lower the back end by thinning the rump with thinning shears.

20. Brush the chest down and the hair on the legs straight down.

21. Brush the tail into a full plume.

22. Spray a protein coat conditioner (with mink oil) lightly from above and allow it to mist over the coat. Brush with a pure bristle brush. The spraying and brushing gives the coat a beautiful gloss and aroma. It should be noted that a coat that has been trimmed in any way must be seriously penalized, and a sculptured coat is a serious fault. The grooming instructions listed above are to make a Bearded Collie a more enjoyable member of the family; they are not intended for show dogs.

GROOMING PROCEDURE

1. Brush the entire coat with a slicker brush, removing any mats with a mat-splitting comb.

2. Clean the ears using medicated ear powder, and lightly pluck any stray hair from the insides.

3. Clean the eyes by wiping them with a cotton ball that has been moistened with eye drops. If the eyes are excessively sticky and watering, snip the stained hair from the corners of the eyes with scissors.

4. Cut the tips of the nails with a nail clipper, being careful not to cut the quick.

5. With a #15 blade on an Oster A-5 clipper, shave the face, starting at the front edge of the ears straight to the outer corners of the eyes. From the outer corners of the eyes, shave straight down to within ½ inch (1 cm) from the corners of the mouth. Next, shave from the back edges (base) of the ears, diagonally down to a point at the base of the throat, thus forming a "V" shape. [Note: When shaving the face, chin, and throat, shave against the grain of the hair.]

6. Shave the entire underjaw.

7. Shave the ears from the base to within 1 inch (2.5 cm) from the center of the edge and down both sides of the ear diagonally from the first point, making an inverted "V" shape.

8. With a #10 blade, shave the anal area, being certain not to put the blade in direct contact with the skin (½ inch [1 cm] on each side).

9. Shave the stomach area from the groin to the navel and down the insides of the thighs.

10. With a #15 blade, shave two-thirds of the tail from the tip, leaving one-third of the hair at the base. Shave the underside of the remaining one-third of the tail.

11. With a #4 or #5 blade on the clipper (according to the length of coat desired), start at the base of the ears and clip diagonally toward the center of the base of the neck, thus making a "V" from the base of the ears down into the neck. Then clip down the back to the base of the tail.

12. Clip down the sides of the neck to the shoulders and blend the hair down into the top of the front legs.

13. Clip down the chest to the breastbone.

14. From the first clip down the back, clip down the sides of the stomach.

continued

Bedlington Terrier

TOOLS AND EQUIPMENT

- Cotton balls
- Eye drops (eye stain remover)
- Mat-splitting comb
- Medicated ear powder
- Metal comb (medium)
- Nail clipper
- Oster A-5 clipper/#4, #5, #10, #15 blades
- Scissors
- Slicker brush

Bedlington Terrier *continued*

15. Blend the hair from the top of the back on the rear end into the top of the thighs.

16. Brush through the hair on the legs, head, and face to remove any excess hair.

17. Put a cotton ball in each ear to prevent any water from entering the ear canal. Bathe the dog and towel dry.

18. Place the dog on the grooming table and fluff dry with a slicker brush, brushing the hair in an upward motion to make it full.

19. Using the same blade on the Oster A-5 clipper as before, repeat the process on the face and body.

20. Scissor the shaved edges of the ears, comb the "tassels" down, and scissor the lower edges into a curve.

21. Scissor the head into the "Roman Arch," i.e., arching from the nose up and over the head and ending in a "V" on the neck. Scissor the sides to curve down and taper into the base of the ears.

22. Scissor the muzzle around so that it is in proportion with the head. When viewed from the front, the head should appear long and straight, arching across the top between the ears, and tapering slightly on the muzzle.

23. Scissor the remaining one-third on the top of the tail into a tubular shape, blending into the body.

24. Scissor around the shave lines on the throat and stomach.

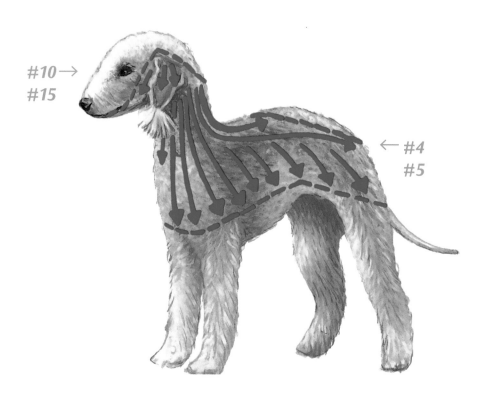

#10 →
#15

← #4
#5

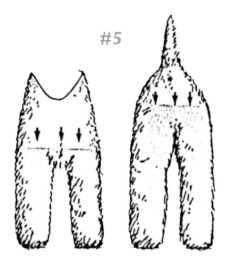

#5

25. Trim the hair from between the pads of the feet, and while the dog is standing, scissor around the edges of the feet to give a round effect. Doing this first will give you a guide for scissoring the legs.

26. Scissor the chest, between the legs, and underneath the stomach.

27. Scissor the front legs into straight, tubular shapes.

28. Scissor the rear legs, following the natural contours. The insides should be straight to the hock joint and taper on up to the shave line.

29. Lightly comb through and fluff up the hair on the legs, head, muzzle, and tail, making sure they are even. Trim any stray hairs as necessary.

The Bedlington Terrier should be groomed every 6 or 8 weeks. Regular brushing and combing by the owner between groomings will help prevent mats. The ears should be checked weekly and cleaned if necessary, and the nails should be checked and cut at the grooming session.

Belgian Malinois

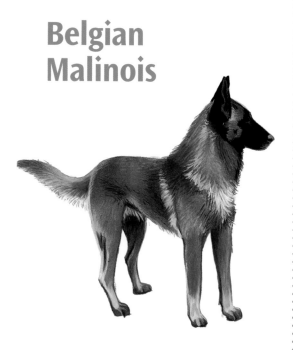

TOOLS AND EQUIPMENT

- Cotton balls
- Ear cleaner
- High-velocity dryer
- Medicated ear powder
- Nail clipper
- Pin brush
- Protein coat conditioner
- Pure boar bristle brush
- Rubber curry brush
- Scissors
- Short-hair molting comb (#564)
- Slicker brush
- Tearless protein shampoo
- Thinning shears
- Undercoat rake

GROOMING PROCEDURE

1. Spray the entire coat with protein coat conditioner. This adds body to the coat and helps repair split ends. Brush through the entire coat with an undercoat rake. This will loosen up the coat and remove dead undercoat. Start at the rear of the dog at the bottom of the skirt area. Work in sections, using your other hand to lift the hair ahead of the section you are working on. Work through the entire dog from the back to the neck area. Then brush through the coat with a slicker brush to remove the top dead coat. If the dog is in a heavy shed, finish with the molting comb, followed by the rubber curry brush. Work vigorously. The more hair you remove now, the less hair you need to wash and dry.

2. Swab the ears with a cotton ball moistened with ear cleaner. This will remove dirt and control ear odor. Follow this with a dry cotton ball, and dust the ears with medicated ear powder.

3. Cut the nails with a guillotine-type nail clipper. Nails should be cut monthly.

4. Check between the foot pads and under the feet for burrs, tar, etc. Scissor the hair under the feet to prevent debris from adhering. Trim any hair around the paw that touches the ground or grows out between the paws with thinning shears.

5. Bathe the dog with a tearless protein shampoo that is pH-alkaline. This will add fullness and body to the coat and restructure damaged hair.

6. Use a high-velocity dryer to blow excess water off the dog while he is still in the tub. This will speed up the drying time and help prevent the coat from becoming overly dry. Cage dry the dog until the hair is damp. Then finish drying on the table using a blow dryer and a pin brush to separate all the hair and remove all of the loose coat.

7. Backbrush the entire coat, but finish the withers and the neck area by rebrushing with the natural lay of the hair. Never leave the withers and the neck backbrushed.

8. Leave the whiskers intact.

9. Spray a boar bristle brush with protein coat conditioner and topbrush the coat to add brilliance and fragrance.

GROOMING PROCEDURE

1. Spray the entire coat with protein coat conditioner. This adds body to the coat and helps repair split ends. Brush through the entire coat with an undercoat rake. This will loosen up the coat and remove dead undercoat. Start at the rear of the dog at the bottom of the skirt area. Work in sections, using your other hand to lift the hair ahead of the section you are working on. Work through the entire dog from the back to the neck area. Then brush through the coat with a slicker brush to remove the top dead coat. Work vigorously. The more hair you remove now, the less hair you need to wash and dry.

2. Swab the ears with a cotton ball moistened with ear cleaner. This will remove dirt and control ear odor. Follow this with a dry cotton ball, and dust the ears with medicated ear powder.

3. Cut the nails with a guillotine-type nail clipper. Nails should be cut monthly.

4. Check between the foot pads and under the feet for burrs, tar, etc. Scissor the hair under the feet to prevent debris from adhering. Trim any hair around the paw that touches the ground or grows out between the paws with thinning shears.

5. Bathe the dog with a tearless protein shampoo that is pH-alkaline. This will add fullness and body to the coat and restructure damaged hair.

6. Use a high-velocity dryer to blow excess water off the dog while he is still in the tub. This will speed up the drying time and help prevent the coat from becoming overly dry. Cage dry the dog until the hair is damp. Then, finish drying on the table using a blow dryer and a pin brush to separate all the hair and remove all of the loose coat

7. Brush the entire coat and be sure to brush down to the skin, using the dryer to style and separate the hair. Follow by combing the entire coat, using the fine part of the comb on the soft hair behind the ears.

Belgian Sheepdog

TOOLS AND EQUIPMENT

- Comb (fine/medium)
- Cotton balls
- Ear cleaner
- High-velocity dryer
- Medicated ear powder
- Nail clipper
- Pin brush
- Protein coat conditioner
- Pure boar bristle brush
- Scissors
- Slicker brush
- Tearless protein shampoo
- Thinning shears
- Undercoat rake

Belgian Tervuren

TOOLS AND EQUIPMENT

- Comb (fine/medium)
- Cotton balls
- Ear cleaner
- High-velocity dryer
- Medicated ear powder
- Nail clipper
- Pin brush
- Protein coat conditioner
- Pure boar bristle brush
- Scissors
- Slicker brush
- Tearless protein shampoo
- Thinning shears
- Undercoat rake

GROOMING PROCEDURE

1. Spray the entire coat with protein coat conditioner. This adds body to the coat and helps repair split ends. Brush through the entire coat with an undercoat rake. This will loosen up the coat and remove dead undercoat. Start at the rear of the dog at the bottom of the skirt area. Work in sections, using your other hand to lift the hair ahead of the section you are working on. Work through the entire dog from the back to the neck area. Then brush through the coat with a slicker brush to remove the top dead coat. Work vigorously. The more hair you remove now, the less hair you need to wash and dry.

2. Swab the ears with a cotton ball moistened with ear cleaner. This will remove dirt and control ear odor. Follow this with a dry cotton ball, and dust the ears with medicated ear powder.

3. Cut the nails with a guillotine-type nail clipper. Nails should be cut monthly.

4. Check between the foot pads and under the feet for burrs, tar, etc. Scissor the hair under the feet to prevent debris from adhering. Trim any hair around the paw that touches the ground or grows out between the paws with thinning shears.

5. Bathe the dog with a tearless protein shampoo that is pH-alkaline. This will add fullness and body to the coat and restructure damaged hair.

6. Use a high-velocity dryer to blow excess water off the dog while he is still in the tub. This will speed up the drying time and help prevent the coat from becoming overly dry. Cage dry the dog until the hair is damp. Then, finish drying on the table using a blow dryer and a pin brush to separate all the hair and remove all of the loose coat.

7. Brush the entire coat and be sure to brush down to the skin, using the dryer to style and separate the hair. Follow by combing the entire coat, using the fine part of the comb on the soft hair behind the ears.

GROOMING PROCEDURE

1. Spray the entire coat with protein coat conditioner. This adds body to the coat and helps repair split ends. Brush through the entire coat with a large pin brush and wood utility comb. Use a slicker brush to break up the matted area. Start at the rear of the dog at the bottom of the skirt area. Work in sections, using your other hand to lift the hair ahead of the section you are working on. Work through the entire dog from the back to the neck area. Comb the entire coat with a molting comb to pull out deep, dead undercoat. Then brush through the coat with a slicker brush to remove the top dead coat. Work vigorously. The more hair you remove now, the less hair you need to wash and dry.

2. Swab the ears with a cotton ball moistened with ear cleaner. This will remove dirt and control ear odor. Follow this with a dry cotton ball, and dust the ears with medicated ear powder.

3. Cut the nails with a guillotine-type nail clipper. Nails should be cut monthly.

4. Wipe the inside corners of the eyes with a water-moistened cotton ball.

5. Bathe the dog with a tearless protein shampoo that is pH-alkaline. This will add fullness and body to the coat and restructure damaged hair.

6. Use a high-velocity dryer to blow excess water off the dog while he is still in the tub. This will speed up the drying time and help prevent the coat from becoming overly dry. Cage dry the dog until the hair is damp. Then, finish drying on the table using a blow dryer and a pin brush to separate all the hair and remove all of the loose coat. Finish with a steel comb through the entire coat, paying special attention to the fine hair behind the ears. Use the fine side of the comb for this area.

7. Scissor any long hair under the tail that hangs over the anus. Be sure the anus is clear, and then thin down under the tail area so it does not collect dirt.

Bernese Mountain Dog

TOOLS AND EQUIPMENT

- Cotton balls
- Ear cleaner
- High-velocity dryer
- Large pin brush
- Long-hair molting comb (#565)
- Medicated ear powder
- Nail clipper (extra large)
- Protein coat conditioner
- Pure boar bristle brush
- Scissors
- Slicker brush
- Steel comb (fine/medium)
- Tearless protein shampoo
- Thinning shears
- Wood utility comb

Bichon Frise

TOOLS AND EQUIPMENT

- Blunt-end scissors
- Coat conditioner
- Comb, 8½ inch (22 cm) stainless steel
- Dematting spray
- Grooming table
- Hair dryer
- Hemostat or tweezers
- Nail clipper
- Pin brush
- Scissors (long, straight grooming shears)
- Slicker brush
- Tearless shampoo (for white dogs)
- Thinning shears
- Towels

GROOMING PROCEDURE

1. Never bathe a matted Bichon because this will only worsen the mats and ruin the coat. The coat must be completely brushed out; if there are mats, pull them apart with your fingers. Use a good dematting spray and a comb as you work, and most important, be patient!

2. Prior to bathing, stray hair should be removed from the ear canals with a hemostat.

3. Nails should be short, so trim them to the pink vein (known as the quick) with a nail clipper.

4. Hair should be trimmed between the foot pads with blunt-end scissors.

5. Bichons should be bathed every 2 weeks, or at least once a month, to keep them clean. Wet the dog completely with water. Shampoo and rinse. Repeat the shampoo step, and rinse well so that no shampoo is left in the coat. Shampoo residue can cause hair breakage or skin problems.

6. Apply coat conditioner now (while the dog is wet) or when he is slightly towel dried. Then start brushing with a very soft slicker brush or pin brush (preferably the slicker).

7. The dog's coat must be brushed while the coat is being fluff dried. This is the only way to achieve the "powder puff" look, whereby the hair stands out away from the body, and it also straightens the Bichon's curly coat. Dry a small area at a time, using a slicker or pin brush. Brush the hair away from the body, making sure the coat is completely dry.

8. After the dog is dry, comb out the hair, lifting it away from the body. Do the entire coat.

9. Keep in mind the "powder puff" look while scissoring, constantly combing the hair away from the body and trimming a little at a time (scissor in front of a mirror, if possible, to help check the overall look). A Bichon coat that is left to grow too long will start to break off and also will part down the middle. The Bichon coat should be scissored every 4 or 5 weeks to achieve and keep that rounded "powder puff" look.

10. Facing the Bichon's head, comb the hair that hangs down in front of his eyes up and toward the nose. Laying the scissors in front of the eyes and across the top part of the nose, cut off that portion of the hair that covers the eyes. Do not extend beyond the outside corners of the eyes.

11. Carefully remove the hair that grows up from the muzzle at the inside corners of the eyes. Part the hair on the dog's muzzle and comb it down.

12. Round off the top part of the head, being careful not to make an indentation at the ear, blending the head into the ears and beard. The result should be a half-moon shape.

13. The beard should not be cut, unless it looks out of proportion to the head.

14. If there is too much hair under the ears, carefully lift each ear and thin the hair slightly with thinning shears. This makes them fall naturally. Continue to round off the head.

15. Turn the dog to check his profile. To achieve that rounded look, trim the hair from the top of the eye up and over the head to the back of the skull. Do the same for the other side.

16. The beard hair begins at the chin and extends back to the dog's throat and around to the back of the ears. Make certain that you scissor the hair on the chest and around the shoulders while blending into the neck. At this time, check the withers to determine where the neck starts and where the back line begins. Begin scissoring the neck and blending— in a curve—into the back of the skull. The hair on the neck is left longer to show the neck.

17. Working from the chest and shoulders, scissor the front legs so that they appear straight when viewed head on, but cylindrical when viewed from a distance.

18. Trim the hair between the legs, so as to create a neat, rounded appearance, blending into a bottom line when viewed from the side. Do not indent at the feet.

19. The topline, which begins at the shoulders and ends at the tail, should be smooth and level. Make sure the hair along the topline is shorter than it is on the neck.

20. Continue scissoring down the sides to create a round look, and blend into the bottom line, curving to follow the line of the body. It is important for the bottom line to look neat.

21. When looking at a Bichon's rear, envision a horseshoe held with the curved side up. Scissor the hindquarters and legs in a rounded horseshoe shape to blend with the rest of the body.

22. The inside of the back legs, when scissored, should resemble the slope of a tent.

23. The hair on the tail should be left long; trim short only the hair around the base of the tail (the anus) for cleanliness.

Keep in mind that the Bichon Frise is not groomed in the same way as a Poodle. With the Bichon, the look to achieve is an all-over rounded "powder puff" look. The Bichon Frise has a coat that does not shed; however, frequent brushing is needed to remove dead hair and to avoid matting. The adult Bichon has a double coat, the outercoat being composed of guard hairs and the undercoat of soft hair. The guard coat starts to appear at about one year of age, and it may take a few months to change completely. During this time, extra attention must be given to brushing the coat so it does not mat.

Black and Tan Coonhound

TOOLS AND EQUIPMENT

- Cotton balls
- Ear cleaner
- Hound glove
- Nail clipper (guillotine or scissor)
- Rubber brush
- Shampoo (all-purpose or dark coat)
- Spray conditioner or coat gloss
- Straight scissors
- Styptic powder

GROOMING PROCEDURE

1. Cut the nails by removing only the tips; avoid cutting into the quick. If the nail bleeds, apply styptic powder to stop the bleeding. Any rough edges may be smoothed with a file.

2. Clean the ears with a liquid ear cleaner. Apply the cleaner to a cotton ball and wipe accumulated dirt and wax from all crevices of both ears.

3. Bathe the dog in a shampoo of your choice. A rubber brush may be used to lather the dog; this removes any dead hair. When cleaning the face and ears, special attention should be given to any folds of skin. Rinse the dog thoroughly. A conditioning rinse may be applied to help cut down on dandruff.

4. Towel dry the dog, and complete the drying in a cage dryer.

5. Brush the dog with a hound glove to remove any remaining dead hair and to help the hair lie smoothly.

6. If desired, the whiskers and eyebrows may be removed with straight scissors.

7. Lightly spray the entire coat with a spray conditioner or coat gloss, and buff with a clean, dry cloth until the coat is shiny.

The coat of a Black and Tan Coonhound should appear shiny, lying close to the body. Grooming should be done every 8 to 12 weeks.

GROOMING PROCEDURE

1. Prior to bathing, the Bloodhound should be brushed to remove all dead coat.

2. The inner ear is cleaned by swabbing with a cotton ball moistened with a good-quality ear cleaner. Check for signs of infection. The Bloodhound's long ears might have crusted edges due to dried-on food debris. These edges can be moistened with mineral oil before bathing.

3. The nails are then cut. Be careful not to cut the quick.

4. The folds of facial skin should be examined for any soreness or debris before bathing.

5. Bathe the dog with proper shampoo for skin type and coat conditioner.

6. The Bloodhound can be cage dried.

7. After drying, the facial wrinkles should be checked again to be certain no dampness remains. An application of baby powder in these areas will prevent them from becoming irritated.

8. Scissor all facial whiskers.

9. Undersides of the foot pads should be checked, and excess hair should be scissored.

10. Elbows, hocks, and pasterns may be sore. Application of aloe cream is helpful.

11. Application of lanolin coat conditioner is the final step. This can be rubbed and brushed into the coat.

TOOLS AND EQUIPMENT

- Aloe cream
- Baby powder
- Cotton balls
- Ear cleaner
- Lanolin coat conditioner
- Mineral oil
- Nail clipper
- Scissors
- Stiff slicker or bristle brush
- Styptic powder

Border Collie

TOOLS AND EQUIPMENT

- Cotton balls
- Eye drops (eye stain remover)
- Matt-splitting comb
- Medicated ear powder
- Metal comb (medium)
- Metal rake
- Nail clipper
- Oster A-5 clipper/#10 blade
- Scissors
- Slicker brush
- Thinning shears

GROOMING PROCEDURE

1. Thoroughly brush the entire coat with a slicker brush, removing any mats or tangles with a mat-splitting comb and/or metal rake.

2. Comb through the coat to remove all loosened hair.

3. Clean the ears using medicated ear powder, and lightly pluck stray hair from the insides.

4. Clean the eyes by wiping them with a cotton ball that has been moistened with eye drops. This will also help remove any stains.

5. Cut the tips of the nails with a nail clipper, being careful not to cut the quick.

6. With scissors, snip the whiskers from the muzzle, under the chin, the sides of the face, and above the eyes. [Note: Clipping the whiskers is a decision to be left to the owner.]

7. With a #10 blade on the Oster clipper, shave the stomach from groin to navel and down the insides of the thighs.

8. Shave the anal area, being certain not to put the blade in direct contact with the skin (⅛ to ¼ inch [0.3 to 0.6 cm] each side).

9. Put a cotton ball in each ear (this prevents water from entering the ear canal), and bathe the dog. Cage dry him.

10. With scissors, cut stray hair from between the pads and toes of the feet and around the edges.

11. With scissors or thinning shears, clip stray hair from around the ankles on the front feet and from the hocks to the feet on the hind legs, thus giving a neat appearance.

12. With scissors, trim the edges of the leg fringes and the lower fringe on the tail.

13. Brush and comb through the coat.

The Border Collie should be groomed every 8 to 10 weeks. The ears should be checked weekly and cleaned if necessary, and the nails should be checked monthly and cut if necessary.

GROOMING PROCEDURE

1. Brush the coat with a pure boar bristle brush to stimulate the growth of new coat and to thin down the undercoat. Use a slicker brush on heavy areas and to help remove dead undercoat. Comb thoroughly with the coarse side of a comb.

2. Swab the ears with a cotton ball moistened with ear cleaner. This will remove dirt and control ear odor. Follow with a dry cotton ball, and dust the ears with medicated ear powder. To remove stray hair inside the ears, pluck with your fingers or use ear forceps.

3. Cut the nails with a guillotine-type nail clipper. Nails should be cut monthly.

4. Check between the foot pads and under the feet for burrs, tar, etc. Scissor the hair under the foot even with the pads to prevent debris from adhering. With thinning shears, trim any hair around the paw that touches the ground or grows out between the toes. Do not expose the nails.

5. Trim the hair around the anus with scissors, and remove any long hair under the tail that hangs over the anus and that may become soiled.

6. Bathe the dog with a tearless terrier shampoo that adds body and texture to the hair and does not soften the coat.

7. Cage dry until damp. Finish drying on the table using a blow dryer and a pure bristle brush. Thoroughly comb the entire dog with a medium comb.

8. Use a stripping knife or thinning shears to remove the hair between the ears and the excess hair on the side of the head and cheeks. The skull should be clean and look broad between the ears, and the hair should blend from the head into the throat without looking clumpy. If you use a stripping knife, use it only for the purpose of gripping the hair and not cutting it. The hair is pulled in the direction of the natural lie of the hair, never against the grain.

9. The ears should look clean and smooth. Remove wisps of hair at the top of the ears, fringes on the ears, and long hair on the edges by pulling with your fingers. Do not cut with scissors. The hair pulls out quite easily.

10. The eyebrow line at the outer corner of the eye should show. Use scissors to trim the eyebrow short. No hair should protrude away from the eye at the outside corner. The eye should have clear vision, so pluck out any hair on the stop that protrudes in front of the eye. Do not strip out in front of the cheeks.

11. Trim straggly hair in the moustache and whiskers.

continued

Border Terrier

TOOLS AND EQUIPMENT

- Cotton balls
- Ear cleaner
- Ear forceps
- Medicated ear powder
- Nail clipper
- Protein coat conditioner
- Pure boar bristle brush
- Slicker brush
- Steel comb (medium/coarse)
- Stripping knife
- Tearless terrier shampoo
- Thinning shears

12. With thinning shears, tip any straggly hair on the neck and back, under the neck, on the brisket, between the front legs, and on the belly. Neaten and define the tuck-up. Point the shears down and angle under the dog toward the feet on the opposite side. Tipping helps the coat stand up and out.

13. Trim inside the thigh on the rear legs and from the crotch down. Tip the rear hock to create a perpendicular line from hock to ground. Comb and remove stray hairs that are down the front portion of the leg, rounding the leg and defining the stifle. The lower portion of the rear leg should form a cylinder when viewed from any angle.

14. Tip straggly hair on the front legs and shape the feet to give a rounded appearance. Blend the feet into the leg furnishings.

15. Thin the tail at the base to make it blend smoothly into the body. Remove any long fringes on the underside of the tail with thinning shears. Taper the tail to a rounded point at the end.

16. Top brush the coat with a pure bristle brush sprayed with protein coat conditioner to add brilliance and fragrance.

GROOMING PROCEDURE

1. Nails should be cut by removing only the tips and avoiding the quick. If the nail bleeds, apply styptic powder to stop the bleeding. Any rough nail edges may be smoothed with a file.

2. Clean the ears with a liquid cleaner. Apply the cleaner to a cotton ball and wipe accumulated dirt and wax from all crevices in both ears.

3. Brush through the entire coat to remove any matted or dead hair.

4. Bathe the dog in a shampoo of your choice. Rinse thoroughly. A conditioning rinse may be used to help cut down on static electricity.

5. Towel dry the dog. A high-velocity dryer may be used at this time to blow off excess water from the coat. Finish drying with a regular blow dryer while brushing the coat in the direction of its growth. When the hair on the very top of the back is just damp dry, complete the drying while brushing the coat against the growth to make the hair stand more erect. This helps to accentuate the distinctive topline. When the dog is dry, comb through the coat to check for any tangles that might have been missed.

6. With scissors, remove hair from between the foot pads and any excess hair on the bottom of the foot. The hair on the pasterns and the hocks may be neatened up also.

7. The whiskers, along with the eyebrows, may be removed if desired, and any tufts of hair sticking out from the ears may also be removed.

8. The hair around the anus may be scissored, too.

The Borzoi should be presented in a natural state. Any grooming should be done only to tidy up the outline. This grooming procedure should be done every 6 to 8 weeks.

TOOLS AND EQUIPMENT

- Comb
- Cotton balls
- Ear cleaner
- High-velocity dryer
- Nail clipper (guillotine or scissor)
- Shampoo (conditioning or whitening)
- Slicker brush
- Spray conditioner or coat gloss
- Straight scissors
- Styptic powder

Boston Terrier

TOOLS AND EQUIPMENT

- Baby powder or talcum powder
- Coarse hand towel
- Cotton balls
- Ear cleaner
- Eye stain cleaner
- Fine thinning shears
- Medicated ear powder
- Mink oil
- Nail clipper
- Pure boar bristle brush
- Scissors
- Tearless protein shampoo

GROOMING PROCEDURE

1. Brush with a pure boar bristle brush.

2. Swab the ears with a cotton ball that has been moistened with ear cleaner. This will remove dirt and control ear odor. Follow with a dry cotton ball, and dust the ears with medicated ear powder.

3. Cut the nails with a guillotine-type nail clipper. Nails should be cut monthly.

4. Check between the foot pads and under the feet for burrs, tar, etc.

5. Wipe inside the corners of the eyes with a water-moistened cotton ball. Remove any eye stains under and around the eyes with a cotton ball that has been moistened with eye stain cleaner.

6. Wrinkles on the face should be cleaned with a water-moistened cotton ball. Dry and powder.

7. Bathe the dog with a tearless protein shampoo that is pH-alkaline. This will add body to the coat and restructure damaged hair.

8. Cage dry until damp. Finish drying on the table using a blow dryer and a pure bristle brush.

9. The whiskers may be removed with scissors to improve expression (optional).

10. Any hair that detracts from the sleek appearance, or any dark hair that overlaps white areas of the coat, can be scissored. Use fine thinning shears. To improve appearance, smooth out any overly heavy patches of hair.

11. Finish with a mist of mink oil to create a brilliant shine. To maintain the dark coat, use mink oil with PABA sunscreen to reduce fading. Polish with a coarse towel.

GROOMING PROCEDURE

Bouvier des Flandres

1. Spray the entire coat with protein coat conditioner. This adds body to the coat and helps repair split ends. Brush through the entire coat with a slicker brush. Start at the rear of the dog, at the bottom of the skirt area. Work in sections through entire coat from the back to the neck area. Comb the entire coat with a molting comb to pull out dead undercoat. Starting at the head, backbrush the entire coat with the pin brush. Then brush it back into place. Brush the legs up and then down.

2. Swab the ears with a cotton ball that has been moistened with ear cleaner. This will remove dirt and control ear odor. Follow this with a dry cotton ball, and dust the ears with medicated ear powder.

3. Cut the nails with a guillotine-type nail clipper. Nails should be cut monthly.

4. Check between the foot pads and under the feet for burrs, tar, etc. Clip the hair between the pads of the feet with a #10 blade. Trim any hair around the paws that touches the ground, and neaten the entire foot.

5. Bathe the dog with a tearless terrier shampoo. This will add texture and body to the coat, yet it won't soften it.

6. Use a high-velocity dryer to blow excess water off the dog while he is still in the tub. This will speed up the drying time and help prevent the coat from becoming overly dry. Cage dry the dog until the hair is damp. Then, finish drying on the table using a blow dryer and a pin brush to separate all the hair and remove all of the loose coat. Finish by combing through the entire coat with a steel comb.

7. Shave the ears on both sides with a #10 blade. Shave from base to tip. Trim the outside edge, using the thumb as a protective guide to prevent nicks. Give a neat appearance, forming a sharply defined line on the outer edge of the ears. Ears should stand out from the ruff of the neck.

8. Shorten the hair on the crown of the head and at the sides of the face so that there is good contrast between the head and ears. Do it with a coarse stripping knife, taking the hair firmly between the thumb and edge of the knife. Turn the blade and pull a few hairs at a time in the direction of hair growth. You may also pluck the hair. Pluck by holding hair between the thumb and index finger, turning your wrist and pulling at the same time. Stripping or plucking keeps the coat uneven and natural looking. Do not use clippers or scissors to shorten this area. Skull hair should be removed just above the eyebrows, back across the skull and blending into the longer hair behind the ears.

continued

TOOLS AND EQUIPMENT

- Cotton balls
- Ear cleaner
- High-velocity dryer
- Large pin brush
- Long-hair molting comb (#565)
- Medicated ear powder
- Mink oil
- Nail clipper (extra large)
- Oster A-5 clipper/#10 blade
- Pure boar bristle brush
- Scissors
- Slicker brush
- Steel comb (medium/coarse)
- Stripping knife
- Tearless protein shampoo
- Thinning shears

73

9. Cheeks should be flattened from the back corner of the eye and the corner of the mouth. Comb and strip, if necessary, the side of the cheeks to avoid protruding cheeks.

10. Eyebrows are long and erect. Comb forward over the eyes. Accentuate by slightly parting with a stripping knife. Eyes should be visible. Shape the eyebrows to give expression. Scissor diagonally from the outside corner to the center of the eye. Do not trim or remove hair between the eyes; comb it down over the muzzle.

11. Brush the Bouvier's beard outward and upward to give width to the muzzle. At the bottom of the beard, divide the hair in half from the middle of the jaw, and comb outward and forward to add width. Neaten the beard but leave it very thick.

12. Comb the throat and chest hair down. Use thinning shears to taper the hair toward the shoulder on either side. This gets the coat to lie smoothly and blend into the shoulders.

13. Comb in the direction the hair grows. Comb the back and upper side to the rear. Comb the lower side down.

14. The brisket is deep, at least to the point of the elbow, with nice tuckup. Use thinning shears to form and neaten the tuckup. Point shears down and angled under the leg toward the feet on the opposite side.

15. With scissors, remove hair that covers the anus and trim hair on the underside of the tail. Shorten the coat at the back of the rump with thinning shears.

16. Scissor around the circumference of the foot to develop a cat's paw.

17. Comb the front legs straight down. Strip out tufts of excess hair at the elbows. Neaten the legs to give a massive, clean line.

18. Comb the rear legs straight down. Thin excess hair at the breeches. Comb hocks back, and remove wild hair with scissors.

Owners requesting a shorter coat and less coat to maintain may ask that this breed be clipped. If so, use an 8½ inch (22 cm) blade on the head, and blend the body down with a #4 blade; or for a longer, nicer look, use a #10 blade and a #1 guard. Clipped areas are blended into patterned areas above to achieve a similar look.

GROOMING PROCEDURE

1. Nails should be cut by removing the tips; avoid cutting the quick. If the nail bleeds, apply styptic powder to stop the bleeding. Any rough nail edges may be smoothed by filing.

2. Clean the ears with a liquid cleaner. Apply cleaner to a cotton ball and wipe accumulated wax and dirt from all crevices in both ears.

3. Bathe the dog in a shampoo of your choice. A whitening shampoo may be used on any white areas. To help remove dead hair while bathing, use a rubber brush to lather the dog. Rinse the dog thoroughly. An after-bath conditioning rinse may be applied to help control dandruff.

4. Towel dry the dog, and place him in a cage dryer until he is completely dry.

5. When the dog is dry, any additional dead hair may be removed with a curry brush. Rub the dog with the curry in circular motions against the lay of hair.

6. With small straight shears, remove hair from the edges of the ears. Whiskers and eyebrows may be removed at an owner's request; otherwise they may be left alone. Hair in the tuckup area and under the tail may be trimmed with straight shears. Any seams (where two different directions of hair growth come together) may be blended with blending shears.

7. As the final step, spray a small amount of spray conditioner or coat gloss on the dog, and buff to a shiny gloss with a clean cloth.

The properly groomed Boxer should have a crisp outline, with a shiny coat that lies smooth and tight to the body. Grooming should be done every 10 to 12 weeks.

TOOLS AND EQUIPMENT

- Blending shears
- Cotton balls
- Ear cleaner
- Hard rubber curry brush
- Nail clipper (guillotine or scissor)
- Rubber brush
- Shampoo (all-purpose or conditioning)
- Spray conditioner
- Straight shears
- Styptic powder

Briard

GROOMING PROCEDURE

1. Spray the entire coat with protein coat conditioner. This adds body to the coat and helps repair split ends. If the coat is matted, spray the matted areas with tangle remover. Let the dog sit 10 to 15 minutes until both products on the coat are absorbed.

2. After 15 minutes, spray the entire coat with coat gloss. This lubricates the coat for easier brushing and combing, and it prevents hair breakage. Brush through the entire coat with a pin brush, using a slicker brush and a utility comb in the matted areas of the coat. Start at the rear of the dog, at the bottom of the skirt area. Work in sections, lifting the hair and brushing it layer by layer. Mist each section with coat gloss as you work. Never brush dry-coated. Work through the entire coat from the back to the neck area. Never bathe the Briard when he has mats in his coat; water will tighten the mats and make them harder to remove.

3. Swab the ears with a cotton ball that has been moistened with ear cleaner. This will remove dirt and control ear odor. Follow this with a dry cotton ball, and dust the ears with medicated ear powder. With your fingers or ear forceps, pull out any dead hair inside the ears.

4. Cut the nails with a guillotine-type nail clipper. Nails should be cut monthly.

5. Wipe the inside corners of the eyes with a water-moistened cotton ball. Remove any eye stains under and around the eyes with a cotton ball that has been moistened with eye stain remover.

6. Check between the foot pads and under the feet for burrs, tar, etc. Scissor the hair under the feet even with the pads to prevent debris from adhering. Trim any hair on which the dog might walk.

7. Scissor any long hair under the tail that hangs over the anus and that may become soiled with fecal matter. Scissor the hair around the anus and be sure it is clear. Trim or blend down under the tail area if the hair there is profuse; otherwise the hair may collect fecal matter.

8. Bathe the dog with a tearless protein shampoo that is pH-alkaline. This will add fullness and body to the coat and restructure damaged hair.

9. Use a high-velocity dryer to blow excess water off the dog while he is still in the tub. This will speed up the drying time and help prevent the coat from becoming overly dry. Cage dry the dog until the hair is damp. Then, finish drying on the table using a blow dryer and a pin brush to separate all the hair and remove all of the loose coat. Finish with a steel comb by combing through the entire coat, paying special attention to the fine hair behind the ears. Use the fine side of the comb for this area.

10. If the neck, base of the tail, or any part of the coat appears clumpy, comb out the excess undercoat rather than trim it with thinning shears.

11. Comb the head with a natural part. If the forelock is profuse, thin it with thinning shears. Comb back from the dog's face and thin underneath the forelock. Do not thin the top layer. The forelock should not obscure the dog's vision nor distort the shape of the head.

12. Brush the tail into a full plume.

13. Spray coat gloss lightly from above and allow it to mist over the coat. Brush with a pure bristle brush to add a beautiful gloss and aroma.

Brittany Spaniel

TOOLS AND EQUIPMENT

- Cotton balls
- Ear cleaner
- High-velocity dryer
- Hound glove
- Medicated ear powder
- Nail clipper
- Oster A-5 clipper/#7, #10 blades
- Pin brush
- Protein coat conditioner
- Pure boar bristle brush
- Scissors
- Short-hair molting comb (#564)
- Slicker brush
- Steel comb (fine/medium)
- Stripping knife
- Tearless protein shampoo
- Thinning shears

GROOMING PROCEDURE

1. Spray the entire coat with protein coat conditioner. This adds body to the coat and helps repair split ends. Brush through the entire coat with a molting comb. This will remove the dead undercoat. Start at the rear of the dog, at the bottom of the skirt area. Work through the entire dog from the back to the neck area. Then brush through the coat with a slicker brush to remove the top dead coat. Work vigorously. The more hair you remove now, the less hair you need to wash and dry.

2. Swab the ears with a cotton ball that has been moistened with ear cleaner. This will remove dirt and control ear odor. Follow this with a dry cotton ball, and dust the ears with medicated ear powder.

3. Cut the nails with a guillotine-type nail clipper. Nails should be cut monthly.

4. Check between the foot pads and under the feet for burrs, tar, etc. Scissor the hair under the feet to prevent debris from adhering. With thinning shears, trim any hair around the paw that touches the ground or grows out between the paws.

5. Use a #10 blade to clip the hair around the anus. Just clear the area and do not use heavy pressure. Scissor any long hair under the tail that hangs over the anus and that may become soiled.

6. Bathe the dog with a tearless protein shampoo that is pH-alkaline. This will add fullness and body to the coat and restructure damaged hair.

7. Use a high-velocity dryer to blow excess water off the dog while he is still in the tub. This will speed up the drying time and help prevent the coat from becoming overly dry. Cage dry the dog until the hair is damp. Then, finish drying on the table using a blow dryer and a pin brush to separate all the hair and remove all of the loose coat.

8. To keep the coat flat and give it a more sleek appearance, pin a large towel around the dog while it is drying. Leave the towel on until the coat is almost completely dry.

9. Brush the entire coat with a pin brush and be sure to brush to the skin, using the dryer to style and separate the hair. Follow by combing the entire coat in the natural direction of the hair growth to encourage a flat, sleek look. Use the fine part of the comb on the soft hair behind the ears.

10. The whiskers may be removed with scissors to improve the expression (optional).

11. Use a stripping knife to remove any straggly hair on the top of the head, around the ears, and under the neck. With thinning shears, blend the hair where the ear joins the skull. Use thinning shears on the underside of the ear to encourage the ear to lie close to the head.

12. Blend the neck and shoulders to lie smoothly. Use the thinning shears to blend the hair under the neck to the breastbone. There should be no thick ruff left, just a smooth taper.

13. Lightly strip any straggly hair on the back. This can also be carded out, holding a #15 blade in your hand and stripping through the coat. Any work on the back should not be noticeable. You should remove only hair that does not conform to the overall desired outline.

14. Use thinning shears if the leg feathering is profuse; scissor the feathering evenly, creating a taper. Remove any long, uneven hair from the hock down to the bottom of the foot.

15. Spray a pure bristle brush with protein coat conditioner and topbrush the coat to add brilliance and fragrance.

Brussels Griffon

TOOLS AND EQUIPMENT

- Blending shears
- Comb
- Cotton balls
- Ear cleaner
- Nail clipper (guillotine or scissor)
- Shampoo (all-purpose or texturizing)
- Slicker brush
- Straight shears
- Stripping knife
- Styptic powder

GROOMING PROCEDURE

1. Nails should be cut by removing only the tips; avoid cutting the quick. If the nail bleeds, apply styptic powder to stop the bleeding. Any rough nail edges may be removed with a file.

2. Using your fingers, pull out any hair that grows in the ear canal. Clean the ears with a liquid cleaner. Apply the cleaner to a cotton ball and wipe accumulated dirt and wax from all crevices in both ears.

3. Brush out the entire coat with a slicker brush to remove any dead coat and to remove any matted hair.

4. With a stripping knife, pluck out all dead and loose hair that grows from the middle of the skull (on top of the head) down to the tail. Strip the hair down over the shoulders to the elbows, over the ribcage to the loin, and down over the thighs. The hair that is left should be of uniform length and lie smoothly.

5. Bathe the dog in a shampoo of your choice, and rinse thoroughly.

6. Towel dry the dog, and place him in a cage dryer to finish drying.

7. With straight scissors, cut any hair that grows in between the foot pads and then round the foot.

8. With blending shears, remove the hair on the outside of the ear leather from base to tip. With straight shears, cut the hair even with the outer edge of the ear leather.

9. With blending shears, slightly shape the face to give a rounded appearance. Any hair growing in the inner corner of the eye may be removed.

10. The legs may be shaped with blending shears to neaten them up yet leave them in a natural look.

11. The hair growing down from the chest should be shaped with blending shears to taper it slightly from the elbow to the loin.

12. The hair around the anus may be scissored. The tail may be neatened up with blending shears.

The Brussels Griffon should look neat and natural and should be groomed every 6 to 8 weeks.

GROOMING PROCEDURE

1. Nails should be cut by removing the tips only; avoid cutting the quick. If the nail bleeds, apply styptic powder to stop the bleeding. Any rough nail edges may be smoothed with a file.

2. Clean the ears with a liquid ear cleaner. Apply the cleaner to a cotton ball and remove accumulated dirt and wax from the crevices of both ears.

3. Bathe the dog in a shampoo of your choice. Special attention should be given to the folds of skin around the face, legs, and body. The rubber brush may be used to lather the dog and to help remove dead hair. Rinse the dog thoroughly.

4. Towel dry the dog, and continue drying him with a blow dryer. The dog may be cage dried.

5. Brush the dog with a hound glove to remove dead hair and to make the coat lie smoothly.

6. Apply a light spray of coat conditioner or coat gloss, and buff with a clean cloth until shiny.

7. Whiskers may be removed with scissors if desired.

The Bulldog should be groomed every 8 to 12 weeks.

TOOLS AND EQUIPMENT

- Cotton balls
- Ear cleaner
- Hound glove
- Nail clipper (guillotine or scissor)
- Rubber brush
- Scissors
- Shampoo (all-purpose or whitening)
- Spray conditioner or coat gloss
- Styptic powder

Bullmastiff

TOOLS AND EQUIPMENT

- Chamois cloth
- Cotton balls
- Eye drops (eye stain remover)
- Lanolin coat conditioner
- Medicated ear powder
- Medicated talcum powder
- Nail clipper
- Scissors
- Sisal (natural bristle) brush

GROOMING PROCEDURE

1. Thoroughly brush the entire coat.

2. Clean the ears using medicated ear powder.

3. Clean the eyes by wiping them with eye stain remover on a cotton ball. This will also help to remove any stains from the corners of the eyes.

4. Cut the tips of the nails with a nail clipper, being careful not to cut the quick.

5. Using a damp cotton ball, clean the insides of the lips, making certain that you remove any trapped food particles.

6. With scissors, clip the whiskers from the muzzle, under the chin, and from the sides of the face and above the eyes. [Note: Clipping the whiskers is a decision to be left to the owner.]

7. Put a cotton ball in each ear (this prevents water from entering the ear canal), and bathe the dog. Cage dry him.

8. Clean the furrows on the face with a cotton ball that has been moistened with eye stain remover; daily use of this product, or medicated talcum powder, on the furrows will keep them clean and help prevent soreness and infection.

9. Put a few drops of lanolin coat conditioner into the palms of your hands, rub them together lightly, and gently massage into the coat.

10. Brush the coat with a sisal brush (to distribute the conditioner), and then rub the coat with a chamois cloth to give it a nice sheen.

The Bullmastiff rarely needs bathing if he is brushed by the owner regularly. The lanolin coat conditioner can be used on a monthly basis to maintain a healthy, shiny coat. The ears should be checked weekly and cleaned if necessary, and the nails should be checked monthly and clipped if needed.

GROOMING PROCEDURE

1. Brush the coat with a rubber brush. Follow with a thorough brushing with a pure bristle brush.

2. Swab the ears with a cotton ball that has been moistened with ear cleaner. This will remove dirt and control ear odor. Follow with a dry cotton ball, and dust the ears with medicated ear powder.

3. Cut the nails with a guillotine-type nail clipper. Nails should be cut monthly.

4. Wipe the inside corners of the eyes with a water-moistened cotton ball. Remove any eye stains under and around the eye with a cotton ball moistened with eye stain cleaner.

5. Bathe the dog with a tearless whitening shampoo that is pH-alkaline balanced to enhance the whiteness of the coat.

6. Cage dry until damp. Finish drying on the table using a blow dryer and a pure bristle brush.

7. The whiskers may be removed with scissors to improve expression (optional).

8. Finish with a mist of mink oil to create a brilliant shine, and brush it in with a pure bristle brush.

TOOLS AND EQUIPMENT

- Cotton balls
- Ear cleaner
- Eye stain cleaner
- Medicated ear powder
- Mink oil
- Nail clipper (extra-large)
- Pure boar bristle brush
- Rubber brush
- Scissors
- Tearless protein shampoo

Bull Terrier, Miniature

TOOLS AND EQUIPMENT

- Chamois cloth
- Cotton balls
- Eye drops (eye stain remover)
- Lanolin coat conditioner
- Medicated ear powder
- Nail clipper
- Scissors
- Sisal (natural bristle) brush

GROOMING PROCEDURE

1. Brush the entire coat vigorously with a sisal brush.

2. Clean the ears using medicated ear powder.

3. Clean the eyes by wiping them with eye stain remover on a cotton ball. This will also help in removing any stains under and around the eyes.

4. Cut the tips of the nails with a nail clipper, being careful not to cut the quick.

5. With scissors, clip the whiskers from the muzzle, under the chin, the sides of the face, and above the eyes. [Note: Clipping the whiskers is optional; the decision should be made by the dog's owner.]

6. Put a cotton ball in each ear to prevent water from entering the ear canal. Next, bathe the dog thoroughly, and cage dry him.

7. Put a few drops of lanolin coat conditioner into the palms of your hands, rub them together lightly, and gently massage into the coat.

8. Brush the coat with a sisal brush to distribute the conditioner; then lightly rub the coat with a chamois cloth, thus giving it a nice sheen.

The Miniature Bull Terrier, because of his coloring, should be groomed every 6 weeks. The ears should be checked weekly, and the nails should be checked and cut at the grooming session.

GROOMING PROCEDURE

1. Brush the entire coat to remove mats and dead hair.

2. Dust the ears with ear powder.

3. Clip the nails, making sure you do not cut too deeply. If the quick bleeds, apply styptic powder.

4. Clip the hair between the foot pads even with the bottom of the foot.

5. With a #10 blade, clip ½ inch (1 cm) on each side of the anus.

6. Clip the bottom half of the stomach.

7. With a #5, #7, or #8½ blade, clip from the base of the neck to the tip of the tail.

8. Using the shoulder as a guide, clip down the side of the dog, blending the hair into the skirt.

9. With the same blade, clip from the base of the neck, blending the hair down to the breastbone.

10. Using a #10 blade, clip from the base of the ear to the tip on both sides.

11. Scissor the edges of the ears to make them look neat.

12. Remove any hair growing at the inside corners of the eyes.

13. With thinning shears, make the face look round.

14. Make sure that in profile view the eyebrows jut out like an awning or canopy; they should not hang over the eyes.

continued

Cairn Terrier

TOOLS AND EQUIPMENT

- Comb
- Ear powder
- Nail clipper
- Oster A-5 clipper/#5, #7, #8½, #10 blades
- Scissors
- Slicker brush
- Styptic powder
- Thinning shears

Cairn Terrier *continued*

15. Scissor around the edges of the feet to make them look round.

16. At the bottom of the tail, where the hair is left hanging, hold the tail up straight and with thinning shears, give it a Christmas-tree shape, tapering from tip to base.

17. Use thinning shears to cut away any hairs in the coat that stick out or are otherwise not in place.

18. Bathe the dog.

19. Fluff dry the dog or put him in a cage to dry.

20. Brush the dog and repeat any of the previous steps from 4 to 17 in case you did not catch all of the stray hairs.

The Cairn Terrier should be groomed every 4 to 8 weeks.

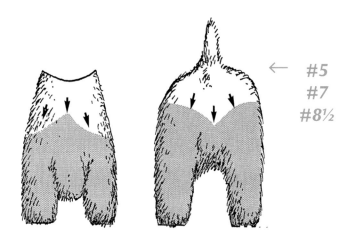

← #5
#7
#8½

← #10

← #5
#7
#8½

GROOMING PROCEDURE

1. Spray the entire coat with protein coat conditioner. This adds body to the coat and helps repair split ends. Brush through the entire coat with a gentle slicker to remove loose hair. Then, to take out loose undercoat, comb with a molting comb made for shorthaired breeds (#564).

2. Swab the ears with a cotton ball that has been moistened with ear cleaner. This will remove dirt and control ear odor. Follow this with a dry cotton ball, and dust the ears with medicated ear powder.

3. Cut the nails with a guillotine-type nail clipper. Nails should be cut monthly.

4. Bathe the dog with a tearless protein shampoo that is pH-alkaline. This will add fullness and body to the coat and restructure damaged hair.

5. Cage dry until damp. Finish drying on the table using a blow dryer and a pure bristle brush. Comb the entire dog thoroughly.

6. Check between the foot pads and under the feet for burrs, tar, etc. Scissor the hair under the feet even with the pads. Trim any hair around the paw that touches the ground and neaten the entire foot. Use thinning shears to trim the hair growing out from between the toes. Be sure to neaten the hair on the back of the rear pasterns.

7. Scissor any long hair under the tail that hangs over the anus. Be sure the anus is clear, and then trim down under the tail area so it does not become soiled.

8. The whiskers may be removed with scissors to improve the expression (optional).

9. Topbrush with a pure bristle brush sprayed with protein coat conditioner to add brilliance and fragrance.

Cardigan Welsh Corgi

TOOLS AND EQUIPMENT

- Cotton balls
- Ear cleaner
- Eye stain remover
- Medicated ear powder
- Nail clipper
- Protein coat conditioner
- Pure boar bristle brush
- Scissors
- Short-hair molting comb (#564)
- Slicker brush (gentle)
- Steel comb (medium/fine)
- Tearless protein shampoo

Cavalier King Charles Spaniel

TOOLS AND EQUIPMENT

- Cotton balls
- Eye drops (eye stain remover)
- Medicated ear powder
- Metal comb (medium)
- Nail clipper
- Oster A-5 clipper/#10 blade
- Scissors
- Slicker brush
- Thinning shears

GROOMING PROCEDURE

1. Brush and comb through the coat with a slicker brush and comb, being certain to remove any tangles.

2. Clean the ears using medicated ear powder and lightly pluck any stray hair from the insides of the ears.

3. Clean the eyes by wiping them with a cotton ball that has been moistened with eye stain remover. This will also help in removing any stains around or under the eyes.

4. Cut the tips of the nails, being careful not to cut the quick.

5. With the scissors, snip the whiskers from the muzzle, under the chin, the sides of the face, and above the eyes. [Note: Clipping the whiskers is a decision to be left to the owner.]

6. Using a #10 blade on an Oster A-5 clipper, shave the anal area, being certain not to put the blade in direct contact with the skin (1½ inches [4 cm] each side). [Note: Shaving this area is a decision best left to the dog's owner.]

7. With a #10 blade, shave the stomach area from groin to navel and down the insides of the thighs. [Note: Again, this is optional, depending on the owner's preference.]

8. Put a cotton ball in each ear to prevent water from entering the ear canal. Bathe the dog and cage dry him.

9. Lightly brush and comb through the coat.

10. With scissors, snip the hair from between the pads and toes of the feet to give a neat appearance.

11. With thinning shears, remove any straggly hair from the hock joints to the feet on the hind legs. Do the same around the ankles on the front legs.

12. Remove straggly hair from the head and the tops of the ears with thinning shears.

13. Comb through the entire coat to remove all loosened hair.

The Cavalier King Charles Spaniel should be groomed every 6 to 8 weeks. The ears should be checked weekly and cleaned if necessary, and the nails should be checked and cut during the grooming session.

GROOMING PROCEDURE

1. Cut the nails by removing only the tips. Avoid cutting the quick. If the nail bleeds, apply styptic powder until the bleeding stops.

2. Clean the ears with a liquid ear cleaner by applying the cleaner to a cotton ball and wiping all accumulated wax and dirt from the crevices of both ears.

3. Brush out the entire dog with a slicker brush to remove any loose or dead hair.

4. Bathe the dog in a shampoo of your choice. Lather well, and rinse the dog thoroughly.

5. Towel off excess water, and finish drying in a cage dryer.

This breed needs no additional grooming, although the whiskers and eyebrows may be removed if desired. A brush may be run through the coat to make it lie close. The Chessie should be groomed every 8 to 12 weeks.

Chesapeake Bay Retriever

TOOLS AND EQUIPMENT

- Cotton balls
- Ear cleaner
- Nail clipper (guillotine or scissor)
- Shampoo (all-purpose)
- Slicker brush
- Styptic powder

Chihuahua, Long Coat

TOOLS AND EQUIPMENT

- Blending shears
- Comb
- Cotton balls
- Ear cleaner
- Nail clipper (guillotine or scissor)
- Shampoo
- Slicker brush
- Styptic powder

GROOMING PROCEDURE

1. Cut the nails by removing the tips only; avoid cutting the quick. If the nail bleeds, apply styptic powder to stop the bleeding. Any rough nail edges may be smoothed with a file.

2. Clean the ears with a liquid ear cleaner. Apply cleaner to a cotton ball and wipe accumulated dirt and wax from the crevices of both ears.

3. Bathe the dog in a shampoo of your choice, and rinse thoroughly. Apply a conditioning rinse to help control static electricity.

4. Towel dry the dog and finish drying him with a dryer while you brush the coat in the direction of its growth. This makes the hair dry smooth and straight.

5. Comb through the entire coat to make sure all tangles are removed.

6. With blending shears, remove the hair that grows in between the toes on the top of the foot.

7. Carefully scissor short the hair around the anus.

The long-coated Chihuahua should have a full ruff around the neck, with long hair on the ears to frame the face. The hair on the tail should be brushed into a full plume. Grooming should be done every 6 to 8 weeks.

GROOMING PROCEDURE

1. Cut the nails by removing the tips only; avoid cutting the quick. If the nail bleeds, apply styptic powder to stop the bleeding. Any rough nail edges may be smoothed with a file.

2. Clean the ears with a liquid ear cleaner. Apply cleaner to a cotton ball and wipe accumulated dirt and wax from the crevices of both ears.

3. Bathe the dog in a shampoo of your choice, and rinse thoroughly. Apply a conditioning rinse if needed. A rubber brush may be used to lather the dog and remove excess dead coat.

4. Towel dry the dog until damp, and continue drying him in a cage with a dryer.

5. With blending shears, remove any stray hairs on the back of the thighs, on the back of the front legs, and on the sides of the neck. Enough hair should be removed only to give the dog a tidy appearance, never enough that it makes the dog look scissored.

The smooth-coated Chihuahua should have a clean outline. Grooming should be done every 6 to 8 weeks.

Chihuahua, Smooth Coat

TOOLS AND EQUIPMENT

- Blending shears
- Bristle brush
- Cotton balls
- Ear cleaner
- Nail clipper (guillotine or scissor)
- Rubber brush
- Shampoo (all-purpose or conditioning)
- Styptic powder

Chinese Crested Dog

TOOLS AND EQUIPMENT

- Aloe-based or baby shampoo
- Baby oil
- Cotton balls
- Eye drops (eye stain remover)
- Medicated ear powder
- Nail clipper
- Soft sisal (natural bristle) brush

GROOMING PROCEDURE

1. Lightly brush the hair tufts.

2. Clean the ears using medicated ear powder, and lightly pluck any stray hair from the inside ear.

3. Clean the eyes by wiping them with a cotton ball that has been moistened with eye stain remover.

4. Cut the tips of the nails with a nail clipper, being careful not to cut the quick.

5. After putting a cotton ball in each ear (this prevents water from entering the ear canal), bathe the dog and gently pat him dry with a soft towel.

6. Fluff dry the tufts of hair.

7. Put a few drops of baby oil into the palms of your hands, rub them together, and gently massage into the skin.

The Chinese Crested Dog may be bathed about every 4 weeks. The owner should use baby oil on the dog twice weekly to keep the skin supple. The ears should be checked weekly and cleaned if necessary, and the nails should be checked monthly and clipped if needed.

GROOMING PROCEDURE

1. Cut the nails by removing the tips; avoid cutting the quick. If the nail bleeds, apply styptic powder to stop the bleeding. Any rough nail edges may be smoothed with a file.

2. Clean the ears with a liquid cleaner. Apply the cleaner to a cotton ball and wipe all accumulated dirt and wax from the crevices of both ears.

3. Bathe the dog in a shampoo of your choice. Lather him with the rubber brush to help remove dead coat. Rinse the dog thoroughly; otherwise, traces of shampoo left on the skin and in the folds of skin may become irritating.

4. Towel dry the dog, and complete the drying with a blow dryer.

5. When the dog is completely dry, brush him with a hound glove to remove any dead or loose hair and to smooth the coat. A light misting of spray conditioner or coat gloss may be applied and buffed shiny with a soft cloth.

6. With the Chinese Shar-Pei, special care should be given to the folds of skin in the wrinkles. Make sure there is no moisture left after the bath and that the folds are completely dry. A light application of baby powder helps keep the wrinkled areas dry and free of irritation.

7. Whiskers may be removed with scissors, if desired.

The completed Chinese Shar-Pei has a well-wrinkled, shiny coat. This grooming procedure should be done every 8 to 12 weeks.

Chinese Shar-Pei

TOOLS AND EQUIPMENT

- Baby powder
- Blow dryer
- Cotton balls
- Ear cleaner
- Hound glove
- Nail clipper (guillotine or scissor)
- Rubber brush
- Scissors
- Shampoo (all-purpose or texturizing)
- Spray coat conditioner or coat gloss
- Styptic powder

Chow Chow

TOOLS AND EQUIPMENT

- Comb (wide-toothed)
- Cotton balls
- Ear cleaner
- High-velocity dryer
- Nail clipper (guillotine or scissor)
- Shampoo (conditioning or all-purpose)
- Slicker brush
- Straight scissors
- Styptic powder

GROOMING PROCEDURE

1. Cut the nails by removing the tips only; avoid cutting the quick. If the nail bleeds, apply styptic powder to stop the bleeding. Any rough nail edges may be smoothed with a file.

2. Clean the ears with a liquid cleaner. Apply the cleaner to a cotton ball and wipe all accumulated dirt and wax from the crevices of both ears.

3. With a slicker brush, brush out the entire coat. As you brush, layer the coat to get down to the skin. This helps remove matting and bunching up of the coat.

4. Bathe the dog with a shampoo of your choice. Rinse thoroughly. A conditioning rinse may be applied to make brushing out the coat easier after the bath.

5. Towel off the dog. A high-velocity dryer may be used at this time to blow off excess water in the coat. Next, use a regular blow dryer while brushing out the coat with a slicker brush. Brush in the direction of hair growth. When the coat is completely dry, comb it through with a wide-toothed comb to check for any bunching of the coat.

6. Carefully scissor the excess hair around the anus.

7. Scissor the hair from underneath the paw and from between the foot pads as well. Any hair that grows in between the toes and on the top of the feet should also be scissored to give a clean, neat appearance. The paws should appear compact and catlike.

8. The whiskers and eyebrows may be removed with scissors if desired.

9. Any excess hair on the back of the hocks should be removed.

Grooming should be done every 4 to 6 weeks.

GROOMING PROCEDURE

1. Nails should be cut by removing the tips only; avoid cutting the quick. If the nail bleeds, apply styptic powder to stop the bleeding. Any rough nail edges may be smoothed by filing.

2. Clean the ears with a liquid cleaner. Apply the cleaner to a cotton ball and wipe all accumulated dirt and wax from the crevices in both ears.

3. Brush the dog thoroughly with a slicker brush to remove any mats or dead coat.

4. Bathe the dog in a shampoo of your choice and rinse him thoroughly. A conditioning rinse may be used after the bath to help cut down on static electricity and to help the coat lie flat.

5. Towel dry the dog, and finish drying with a blow dryer while you brush the hair in the direction of its growth so that it lies smooth.

6. With straight scissors, carefully scissor off the excess hair that grows in between the paw pads.

7. With blending shears remove the hair that grows in between the toes and on the top of the foot. To show the natural outline, the foot should look tidy and compact.

8. Remove excess hair from the backs of the hocks.

9. Ears may be neatened up with blending shears. The hair may be thinned out directly under the ear leather to help the ear lie flat. The hair directly in front of the ear opening also may be removed to increase the air circulation to the ear canal.

10. Excess hair on top of the skull may be smoothed down to give a rather broad and neat appearance. Any "fuzzies" may be removed from the face and muzzle.

11. Excess hair or tufts may be removed from the end of the tail.

12. Remove any stray hairs from the body and legs—not to make them look scissored, but just enough to neaten the appearance.

Clumber Spaniel

TOOLS AND EQUIPMENT

- Blending shears
- Comb
- Cotton balls
- Ear cleaner
- Nail clipper (guillotine or scissor)
- Shampoo (all-purpose or whitening)
- Slicker brush
- Straight shears
- Styptic powder

Cocker Spaniel, American

TOOLS AND EQUIPMENT

- Nail clipper
- Oster A-5 clipper/#5F, #7F, #8½, #10, #15 blades
- Scissors
- Slicker brush
- Steel comb (¼ inch [0.6 cm] spaced teeth)
- Stripping knife
- Thinning shears

GROOMING PROCEDURE

1. Brush the coat with a slicker brush. If the dog has mats under the elbows and inside the hind legs, shave them out with a #10 or #15 blade.

2. Clean the ears.

3. Bathe the dog. Use protein shampoo and conditioning rinse. If the coat is matted, soak all mats well.

4. Cage dry the dog until half dry. Finish drying on the table, blowing him dry while brushing and combing. Dry the shortest hair first. The dog should be completely combed out before clipping.

5. Clip the face with a #10 blade against the grain on the jawbone and cheeks. Clean all hair off the lower jaw, including the creases of the lips. It is necessary to insert your finger into the corner of the mouth, pull the skin taut, and clip off all the hair. Use a #15 blade in this area. Pull down the chin flesh and clean off all hairs. This is very visible when the mouth is open. It is important to clean this off for hygienic reasons.

6. Make a reverse "V" in the stop with a #10 a blade. Clip the top of the nose and under the eyes.

7. Trim the back of the head, starting slightly forward from where the ears set on, with a #10 blade and blend this gradually into the neck. If the hair over the eyes is very long, use a #5F or #7F to trim it. Thinning shears or straight scissors can be used to blend hair into the top of the head.

8. Ears are clipped with a #10 or #15 blade. Hair is clipped either up or down to remove as much hair as possible, inside and outside the ear. One-third the length of the ear hair is removed, usually about 2½ inches (6 cm) down the ear.

9. Go over the body with a stripping knife to determine whether the dog is shedding his undercoat. This will minimize clipper marks.

10. Clip the body, including the tail, with a #7F. Clip with the direction of hair growth, gradually coming off the side and blending into the longer hair. Do not make a straight line (hula skirt effect). The line can be dropped for a slimming effect on overweight dogs.

11. Clean off the whole tail, top and bottom. Clip under the tail area, down about 2 to 3 inches (5 to 8 cm), and blend into the feathering.

12. The neck should be clipped with a #10 blade on the front and sides. Clip to the breastbone.

13. Go over the neck and back with a stripping knife.

14. Clip the nails at this time.

15. Scissor the hair around the foot flush with the pads. Feel around to see if there are mats between the foot pads. If necessary, shave out any mats with a #15 blade.

16. Cocker feet should be round. Use the dog's nails as a guide, lining up the scissors vertically against the nails, and then cut. Nails should not be seen. Sometimes it is necessary to lift the long leg coat just to see the front of the foot. Lift up the hair and make the first circle of the foot with scissors. Comb over and over, down and out. Keep correcting your circle.

17. Uneven hair on the legs should be scissored to blend in and give a tidy look. Scissor the tips of the hair for a full-coated look, or remove 1 to 2 inches (2.5 to 5 cm) by scissoring for a "puppy cut."

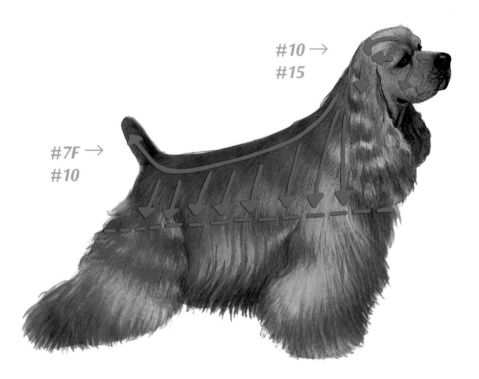

Cocker Spaniel, English

TOOLS AND EQUIPMENT

- Blending shears
- Comb
- Cotton balls
- Ear cleaner
- Nail clipper (guillotine or scissor)
- Oster A-5 clipper/#7, #10, #15 blades
- Shampoo (all-purpose or conditioning)
- Slicker brush
- Straight shears
- Styptic powder

GROOMING PROCEDURE

1. Nails should be cut by removing the tips only; avoid cutting into the quick. If the nail bleeds, apply styptic powder to stop the bleeding. Any rough nail edges may be smoothed with a file.

2. Clean the ears by moistening a cotton ball with liquid ear cleaner and wiping accumulated dirt and wax from all crevices in both ears.

3. Cut the hair under the paw and between the pads with a clipper and a #15 blade.

4. Cut the hair on the abdomen, from the groin to the navel, with a #10 blade. Clip with the growth of the hair.

5. Brush out the entire dog to remove any matting and/or dead coat.

6. Bathe the dog in a shampoo of your choice and rinse him well. A conditioning rinse may be used to help cut down on static electricity and to make the coat more manageable.

7. Towel dry the dog until he is damp, and then fluff dry with a dryer while brushing the coat in the direction of its growth. This helps the hair lie flat.

8. With a #10 blade, clip the muzzle in the direction of hair growth and continue clipping over the cheek to the front of the ear opening. Clip the hair from the chin down to the throat. Continue to the top of the breastbone and inside the "V" of the throat seams (where the hair growing in two different directions comes together).

9. The top of the skull should be clipped, starting about ½ inch [1 cm] behind the eyebrows to the back of the skull. The top third of each ear should be clipped on both the inner and outer side of the ear leather. The hair just in front of the ear opening should be carefully clipped as well to allow air to circulate in the ear canal.

10. With a #7 blade, clip from just under the ear flap down the side of the neck to the shoulder.

11. The top body coat may also be cut with the #7 blade. Start at the base of the skull and work to the tip of the tail. Clip from the spine down, over the sides of the dog, to just past the widest part of the rib cage. This line is almost straight across the side of the dog, except in the shoulder area, where it goes down to where the front leg joins the body on the front side. On the back leg, the clipper line goes a little lower to expose the muscle on the top of the outer thigh.

12. An optional method for the top coat, and, actually, the more correct way, is to leave the coat natural but to thin it out. This helps it lie flat against the dog. The lines for this method are the same as for clipping the dog.

13. The English Cocker should not be left with too much coat on the legs or abdomen. This hair should be shortened up with blending shears so as to look natural.

14. With blending shears, remove the hair growing out between the toes and on top of the feet to give the foot a tight compact look.

15. Again, with blending shears, blend in the eyebrows to give the skull a long, lean look without a pronounced stop.

The completed English Cocker Spaniel should give the appearance of a short-bodied, strong-limbed dog with a distinctive head. This breed should be groomed every 6 to 8 weeks.

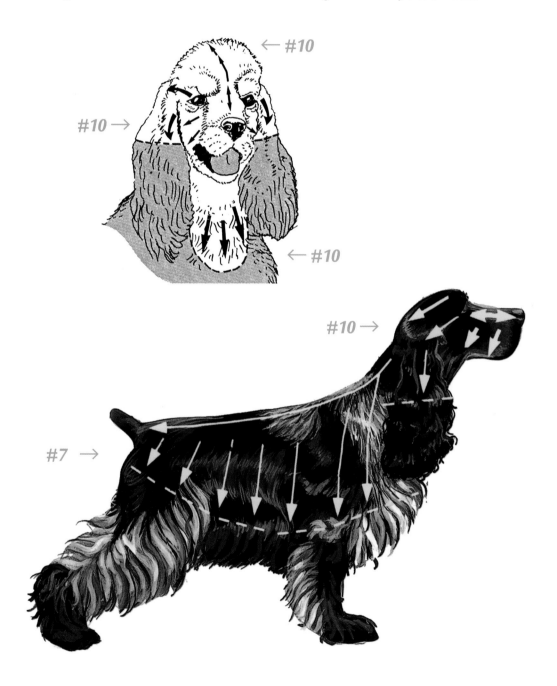

Collie, Rough Coat

TOOLS AND EQUIPMENT

- Cotton balls
- Ear cleaner
- High-velocity dryer
- Large pin brush
- Long-hair molting comb (#565)
- Medicated ear powder
- Nail clipper
- Oster A-5 clipper/#10 blade
- Protein coat conditioner
- Pure boar bristle brush
- Scissors
- Slicker brush
- Steel comb (fine/medium)
- Tearless protein shampoo
- Thinning shears
- Wood utility comb

GROOMING PROCEDURE

1. Spray the entire coat with protein coat conditioner to add body and help repair split ends. Brush through the entire coat with a large pin brush, alternating with a slicker brush in matted areas and a molting comb as needed. Work layer by layer—alternating brush and comb. Lift the coat up with your hand, working on thin layers at a time. Brush down and out until all mats and loose hair are removed. Work deep into the coat, but do not brush to the skin or you will cause abrasion. Start at the rear of the dog, at the bottom of the skirt area. Work through the entire coat until the outer coat is separated well and combs smoothly. Work vigorously. The more hair you remove now, the less hair you'll need to wash and dry.

2. Comb through the entire coat with a wide-toothed utility comb. Use a fine steel comb on the soft hair behind the ears. With your fingers, strip out dead hair behind the ears.

3. Swab the ears with a cotton ball moistened with ear cleaner to remove dirt and control ear odor. Follow this with a dry cotton ball, and dust the ears with medicated ear powder.

4. Cut the nails with a guillotine-type nail clipper. Nails should be cut monthly.

5. Check between the foot pads and under the feet for burrs, tar, etc. Scissor the hair under the foot even with the pads. Trim any hair around the paw that touches the ground and neaten the entire foot. Trim the hair growing out from between the toes with thinning shears. The toes should lie close, like those on a cat's foot.

6. Bathe the dog with a tearless protein shampoo that is pH-alkaline. This will add fullness and body to the coat and restructure damaged hair.

7. Use a high-velocity dryer to blow excess water off the dog while he is still in the tub to speed up drying time and prevent the coat from becoming overly dry. Cage dry until the hair is damp. Finish drying on the table using a blow dryer and a pin brush to separate all the hair and remove all of the loose coat.

8. Brush the entire coat to the skin, using the dryer to style and separate the hair. Follow by combing the entire coat.

9. Use a fine steel comb to finish the head and the ears. Comb straight back. Keep the muzzle smooth. The excess hair behind the ears may be thinned with thinning shears. The whiskers may be removed with scissors to improve the expression (optional).

10. Comb out the leg feathering. Trim excess hair on the feet and hocks. The hind legs are to be smooth below the hock joint, with a perpendicular line from the hock to the ground. Leave feathering on the forelegs full, but trim it so that it naturally meets the pastern and does not touch the ground.

11. Scissor any long hair under the tail that hangs over the anus to be sure it is clear, then use a #10 blade to blend down under the tail.

12. Lightly mist the coat with protein coat conditioner to add brilliance and fragrance. Back brush with a pin brush so the coat stands out away from the body.

GROOMING PROCEDURE

1. Spray the entire coat with a protein coat conditioner. This adds body to the coat and helps repair split ends. Brush through the entire coat with a gentle slicker to remove loose or dead hair. Then comb with a molting comb made for shorthaired breeds (#564) to take out loose undercoat.

2. Swab the ears with a cotton ball that has been moistened with ear cleaner. This will remove dirt and control ear odor. Follow this with a dry cotton ball, and dust the ears with medicated ear powder.

3. Cut the nails with a guillotine-type nail clipper. Nails should be cut monthly.

4. Bathe the dog with a tearless protein shampoo that is pH-alkaline. This will add fullness and body to the coat and at the same time restructure damaged hair.

5. Use a high-velocity dryer to blow excess water off the dog while he is still in the tub. This will speed up the drying time and help prevent the coat from becoming overly dry. Cage dry the dog until the hair is damp. Finish drying him on the table using a blow dryer and a pin brush to separate all of the hair and remove all of the loose coat. Finish with a steel comb through the entire coat, paying special attention to the fine hair behind the ears. Use the fine side of the comb for this area.

6. With scissors, neaten the hair at the base and on the inside of the ear.

7. Check between the foot pads and under the feet for burrs, tar, etc. Scissor the hair under the foot even with the pads. Trim any hair around the paw that touches the ground and neaten the entire foot. Use thinning shears to trim the hair growing out between the toes. Be sure to neaten the hair on the back of the rear pasterns.

8. The whiskers may be removed with scissors to improve the expression (optional).

9. Under the body should be natural, but remove all straggly hair with thinning shears to create a smooth line.

10. Use thinning shears to give a nice rounded look to the rump. Never trim to excess or until noticeable. The coat should appear smooth but natural.

11. Topbrush the coat with a pure bristle brush that has been sprayed with protein coat conditioner. This adds brilliance and fragrance to the coat.

Collie, Smooth Coat

TOOLS AND EQUIPMENT

- Cotton balls
- Ear cleaner
- Eye stain remover
- Medicated ear powder
- Nail clipper
- Protein coat conditioner
- Pure boar bristle brush
- Scissors
- Short-hair molting comb (#564)
- Slicker brush (gentle)
- Steel comb (medium/fine)
- Tearless protein shampoo

Curly-Coated Retriever

TOOLS AND EQUIPMENT

- Blending shears
- Cotton balls
- Ear cleaner
- Nail clipper (guillotine or scissor)
- Shampoo (all-purpose)
- Slicker brush
- Straight shears
- Styptic powder

GROOMING PROCEDURE

1. Nails should be cut by removing only the tips; avoid cutting the quick. If the nail bleeds, apply styptic powder to stop the bleeding. Any rough nail edges may be smoothed with a file.

2. Ears should be cleaned with a liquid cleaner. Apply the cleaner to a cotton ball and wipe clean accumulated wax and dirt from all crevices in both ears.

3. Brush through the entire coat to remove any dead or loose hair.

4. Bathe the dog with a shampoo of your choice. Lather well and rinse thoroughly.

5. Towel dry the dog, and finish drying in a cage dryer.

6. With blending shears, remove any fuzz from the dog's face. The face should be smooth.

7. With straight shears, remove any wispy or fuzzy hairs that are sticking out from the coat. As the breed name implies, the coat should be curly, so do not brush after the bath.

GROOMING PROCEDURE

1. Brush the entire coat with a slicker brush, removing any mats with a metal comb.

2. Clean the ears using medicated ear powder, and lightly pluck any stray hairs from the insides.

3. Clean the eyes by wiping them with a cotton ball that has been moistened with eye drops. This will also help to remove any stains around the eyes.

4. Cut the tips of the nails with a nail clipper, being careful not to cut the quick.

5. Using a #10 blade, shave the anal area, being certain not to put the blade in direct contact with the skin. [Note: Shaving this area is a decision to be left to the dog's owner.]

6. Using a #10 blade, shave the stomach area from groin to navel and down the insides of the thighs. [Note: Again, this depends on the dog owner's preferences.]

7. With scissors, clip the whiskers from the muzzle, under the chin, from the sides of the face, and above the eyes. [Note: Whiskers should be clipped only if the dog's owner wants this done.]

8. Put a cotton ball in each ear (this prevents water from entering the ear canal), and bathe the dog. Fluff dry him.

9. Brush the coat with a slicker brush and comb with a metal comb, paying special attention to the feathering on the legs, tail, and ears.

10. With scissors, snip any stray hair from the feet and between the foot pads and toes, thus giving a neat appearance.

The long-coated Dachshund should be groomed about every 8 weeks.

Dachshund, Long Coat

TOOLS AND EQUIPMENT

- Cotton balls
- Eye drops (eye stain remover)
- Medicated ear powder
- Metal comb (medium)
- Nail clipper
- Oster A-5 clipper/#10 blade
- Scissors
- Slicker brush

Dachshund, Smooth Coat

TOOLS AND EQUIPMENT

- Chamois cloth
- Cotton balls
- Eye drops (eye stain remover)
- Lanolin coat conditioner
- Medicated ear powder
- Nail clipper
- Scissors
- Sisal (natural bristle) brush

GROOMING PROCEDURE

1. Brush the coat briskly with a sisal brush.

2. Clean the ears using medicated ear powder.

3. Clean the eyes by wiping them with a cotton ball that has been moistened with eye drops. This will also help remove any stains around the eyes.

4. Cut the tips of the nails with a nail clipper, being careful not to cut the quick.

5. With scissors, clip the long whiskers from the muzzle, under the chin, from the sides of the face, and above the eyes. [Note: Clipping the whiskers is a decision to be left to the dog's owner.]

6. Put a cotton ball in each ear (this prevents water from entering the ear canal), and bathe the dog. Cage dry him.

7. Put a few drops of lanolin coat conditioner into the palms of your hands, rub them together lightly, and gently massage into the coat.

8. Brush the coat with a sisal brush to distribute the conditioner, and then lightly rub over the coat with a chamois cloth, thus giving it a nice sheen.

The smooth-coated Dachshund should be bathed every 8 weeks. Between baths, the dog should be brushed regularly by the owner to help maintain a healthy, shiny coat. The ears should be checked weekly; the nails should be checked monthly and clipped if necessary.

GROOMING PROCEDURE

1. Brush the coat thoroughly with a sisal brush.

2. Comb through the coat to remove all loosened hair.

3. Clean the ears using medicated ear powder, and lightly pluck any stray hair from the insides.

4. Clean the eyes by wiping them with a cotton ball that has been moistened with eye stain remover.

5. Cut the tips of the nails with a nail clipper, being careful not to cut the quick.

6. With a #10 blade on the Oster A-5 clipper, shave the stomach from groin to navel and down the insides of the thighs.

7. Shave the anal area, being certain not to put the blade in direct contact with the skin (½ inch [1 cm] each side).

8. Put a cotton ball in each ear (this prevents water from entering the ear canal), and bathe the dog. Cage dry him.

9. With scissors, snip hair from between the pads and toes of the feet and around the edges for a neat effect.

10. With scissors or thinning shears, trim straggly hairs from around the ankles on the front feet and from the hocks down to the feet on the hind legs.

11. Comb the hair on the face downward, and with scissors or thinning shears, trim the lower edge evenly.

12. With scissors or thinning shears, trim the lower edge of the belly fringe evenly.

13. Comb through the coat, and remove all loosened hair.

Dachshund, Wire Coat

TOOLS AND EQUIPMENT

- Cotton balls
- Eye drops (eye stain remover)
- Medicated ear powder
- Metal comb (medium)
- Nail clipper
- Oster A-5 clipper/#10 blade
- Scissors
- Sisal (natural bristle) brush
- Thinning shears

Dalmatian

TOOLS AND EQUIPMENT

- Cotton balls
- Ear cleaner
- Hound glove
- Nail clipper (guillotine or scissor)
- Rubber brush
- Shampoo (all-purpose or whitening)
- Spray conditioner or coat gloss
- Straight scissors
- Styptic powder

GROOMING PROCEDURE

1. Nails should be cut by removing the tips only; avoid cutting the quick. If the nail bleeds, apply styptic powder to stop the bleeding. Any rough nail edges may be removed with a file.

2. Clean the ears with a liquid cleaner. Apply the cleaner to a cotton ball and wipe accumulated dirt and wax from all crevices in both ears.

3. Bathe the dog in a shampoo of your choice. Lather him using a rubber brush to remove dead hair. Rinse him thoroughly.

4. Towel dry the dog and complete the drying by placing him in a cage to which a dryer has been attached.

5. When the dog is completely dry, brush the coat with a hound glove to remove any remaining dead hair and to make the hair lie flat.

6. Lightly spray the coat with a conditioner or coat gloss, and buff it with a clean, dry cloth.

7. The whiskers and eyebrows may be removed if desired.

The Dalmatian should be groomed every 8 to 12 weeks.

GROOMING PROCEDURE

1. Spray the entire coat with protein coat conditioner. This adds body to the coat and helps repair split ends. If the coat is matted in areas, spray the mats with tangle remover. Let the dog sit 10 to 15 minutes with both products on the coat until they are absorbed and become partially dry.

2. After 15 minutes, spray the entire coat with coat gloss. This lubricates the coat for easier brushing and combing and prevents hair breakage. Brush through the entire coat with a pin brush, using a slicker brush and a utility comb in the matted areas of the coat. Start at the rear of the dog, at the bottom of the skirt area. Work in sections, lifting the hair and brushing it layer by layer. Mist each section with coat gloss as you work. Never brush dry-coated. Work through the entire coat from the back to the neck area. Never bathe this breed with mats in the coat because water will tighten the mats and make them harder to remove.

3. Swab the ears with a cotton ball that has been moistened with ear cleaner. This will remove dirt and control ear odor. Follow this with a dry cotton ball, and dust the ears with medicated ear powder. With your fingers or ear forceps, pull out any dead hair inside the ears.

4. Cut the nails with a guillotine-type nail clipper. Nails should be cut monthly.

5. Wipe the inside corners of the eyes with a water-moistened cotton ball. Remove any eye stains under and around the eyes with a cotton ball that has been moistened with eye stain remover.

6. Check between the foot pads and under the feet for burrs, tar, etc. Scissor the hair under the foot even with the pads to prevent debris from adhering. Trim any hair on which the dog might walk.

7. Scissor any long hair under the tail that hangs over the anus and that may become soiled with fecal matter. Scissor the hair around the anus itself, and be sure it is clear.

8. Bathe the dog with a tearless protein shampoo that is pH-alkaline. This will add fullness and body to the coat and restructure damaged hair.

9. Cage dry the dog until the hair is damp. Then finish drying on the table using a blow dryer and a pin brush to separate all the hair. Spray with coat gloss to eliminate flyaway hair and static. Finish by combing through the entire coat with a steel comb, making certain that you comb to the skin.

10. Clip the stomach with a #10 blade, going with the grain.

continued

Dandie Dinmont Terrier

TOOLS AND EQUIPMENT

- Cotton balls
- Ear cleaner
- Ear forceps
- Eye stain remover
- Large pin brush
- Long-hair molting comb (#565)
- Medicated ear powder
- Nail clipper
- Protein coat conditioner
- Pure boar bristle brush
- Scissors
- Slicker brush
- Steel comb (fine/medium)
- Tangle remover
- Tearless protein shampoo
- Thinning shears
- Wood utility comb

11. The body coat should be maintained at a length of no more than 2 inches (5 cm). This may be accomplished by stripping the coat with thinning shears or by top scissoring. If you must use a clipper, use a #4 blade or a #10 with a #1 guard.

12. Chest hair should be combed straight down and shortened to a length of 2 inches (5 cm).

13. On the front legs, comb out the hair, and scissor it to 2 inches (5 cm) on all sides. Then comb the hair down and thin it to achieve a straight line from shoulder to leg. Neaten the front feet.

14. On the rear legs, thin the hair so that the fringe from tuckup to rear stifle is no longer than 2 inches (5 cm). Neaten the hind feet.

15. Remove any long hair that extends past the tip of the tail. Use thinning shears to shape the tail, tapering the tip with no more than 2 inches (5 cm) at the longest point. The completed tail should curve up like a scimitar.

16. Use thinning shears to shorten a strip from between the inside corners of the eyes to the stop. This strip of hair should be almost as wide as the dog's nose.

17. Pluck the hair at the inside corners of the eyes.

18. Pluck the long hair on the inside and outside of the ear. Leave hair above the fold line of the ear since it will become part of the topknot. Leave a tassel of hair at the tip of the ear. The bottom of the tassel should come to a point.

19. Back comb the outside of the ear flap. Lay thinning shears against the skin at the ear tip. Point the shears toward the fold and angle them out so that the hair, when cut, will be shorter at the tip than at the fold. Hair at the fold should be the same length as the hair on top of the skull.

20. Scissor a line from the outside corner of the eye to the ear canal. Scissor another line from the outside corner of the eye to the point of the jawbone. Use thinning shears to shorten the hair in this triangular section.

21. Brush the topknot forward. Scissor the front to make a topknot effect above the eyes. Shape the sides and back to finish the topknot. The back of the topknot should be a continuation from the back edge of the ear. Eyes should be clear, so trim hair that falls in front of them.

GROOMING PROCEDURE

1. Nails should be cut by removing tips only; avoid cutting the quick. If the nail bleeds, apply styptic powder to stop the bleeding. Any rough nail edges may be smoothed by filing.

2. Clean the ears by moistening a cotton ball with liquid ear cleaner and wiping accumulated wax and dirt from all crevices in both ears.

3. Bathe the dog by lathering with a shampoo of your choice. Rinse him thoroughly. An after-bath conditioner or a hot oil treatment may be applied to the coat and then rinsed off. This helps control dandruff.

4. Towel dry the dog, and then place him in a cage with a dryer until he is completely dry.

5. A rubber brush may be used to remove any dead hair.

6. Pet Dobermans generally do not need much trimming unless the owner specifies this. Areas to be trimmed are the edges of the ears, the ear opening, the whiskers, and the eyebrows. Any areas where there are seams (where two different directions of hair growth come together) may be blended with blending shears. Any excess hair on the back of the front legs may be removed, as well as the hair on the back of the thighs. The sides of the neck may need attention also.

7. To give the Doberman a final touch, a small amount of spray conditioner or coat gloss should be lightly misted over the coat. Then polish with a clean cloth or a hound glove.

Doberman Pinscher

TOOLS AND EQUIPMENT

- Blending shears
- Cotton balls
- Ear cleaner
- Hound glove
- Nail clipper (guillotine or scissor)
- Rubber brush
- Shampoo (all-purpose, dark coat, or conditioning)
- Spray conditioner or coat gloss
- Straight shears
- Styptic powder

English Setter

TOOLS AND EQUIPMENT

- Blending shears
- Comb
- Conditioning rinse
- Cotton balls
- Ear cleaner
- Nail clipper (guillotine or scissor)
- Oster A-5 clipper/#7, #10, #15 blades
- Shampoo (all-purpose or whitening)
- Slicker brush
- Straight shears
- Styptic powder

GROOMING PROCEDURE

1. Nails should be cut by removing the tips only; avoid cutting the quick. If the nail bleeds, apply styptic powder to stop the bleeding. Any rough nail edges may be smoothed out with a file.

2. Clean the ears with a liquid ear cleaner. Apply this to a cotton ball and wipe accumulated wax and dirt from all crevices in both ears.

3. With a #15 blade, cut the hair under the foot and between the pads. If desired, this hair may be scissored off instead.

4. Cut the hair on the abdomen from groin to navel with a #10 blade, going with the growth of the hair.

5. Brush out the entire coat to remove dead hair and any mats that have formed.

6. Bathe the dog in a shampoo of your choice and rinse him thoroughly. After the bath, apply conditioner to the coat and rinse well.

7. Towel dry the dog until he is damp, and then fluff dry the rest of the way. Use a slicker brush to brush the hair while it is drying. While drying, always brush with the growth of the hair so that it lies flat. Continue until the dog is completely dry.

8. With a #10 blade, clip the muzzle in the direction of hair growth, and continue clipping over the cheeks to in front of the ear opening. Clip the hair on the chin, and continue down the throat to the top of the breastbone, staying inside the "V" of the neck seams and clipping with the growth of the hair. The top of the head may be clipped with a #10 blade also, or it may be smoothed out with blending shears.

9. The ears should be clipped with a #10 blade about one-third of the way down from the top, where the ears join the skull. Leave some hair on the front edge of the ear to soften the expression.

10. With a #7 blade, clip down the sides of the neck from under the ear to the shoulder.

11. If the top body coat is thick, this area may also be clipped off with a #7 blade. Start at the base of the skull and continue to the root of the tail. Clip down over the sides of the ribcage to just below the widest part of the ribs. This line is almost straight across the side of the dog, except in the shoulder area, where it slopes down to the point at which the front leg joins the body on the front side. On the back leg, the clipper line goes a little lower to expose the muscle on the top of the outer thigh. [Note: An optional method, and actually the correct way, would be to use a stripping knife and thinning shears to card out the back of the dog in order to make the hair lie smooth and flat naturally. The same lines would apply.]

12. The hair on top of the feet that grows between the toes should be removed to give a tidy, compact, and well-knuckled look.

13. Excessive hair on the back of the hocks should be removed.

14. The tail should be trimmed into a triangular flag shape (plume). The tip should be long enough to just reach the hock.

The completed English Setter should possess a noble look with a graceful, flowing coat. This complete grooming should be done every 4 to 6 weeks.

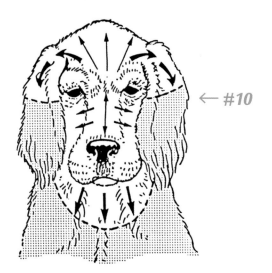

← *#10*

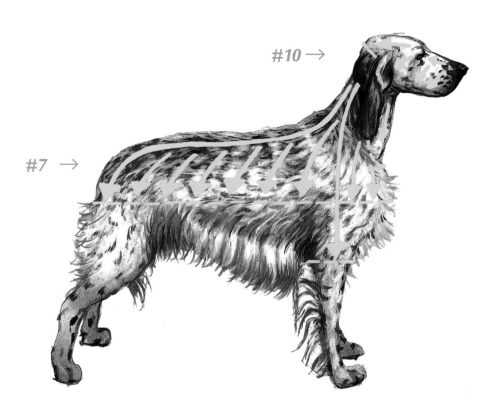

#10 →

#7 →

English Springer Spaniel

TOOLS AND EQUIPMENT

- Comb (fine/medium)
- Cotton balls
- Ear cleaner
- High-velocity dryer
- Medicated ear powder
- Nail clipper
- Oster A-5 clipper/#7, #7F, #10 blades
- Pin brush
- Protein coat conditioner
- Pure boar bristle brush
- Scissors
- Short-hair molting comb (#564)
- Slicker brush
- Tearless protein shampoo
- Thinning shears

GROOMING PROCEDURE

1. Spray the entire coat with protein coat conditioner. This adds body to the coat and helps repair split ends. Comb through the entire coat with a molting comb; this will remove dead undercoat. Start at the rear of the dog, at the bottom of the skirt area. Work in sections, using your other hand to lift the hair ahead of the section you are working on. Work through the entire dog from the back to the neck area. Then brush through the coat with a slicker brush to remove the top dead coat. Work vigorously. The more hair you remove now, the less hair you need to wash and dry later.

2. Swab the ears with a cotton ball that has been moistened with ear cleaner. This will remove dirt and control ear odor. Follow this with a dry cotton ball, and dust the ears with medicated ear powder.

3. Cut the nails with a guillotine-type nail clipper. Nails should be cut monthly.

4. Check between the foot pads and under the feet for burrs, tar, etc. With a #10 blade, clip the hair under the feet and between the pads.

5. Bathe the dog with a tearless protein shampoo that is pH-alkaline. This will add fullness and body to the coat and restructure damaged hair.

6. Use a high-velocity dryer to blow excess water off the dog while he is still in the tub. This will speed up the drying time and help prevent the coat from becoming overly dry. Cage dry the dog until the hair is damp. Then, finish drying on the table using a blow dryer and a pin brush to separate all the hair and remove all of the loose coat.

7. Brush the entire coat and be sure to brush to the skin, using the dryer to style and separate the hair. Follow by combing the entire coat, using the fine side of the comb on the soft hair behind the ears.

8. Use a #10 blade to clip the hair around the anus. Just clear the area and do not use heavy pressure. Scissor any long hair under the tail that hangs over the anal area and that may become soiled.

9. Shave the stomach area with a #10 blade, going with the lay of the hair.

10. Clip the head and muzzle, from above the brow to the base of the skull, with a #10 blade.

11. Use a #10 blade to shave the cheek to the outer corner of the ear. Shave the folds in the lower jaw area—under the jaw and the throat—to approximately 1 or 2 inches (2.5 or 5 cm) above the breastbone. Taper into the unclipped area of the apron. Make a deep "U" shape from ear to ear, always working with the grain of the hair. If you have trouble getting the flews of the lips

clean, carefully stretch the skin and go lightly against the grain. The chest should be left full to accentuate the depth of the chest.

12. Clip the front and back of the ears with a #10 blade about one-third of the way down the ear leather. Ear furnishings should be long: Do not shorten! Just neaten uneven bottoms with scissors. The bottom edges of the ears should be curved, not square. [Note: One-third refers to one-third of the overall ear, including the feathering.]

13. Clip the body with a #7F blade. The body blades you use will vary, depending on the type of Springer coat and skin sensitivity. Clip from the base of the skull to the end of the tail (depending on coat texture, a #7F blade may be changed to a #7, #9, or #10). Clip both sides of the body, from the sides of the neck to the shoulder joint in the front leg and down to the thigh on the rear leg. Looking at the dog from the side, you should have blended from the front elbow up gradually to about 1 inch (2.5 cm) under the tail. Do not clip below the area where the coat begins to hang down naturally. Follow the contour of the body, directing your clipper in the direction the hair grows. Do not go against the grain or across the grain. Lift your clipper slightly as you near the end of your clipped area, so as to blend the clipped area into the nonclipped area of the skirt and leg. It takes a slight twist of the wrist to accomplish this, as if you were using the end of the clipper as a shovel. You must work to blend the clipped area into the fringe area, leaving no uneven lines or ridges.

14. Clip the tail with a #7F blade. Always clip with the grain—the way the hair grows—and never against the growth. To prevent irritation, use very light pressure on the underside of the tail. Blend the area under the tail into the skirt.

15. Use thinning shears to shape the legs so that they appear even and tapered. Remove all straggly hair, and thin and shorten excess feathering, especially from the hocks to the feet.

16. Use thinning shears to blend in any uneven lines between shaved and unshaved areas.

17. Feet should be neat, rounded, and blended into the legs.

18. Topbrush the coat with a pure bristle brush that has been sprayed with protein coat conditioner. This adds brilliance and fragrance.

#10 →

#7 →

English Toy Spaniel

TOOLS AND EQUIPMENT

- Cotton balls
- Ear cleaner
- Ear forceps
- Eye stain remover
- High-velocity dryer
- Medicated ear powder
- Nail clipper
- Oster A-5 clipper/#10 blade
- Protein coat conditioner
- Pure boar bristle brush
- Scissors
- Skin cream
- Slicker brush (gentle)
- Steel comb (medium/coarse)
- Tearless protein shampoo
- Thinning shears

GROOMING PROCEDURE

1. Spray the entire coat with protein coat conditioner. This adds body to the coat and helps repair split ends. Brush through the entire coat with a gentle slicker brush.

2. Swab the ears with a cotton ball that has been moistened with ear cleaner. This will remove dirt and control ear odor. Follow with a dry cotton ball, and dust the ears with medicated ear powder. With your fingers or ear forceps, pluck the hair inside the ears.

3. Wipe inside the corners of the eyes with a water-moistened cotton ball. Remove any stains under and around the eye with a cotton ball that has been moistened with eye stain remover.

4. Cut the nails with a guillotine-type nail clipper. Nails should be cut monthly.

5. Check between the foot pads and under the feet for burrs, tar, etc. Scissor the hair under the foot even with the pads to prevent debris from adhering. With thinning shears, trim any hair around the paw that touches the ground or grows out between the toes.

6. Use a #10 blade to clip the hair around the anus. Just clear the area and do not use heavy pressure. Scissor any long hair under the tail that hangs over the anus and that may become soiled.

7. Shave the stomach area with a #10 blade, going with the lay of the hair.

8. Bathe the dog with a tearless protein shampoo that is pH-alkaline. This will add fullness and body to the coat and restructure damaged hair. Solid-colored dogs (who are show dogs) should not be washed the day before a dog show; instead, wash them several days ahead to allow the natural oil and gloss to return to the coat.

9. Use a high-velocity dryer to blow excess water off the dog while he is still in the tub. This will speed up the drying time and help prevent the coat from becoming overly dry. Cage dry the dog until the hair is damp. Then, finish drying on the table using a blow dryer and a pin brush to separate all the hair and remove all of the loose coat. Comb with the fine side of the steel comb to separate all the hair down to the skin.

10. Use thinning shears to thin out any heavy areas, to remove straggly hair, and to give the dog an overall well-sculptured look.

11. The whiskers may be removed with scissors to improve expression (optional).

12. Spray a pure bristle brush with protein coat conditioner and topbrush the coat to add brilliance and fragrance. For show dogs, there is to be no scissoring of any kind.

[Note: In Great Britain, this breed is known as the King Charles Spaniel.]

GROOMING PROCEDURE

1. Brush the coat vigorously with a sisal brush, using long deep strokes.

2. Clean the ears using medicated ear powder.

3. Clean the eyes by wiping them with a cotton ball that has been moistened with eye stain remover.

4. Cut the tips of the nails with a nail clipper, being careful not to cut the quick.

5. With scissors, snip the whiskers from the muzzle, under the chin, the sides of the face, and above the eyes. [Note: Clipping the whiskers is a decision to be left to the dog's owner.]

6. Put a cotton ball in each ear (this prevents water from entering the ear canal), and bathe the dog. Cage dry him.

7. Put a few drops of lanolin coat conditioner into the palms of your hands, rub them together lightly, and massage into the coat.

8. Brush the coat with a sisal brush to distribute the conditioner, and then lightly rub over the coat with a chamois cloth, thus giving it a nice sheen.

The English Toy Terrier (Black and Tan) should be groomed every 8 to 10 weeks. The ears should be checked weekly and cleaned if necessary, and the nails should be checked monthly and cut if necessary.

English Toy Terrier
(Black and Tan)

TOOLS AND EQUIPMENT

- Chamois cloth
- Cotton balls
- Eye drops (eye stain remover)
- Lanolin coat conditioner
- Medicated ear powder
- Nail clipper
- Scissors
- Sisal (natural bristle) brush

Eskimo Dog

TOOLS AND EQUIPMENT

- Cotton balls
- Eye drops (eye stain remover)
- Mat-splitting comb
- Medicated ear powder
- Metal comb (wide-toothed)
- Metal rake
- Nail clipper
- Scissors
- Slicker brush
- Thinning shears

GROOMING PROCEDURE

1. Starting at the head, brush the entire coat and tail with a slicker brush.

2. With a metal rake, gently rake through the coat. During the nonshedding season, do not rake out the undercoat; just untangle it with a metal rake and/or mat-splitting comb. Comb through the coat to remove all loosened hair.

3. Clean the ears using medicated ear powder.

4. Clean the eyes by wiping them with eye stain remover applied to a cotton ball. This product will also help to remove stains under and around the eyes.

5. Cut the tips of the nails with a nail clipper, being careful not to cut the quick.

6. With scissors, clip the whiskers from the muzzle, under the chin, the sides of the face, and above the eyes. [Note: Clipping the whiskers is a decision to be left to the dog's owner.]

7. Put a cotton ball in each ear to prevent water from entering the ear canal. Bathe the dog, and cage or fluff dry him.

8. With scissors, snip the hair between the pads and toes on the feet and around the edges to give a neat appearance.

9. With thinning shears, remove any straggly hair from the hock joints to the feet on the hind legs and from around the ankles on the front legs.

10. Brush and comb through the entire coat.

The Eskimo Dog should be groomed every 10 to 12 weeks. Regular brushing by the owner will help to keep the coat healthy and the undercoat free of tangles. The ears should be checked weekly and cleaned if necessary.

GROOMING PROCEDURE

1. Thoroughly brush the entire coat with a slicker brush, removing any mats or tangles with a mat-splitting comb and/or metal rake.

2. Comb through the coat to remove all loosened hair.

3. Clean the ears using medicated ear powder, and lightly pluck any stray hair from the insides without removing any of the outer protective hair.

4. Clean the eyes by wiping them with a cotton ball that has been moistened with eye stain remover.

5. Cut the tips of the nails with a nail clipper, being careful not to cut the quick.

6. Using a damp cotton ball, clean the insides of the lips, removing any trapped food particles.

7. With scissors, snip the whiskers from the muzzle, under the chin, the sides of the face, and above the eyes. [Note: Clipping the whiskers is a decision to be left to the owner if the dog is not a show dog.]

8. Place a cotton ball in each ear (this prevents water from entering the ear canal), and bathe the dog. Cage dry or fluff dry him.

9. With scissors, snip hair between the pads and toes of the feet and around the edges.

10. With scissors or thinning shears, trim straggly hair from around the ankles on the front feet and from the hocks to the feet on the hind legs, thus giving a neat appearance.

11. Brush and comb through the entire coat.

The Estrela Mountain Dog should be groomed every 10 to 12 weeks. The ears should be checked weekly and cleaned if necessary.

Estrela Mountain Dog

TOOLS AND EQUIPMENT

- Cotton balls
- Eye drops (eye stain remover)
- Mat-splitting comb
- Medicated ear powder
- Metal comb (wide-toothed)
- Metal rake
- Nail clipper
- Scissors
- Slicker brush
- Thinning shears

Field Spaniel

TOOLS AND EQUIPMENT

- Blending shears
- Comb
- Cotton balls
- Ear cleaner
- Nail clipper (guillotine or scissor)
- Oster A-5 clipper/#10, #15 blades
- Shampoo (all-purpose or dark coat)
- Slicker brush
- Straight shears
- Styptic powder

GROOMING PROCEDURE

1. Nails should be cut by removing the tips only. Avoid cutting into the quick. If the nail bleeds, apply styptic powder to stop the bleeding. Any rough edges may be smoothed with a file.

2. Clean the ears with a liquid cleaner. Apply cleaner to a cotton ball and wipe accumulated dirt and wax from all crevices in both ears.

3. Remove hair from between the foot pads and on the bottom of the foot with a #15 blade.

4. Cut the hair on the abdomen (from groin to navel) with a #10 blade, clipping with the direction of hair growth.

5. Brush out the dog's entire coat to remove any matting and/or dead coat.

6. Bathe the dog in a shampoo of your choice and rinse him thoroughly. A conditioning rinse may be used to help cut down on static electricity and make the coat lie more smoothly.

7. Towel dry the dog. Finish drying him with a blow dryer while brushing the coat in its natural direction of growth. The coat should be encouraged to lie flat.

8. With blending shears, remove hair that grows out from between the toes and on top of the foot to give the foot a tidy, compact look.

9. With blending shears, remove any "fuzz" from the face and muzzle.

10. With a #10 blade, remove the hair from the top one-third of the ear on both the outer and inner side of the ear flap. The hair should also be removed from in front of the ear opening to increase air circulation to the ear canal. With blending shears, blend at the top of the ear where the clipper line begins at the skull. You should not be able to see a clipper line. The top of the head may be blended, as well, to give the skull a smooth appearance.

11. Remove any excess hair from the back of the hocks.

12. Remove any stray hair that may be giving the outline an uneven appearance.

The completed Field Spaniel should look tidy yet present a neat and natural look. This grooming procedure should be done every 8 to 10 weeks.

GROOMING PROCEDURE

1. Starting at the head, brush the entire coat.

2. With a metal rake, gently rake through the coat. In the nonshedding season, do not rake out the undercoat; only untangle it with a rake and/or mat-splitting comb. Comb through the coat to remove all loosened hair.

3. Clean the ears using medicated ear powder.

4. Clean the eyes by wiping them with a cotton ball that has been moistened with eye drops. This will also help in removing any stains around the eyes.

5. Cut the tips of the nails with a nail clipper, being careful not to cut the quick.

6. With scissors, cut the whiskers from the muzzle, under the chin, the sides of the face, and above the eyes. [Note: Clipping the whiskers is a decision to be left to the dog's owner.]

7. Put a cotton ball in each ear (to keep water out of the ear canal), and bathe the dog. Cage dry or fluff dry. (Fluff drying may be preferable if the undercoat is excessively heavy.)

8. With scissors, snip the hair from between the pads and toes on the feet and around the edges to give a neat appearance.

9. With thinning shears, remove any straggly hair from the hock joint to the feet on the hind legs.

10. Brush and comb through the entire coat.

The Finnish Spitz should be groomed every 8 to 10 weeks. Regular brushing by the owner will help to keep the coat healthy and the undercoat free of tangles. The ears should be checked weekly and cleaned if necessary, and the nails should be checked monthly and cut if needed. The hair on the ears of these dogs is a natural protection and should not be touched; however, hair may be removed from the ear canals for hygienic reasons.

Finnish Spitz

TOOLS AND EQUIPMENT

- Cotton balls
- Eye drops (eye stain remover)
- Mat-splitting comb
- Medicated ear powder
- Metal comb (wide-toothed)
- Metal rake
- Nail clipper
- Scissors
- Slicker brush
- Thinning shears

Flat-Coated Retriever

TOOLS AND EQUIPMENT

- Blending shears
- Comb
- Cotton balls
- Ear cleaner
- Nail clipper (guillotine or scissor)
- Shampoo (all-purpose or conditioning)
- Slicker brush
- Straight scissors
- Styptic powder

GROOMING PROCEDURE

1. Cut the nails by removing only the tips; avoid cutting the quick. If the nail bleeds, apply styptic powder to stop the bleeding. Any rough nail edges may be smoothed with a file.

2. Clean the ears with a liquid ear cleaner. Moisten a cotton ball with cleaner and wipe all accumulated wax and dirt from the crevices in both ears.

3. Brush out the entire coat to remove any mats and/or dead coat.

4. Bathe the dog in a shampoo of your choice and rinse him thoroughly. A conditioning rinse may be used to help cut down on static electricity and to give the coat a shine.

5. Towel dry the dog. Use a dryer to complete the drying process. While blow drying, brush the coat in the direction of its growth to make it lie smoothly. After drying, comb through the coat to remove any tangles.

6. With straight scissors, cut the hair from the bottom of the foot and between the pads. Remove the hair on the outer edge of the foot by the pads to round the foot. With blending shears, remove the hair that grows from between the toes and on the top of the feet.

7. The hair directly under the ear flap may be thinned out to allow the ear to lie close to the skull. The edge of the ear may be neatened with blending shears.

8. Excess hair on the back of the hock should be neatened.

9. The tail may be neatened. It should be carried straight out as a smooth extension of the topline. At rest, the tip of the tail should reach the hock joint, but not any further.

This breed should not be overly groomed but should maintain a natural appearance. Grooming should be done every 8 to 12 weeks.

GROOMING PROCEDURE

1. Thoroughly brush the entire coat with a sisal brush.

2. Clean the ears using medicated ear powder.

3. Clean the eyes by wiping them with a cotton ball that has been moistened with eye drops. This will also help to remove any stains around the eyes.

4. Clip the tips of the nails with a nail clipper, being careful not to cut the quick.

5. Using scissors, clip the whiskers from the muzzle, the chin, the sides of the face, and above the eyes. [Note: Clipping the whiskers is a decision to be left to the dog's owner.]

6. Put a cotton ball in each ear (this prevents water from entering the ear canal). Bathe the dog, paying special attention to the white areas of the coat. Cage dry him.

7. Put a few drops of lanolin coat conditioner into the palms of your hands, rub them together lightly, and gently massage this into the coat.

8. Brush the coat with a sisal brush (to distribute the conditioner), and then lightly rub over the coat with a chamois cloth, thus giving it a nice sheen.

The American Foxhound needs to be bathed only once every 3 to 4 months. Regular brushing by the owner between baths helps maintain a healthy, shiny coat. The ears should be checked weekly and the nails should be checked monthly—the former cleaned and the latter clipped, if necessary.

Foxhound, American

TOOLS AND EQUIPMENT

- Chamois cloth
- Cotton balls
- Eye drops (eye stain remover)
- Lanolin coat conditioner
- Medicated ear powder
- Nail clipper
- Scissors
- Sisal (natural bristle) brush

Foxhound, English

TOOLS AND EQUIPMENT

- Chamois cloth
- Cotton balls
- Eye drops (eye stain remover)
- Lanolin coat conditioner
- Medicated ear powder
- Nail clipper
- Scissors
- Sisal (natural bristle) brush

GROOMING PROCEDURE

1. Thoroughly brush the entire coat with a sisal brush.

2. Clean the ears using medicated ear powder.

3. Clean the eyes by wiping them with a cotton ball that has been moistened with eye drops. This will also help to remove any stains under and around the eyes.

4. Clip the tips of the nails with a nail clipper, being careful not to cut the quick.

5. Using scissors, clip the whiskers from the muzzle, the chin, the sides of the face, and above the eyes. [Note: Clipping the whiskers is a decision to be left to the owner—if the dog is not a show dog.]

6. Put a cotton ball in each ear (this prevents water from entering the ear canal). Bathe the dog, paying special attention to the white areas of the coat. Cage dry him.

7. Put a few drops of lanolin coat conditioner into the palms of your hands, rub them together lightly, and gently massage into the coat.

8. Brush the coat with a sisal brush (to distribute the conditioner), and then lightly rub over the coat with a chamois cloth, thus giving it a nice sheen.

The English Foxhound needs to be bathed only once every 3 to 4 months. Regular brushing by the owner between baths helps maintain a healthy, shiny coat. The ears should be checked weekly and cleaned if needed, and the nails should be checked monthly and clipped if necessary.

GROOMING PROCEDURE

1. Brush the entire coat with a pure boar bristle brush, followed with a rubber curry brush.

2. Swab the ears with a cotton ball that has been moistened with ear cleaner. This will remove dirt and control ear odor. Follow with a dry cotton ball, and dust the ears with medicated ear powder.

3. Cut the nails with a guillotine-type nail clipper. Nails should be cut monthly.

4. Check between the foot pads and under the feet for burrs, tar, etc.

5. Bathe the dog with a tearless protein shampoo that is pH-alkaline. This will add body to the coat and restructure damaged hair.

6. Cage dry until damp. Finish drying on the table using a blow dryer and a pure bristle brush.

7. The whiskers may be removed with scissors to improve expression, although this is optional.

8. Trim with scissors any stray hair on the edges of the ears.

9. Smooth any hair that detracts from an overall sleek look. Use a fine stripping knife to remove rough ridges and to get the coat to lie close to the skin.

10. Trim any hair around the paw that looks long. The foot should be compact and neat

11. Finish with a mist of mink oil to create a brilliant shine, and brush this in with a pure bristle brush.

Fox Terrier, Smooth

TOOLS AND EQUIPMENT

- Cotton balls
- Ear cleaner
- Medicated ear powder
- Mink oil
- Nail clipper
- Pure boar bristle brush
- Rubber curry brush
- Scissors
- Stripping knife, fine
- Tearless protein shampoo
- Thinning shears

Fox Terrier, Wire

TOOLS AND EQUIPMENT

- Cotton balls
- Eye drops (eye stain remover)
- Medicated ear powder
- Metal comb (medium)
- Nail clipper
- Oster A-5 clipper/#8½ (or #7 or #5), #10 blades
- Scissors
- Slicker brush
- Thinning shears

GROOMING PROCEDURE

1. Brush the entire coat and tail with a slicker brush. Comb through with a metal comb, paying special attention to any tangles.

2. Clean the ears using medicated ear powder, and lightly pluck any stray hair from inside the ears.

3. Clean the eyes by wiping them with a cotton ball that has been moistened with eye drops. Use the same product to remove any stains under or around the eyes.

4. Cut the tips of the nails with a nail clipper, being especially careful not to cut the quick.

5. With a #10 blade on an Oster A-5 clipper, shave the anal area, being certain not to put the blade in direct contact with the skin (½ inch [1 cm] each side).

6. Shave the stomach area from groin to navel and down the insides of the thighs.

7. With a #10 blade, shave the head, starting at the center of the eyebrows and working back to the base of the skull. Then shave from the center again to the outer corners of the eyes. This line should be about ¾ inch (2 cm) above the inner corner of the eye, and it should taper into the outer corner, thus making a triangle. Next, shave down from the outer corners of the eyes to within ¾ inch (2 cm) from the corners of the mouth, and continue this line across and under the chin.

8. Shave both sides of the ears, and from the back edges of the ears shave down diagonally to a point at the base of the throat, thus forming a "V" shape.

9. With a #8½, #7, or #5 blade on an Oster A-5 clipper (according to the length of the coat desired), start at the base of the skull and dip down the back to the base of the tail.

10. Clip the top half of the tail and blend down either side of the bottom fringe. Comb the fringe downward, and scissor the lower edge, making a close feather shape.

11. With the clipper, clip down the sides of the neck to the shoulder and then down to the elbow.

12. Clip down the chest to the breastbone, and slope the pattern down diagonally to the center front of the legs.

13. From the first clip down the back, clip down the sides of the stomach, arching the pattern over the hips. (From the side, the pattern line should slope down diagonally from the breastbone, straight across the tops of the front legs, sloping up across the stomach, arching up over the hips, and down to a point in the rear.)

14. Comb through the coat to remove all loosened hair.

15. Put a cotton ball in each ear (this prevents water from entering the ear canal), and bathe the dog. Cage dry him.

16. Brush and comb through the coat.

17. Using the same blade on the Oster A-5 clipper as before, repeat the process for the pattern, blending the hair down from the pattern with the blade.

18. Scissor around the edges of the ears.

19. Comb the eyebrows forward and scissor a "V" in the center.

20. Comb the hair on the face and eyebrows forward and downward. Align the base of your scissors at the nose and the tip of the scissors at the outer corners of the eyes. Scissor the eyebrows from this angle, thus making a deep triangle, and be careful not to cut any hair from the top of the muzzle.

21. Lightly scissor any stray hairs from around the edges and sides of the beard. Use thinning shears to shape the beard, which should be long and barrel-shaped.

22. Use thinning shears to trim any stray hairs from the top of the muzzle.

23. With scissors, snip the hair from between the pads of the feet; while the dog is standing, scissor around the edges to give a neat effect (doing this first will give you a guide for shaping the legs).

24. Scissor the front legs into straight, tubular shapes.

25. Scissor evenly the bottom of the chest fringe.

26. Scissor the bottom of the belly fringe, following the contour of the dog's body and tapering up from the elbows on the front legs to the flanks at the rear.

27. Scissor the hind legs, following the natural contours. From the back view, the legs should be straight on the outside edges; on the inside edges, the legs should be straight, up to the thighs, and then they should arch up and into the shave line.

28. Lightly comb through the legs, fringe areas, and face, removing all excess hair and trimming any stray hairs as necessary.

The Wire Fox Terrier should be groomed every 6 to 8 weeks. The ears should be checked weekly and cleaned if necessary, and the nails should be checked and cut at the grooming session.

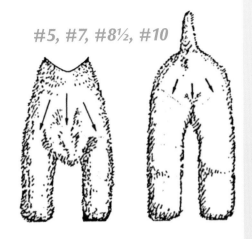

#5, #7, #8½, #10

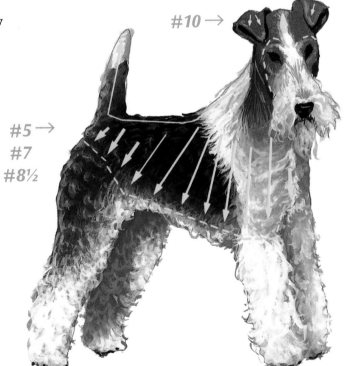

#10 →

#5 →
#7
#8½

French Bulldog

TOOLS AND EQUIPMENT

- Cotton balls
- Ear cleaner
- Hound glove
- Nail clipper (guillotine or scissor)
- Rubber brush
- Shampoo (all-purpose or whitening)
- Straight scissors (small)
- Styptic powder

GROOMING PROCEDURE

1. Cut the nails by removing only the tips; avoid cutting the quick. If the nail bleeds, apply styptic powder to stop the bleeding. Any rough nail edges may be smoothed with a file.

2. Ears should be cleaned with a liquid cleaner. Apply the cleaner to a cotton ball and wipe accumulated dirt and wax from all crevices in both ears.

3. Bathe the dog in a shampoo of your choice. Lather the dog using a rubber brush to remove any dead coat. Special attention should be paid to the folds in the skin and around the eyes. Rinse the dog thoroughly.

4. Towel dry the dog, and complete the drying with a blow dryer. The French Bulldog may also be cage dried.

5. When the dog is completely dry, brush the coat with a hound glove to remove dead coat and to make the hair lie smoothly.

6. With straight scissors, scissor the hair around the edges of the ears. The whiskers and eyebrows may be removed if desired.

The French Bulldog should be groomed every 8 to 12 weeks.

GROOMING PROCEDURE

1. Starting at the head, brush the entire coat and tail with a slicker brush.

2. During the shedding season, use a shedding blade (work from the rear to the front) and remove any mats in the undercoat (i.e., neck, chest, thighs) with a metal rake.

3. Clean the ears using medicated ear powder, and lightly pluck any stray hair from the insides of the ears.

4. Clean the eyes by wiping them with a cotton ball that has been moistened with eye drops. This will also help to remove any stains around the eyes.

5. Cut the tips of the nails with a large nail clipper, being careful not to cut the quick.

6. With scissors, clip the whiskers from the muzzle, chin, sides of the face, and above the eyes. [Note: Clipping the whiskers is a decision to be left to the dog's owner.]

7. Put a cotton ball in each ear to prevent water from entering the ear canal. After doing this, bathe the dog and cage dry him.

8. Brush through the coat briskly with a slicker brush, and then comb through with the metal comb to remove the loosened hair.

9. With scissors, snip the hair from between the pads and toes on the feet to give a neat appearance.

The German Shepherd Dog should be groomed every 8 or 10 weeks. Regular brushing by the owner with a slicker brush will help to keep the undercoat free of tangles. The ears should be checked weekly and cleaned if necessary, and the nails should be checked and cut at the grooming session.

German Shepherd Dog

TOOLS AND EQUIPMENT

- Cotton balls
- Eye drops (eye stain remover)
- Medicated ear powder
- Metal comb (wide-tooth)
- Metal rake (wide-tooth)
- Nail clipper (large)
- Scissors
- Shedding blade
- Slicker brush

German Shorthaired Pointer

TOOLS AND EQUIPMENT

- Cotton balls
- Ear cleaner
- Hound glove
- Nail clipper (guillotine or scissor)
- Rubber brush
- Shampoo (all-purpose)
- Spray conditioner or coat gloss
- Styptic powder

GROOMING PROCEDURE

1. Nails should be cut by removing only the tips; avoid cutting the quick. If the nail bleeds, apply styptic powder to stop the bleeding. Any rough edges may be smoothed with a file.

2. Clean the ears by applying liquid cleaner to a cotton ball and wiping accumulated wax and dirt from all crevices in both ears.

3. Bathe the dog in a shampoo of your choice. Lather him well using a rubber brush to remove dead hair and dirt. Rinse the dog thoroughly.

4. Towel dry the dog. Complete the drying with a cage dryer.

5. When the dog is fully dry, brush the coat with a soft bristle brush or a hound glove to remove any remaining dead hair. This also makes the coat lie smoothly.

6. Lightly spray the coat with a conditioner or coat gloss, and buff with a dry clean cloth.

The German Shorthaired Pointer should be groomed every 12 weeks.

GROOMING PROCEDURE

1. Starting at the head, brush the entire coat and tail with a slicker brush.

2. With a metal rake, gently rake through the coat. During the nonshedding season, do not rake out the undercoat; just untangle it with a rake and/or mat-splitting comb. Comb through the coat to remove all loosened hair.

3. Clean the ears using medicated ear powder.

4. Clean the eyes by wiping them with a cotton ball that has been moistened with eye drops. This will also help to remove stains around the eyes.

5. Cut the tips of the nails with a nail clipper, being careful not to cut the quick.

6. With scissors, cut the whiskers from the muzzle, under the chin, the sides of the face, and above the eyes. [Note: Clipping the whiskers is optional and should be left to the discretion of the dog's owner.]

7. Put a cotton ball in each ear and bathe the dog. Cage dry or fluff dry him. (Fluff drying may be preferable if the undercoat is excessively heavy.)

8. With scissors, snip the hair between the pads and toes on the feet and around the edges of the feet to give a neat appearance.

9. With thinning shears, remove any straggly hair from the hock joint to the feet on the hind legs.

10. Brush and comb through the entire coat.

The German Spitz should be groomed every 8 to 10 weeks. Regular brushing by the owner will help to keep the coat healthy and the undercoat free of tangles. The ears should be checked weekly and cleaned if necessary, and the nails should be checked monthly and cut if necessary.

TOOLS AND EQUIPMENT

- Cotton balls
- Eye drops (eye stain remover)
- Mat-splitting comb
- Medicated ear powder
- Metal comb (wide-toothed)
- Metal rake
- Nail clipper
- Scissors
- Slicker brush
- Thinning shears

German Wirehaired Pointer

TOOLS AND EQUIPMENT

- Comb
- Cotton balls
- Ear cleaner
- Nail clipper (guillotine or scissor)
- Oster A-5 clipper/#7 blade
- Shampoo (all-purpose or texturizing)
- Slicker brush
- Straight scissors
- Stripping knife
- Styptic powder

GROOMING PROCEDURE

1. Nails should be cut by removing only the tips; avoid cutting the quick. If the nail bleeds, apply styptic powder to stop the bleeding. Any rough nail edges may be removed with a file.

2. Ears should be cleaned with a liquid cleaner. Apply the cleaner to a cotton ball and wipe accumulated wax and dirt from all crevices in both ears.

3. Brush through the entire coat to remove dead coat and accumulated dirt.

4. The coat should be plucked, with the help of a stripping knife, to a length of about 1½ inches (4 cm). The coat on the cheeks, ears, and top of the head should be plucked closer than 1½ inches (4 cm) in order to give a smooth appearance. A beard should be left, as well as eyebrows, which should be longer at the inside corner of the eye and taper to the outer corner. Any long hairs on the body should be plucked, with the neck and shoulder areas being slightly shorter than the back area so as to accentuate the length of the neck. Any long hairs on the legs should be removed, except for some feathering on the back of the front legs. For a shorter pet clip, use a clipper with a #7 blade to cut the hair from the top of the head, the cheeks, and the ears. Continue down the throat and neck, over the back, and down to the tail. Clip the sides down over the ribs, leaving some hair at the bottom of the ribcage to accentuate depth of chest. All clipper lines should be feathered off or blended so that no line between the clipped and nonclipped areas may be detected. The top and bottom of the tail may be clipped as well.

5. The hair between the foot pads should be cut short with straight scissors. The hair from the top of the foot that grows between the toes also should be cut short.

6. Bathe the dog in a shampoo of your choice.

7. Towel dry the dog until damp. Brush the coat flat with the direction of hair growth. Let the dog air dry if it is warm enough; otherwise, finish drying him in a cage dryer.

8. When the dog is dry, go over the coat and remove any hairs that are sticking out.

The German Wirehaired Pointer should have a clean outline and be groomed every 8 to 12 weeks.

GROOMING PROCEDURE

1. Brush the entire coat with a slicker brush. Comb through with a metal comb.

2. Clean the ears using medicated ear powder, and lightly pluck any stray hair from the insides.

3. Clean the eyes by wiping them with a cotton ball that has been moistened with eye drops. This will also help to remove stains around the eyes.

4. Cut the tips of the nails with a nail clipper, being careful not to cut the quick

5. With a #10 blade on an Oster A-5 clipper, shave the head, starting at the center of the eyebrows and continuing back to the base of the skull. Then from the center again, shave to the outer corners of the eyes. This line should be about ¾ inch (2 cm) above the inner corner of the eye, and it should taper into the outer corner, thus making a triangle. Next, shave down from the outer corners of the eyes to within ¾ inch (2 cm) from the corner of the mouth and continue this line across and under the chin. [Note: When shaving the head and face, shave with the hair grain.]

6. Shave both sides of the ears. From the back edges of the ears, shave down diagonally to a point at the base of the throat, thus forming a "V" shape. Shave with the grain of the neck hair.

7. Shave the anal area, being certain not to put the blade in direct contact with the skin (½ inch [1 cm] on each side).

8. Shave the abdomen (from groin to navel) and down the insides of the thighs.

9. With a #10, #8½, or #7 blade on the Oster A-5 clipper (according to the length of coat desired), start at the base of the skull and clip down the back to the base of the tail.

10. Clip the entire tail.

11. With the clipper, clip down the sides of the neck to the shoulder and down to the elbow.

12. Clip down the chest to the breastbone, and slope the pattern down diagonally to the center front of the legs.

13. From the first clip down the back, clip down the sides of the abdomen to the flank. From the flank, clip straight down to the hock joint

14. Continue clipping the entire rear end. (From the side view, the pattern line should slope down diagonally from the breastbone, continue straight across the tops of the front legs, slope up across the abdomen, and slope down sharply to the hock joint—creating a large "V" on the rear leg.)

continued

Giant Schnauzer

TOOLS AND EQUIPMENT

- Cotton balls
- Eye drops (eye stain remover)
- Medicated ear powder
- Metal comb (medium)
- Nail clipper (large)
- Oster A-5 clipper/#7, #8½, #10 blades
- Scissors
- Slicker brush

Giant Schnauzer *continued*

15. Brush through the coat with a slicker brush to remove any excess hair.

16. Put a cotton ball in each ear to prevent water from entering the ear canal. After you have done this, bathe and cage dry the dog.

17. Brush and comb through the coat.

18. Using the same blade on the Oster A-5 clipper as before, repeat the process for the pattern, blending the hair down on the top of the pattern with the blade.

19. Scissor around the edges of the ears.

20. Scissor a "V" in the center of the eyebrows for the separation.

21. Make a part down the center of the muzzle and comb downward. Trim the edges to taper into the outer corners of the eyes.

22. Comb the eyebrows forward. Align the base of your scissors with the nose and the tip of your scissors with the outer corner of the eye. Scissor the eyebrows from this angle, thus making a deep triangle (be careful not to cut any hair from the top of the muzzle).

23. Trim the hair between the pads of the feet; while the dog is standing, scissor around the edges to give a round effect. (Doing this first will give you a guide for scissoring the legs.)

24. Scissor the front legs into straight, tubular shapes.

25. Scissor the bottom of the chest fringe evenly.

26. Scissor the belly fringe, following the contour of the dog's body and tapering up from the elbows on the front legs to the flanks at the rear.

27. Scissor the rear legs, following the natural contours. The insides should be straight to the hock joint and taper up to the shave line.

GROOMING PROCEDURE

1. Brush the coat thoroughly with a slicker brush.

2. Comb through the coat to remove all loosened hair.

3. Clean the ears using medicated ear powder, and lightly pluck any stray hair from the insides.

4. Clean the eyes by wiping them with a cotton ball that has been moistened with eye drops.

5. Cut the tips of the nails with a nail clipper, being careful not to cut the quick.

6. With a #10 blade on the Oster A-5 clipper, shave the abdomen from groin to navel and down the insides of the thighs.

7. Shave the anal area, being certain not to put the blade in direct contact with the skin (½ inch [1 cm] on either side).

8. Place a cotton ball in each ear (this prevents water from entering the ear canal), and bathe the dog. Cage dry him.

9. With scissors, snip hair from between the pads and toes of the feet and around the edges for a neat effect.

10. With scissors or thinning shears, trim straggly hairs from around the ankles on the front feet and from the hocks down to the feet on the hind legs.

11. Comb through the entire coat to remove all loosened hair.

The Glen of Imaal Terrier should be groomed every 8 to 10 weeks. The ears should be checked weekly and cleaned if necessary, and the nails should be checked monthly and cut if necessary.

Glen of Imaal Terrier

TOOLS AND EQUIPMENT

- Cotton balls
- Eye drops (eye stain remover)
- Medicated ear powder
- Metal comb (medium)
- Nail clipper
- Oster A-5 clipper/#10 blade
- Scissors
- Slicker brush
- Thinning shears

Golden Retriever

TOOLS AND EQUIPMENT

- Blending shears
- Comb
- Cotton balls
- Ear cleaner
- Nail clipper (guillotine or scissor)
- Shampoo (all-purpose or conditioning)
- Slicker brush
- Straight scissors
- Styptic powder

GROOMING PROCEDURE

1. Nails should be cut by removing only the tips; avoid cutting the quick. If the nail bleeds, apply styptic powder to stop the bleeding. Any rough nail edges may be smoothed with a file.

2. Clean the ears with a liquid cleaner. Apply the cleaner to a cotton ball and wipe accumulated dirt and wax from the crevices in both ears.

3. To remove dead coat and any matted hair, brush out the entire dog with a slicker brush.

4. Bathe the dog in a shampoo of your choice and rinse him thoroughly. A conditioning rinse may be used to help cut down on static electricity.

5. Towel dry the dog. Use a dryer to complete the drying as you brush the coat in the direction of its growth. After drying, comb through the coat to remove any tangles.

6. With straight scissors, remove the hair on the bottom of the foot and between the pads. Remove the hair on the outer edge and underside of the paw to round the foot. With blending shears, remove the hair that grows out between the toes on the top side of the foot. The foot should have a round, well-knuckled-up, compact look.

7. Excessive hair should be removed from the back of the hock to even up the hairs.

8. The hair directly under the flap may be thinned out to allow the ear to hang close to the side of the head. The edge of the ear may be neatened up with blending shears.

9. The Golden's plume-like tail, when extended to the hock joint, should not exceed it. The tail should be trimmed so that it just touches the hock.

10. Any hair around the anus may be carefully trimmed away.

The completed Golden Retriever should have a neat outline without looking scissored. This breed should be natural looking. Grooming should be done every 6 to 8 weeks.

GROOMING PROCEDURE

1. Spray the entire coat with protein coat conditioner. This adds body to the coat and helps repair split ends. Brush through the entire coat with a pin brush. Then comb with a molting comb to take out loose, dead undercoat. Use a slicker brush to loosen up matted areas.

2. Swab the ears with a cotton ball that has been moistened with ear cleaner. This will remove dirt and control ear odor. Follow this with a dry cotton ball, and dust the ears with medicated ear powder.

3. Cut the nails with a guillotine-type nail clipper. Nails should be cut monthly.

4. Check between the foot pads and under the feet for burrs, tar, etc. Scissor the hair under the feet to prevent debris from adhering. Trim any hair around the paw that touches the ground. Do not take out any hair between the toes.

5. Scissor any long hair under the tail that hangs over the anus. Be sure the anus is clear, and then trim down under the tail area so it does not collect fecal matter.

6. The whiskers may be removed with scissors to improve the expression, although this is optional.

7. Bathe the dog with a tearless protein shampoo that is pH-alkaline. This will add fullness and body to the coat and restructure damaged hair.

8. Use a high-velocity dryer to blow excess water off the dog while he is still in the tub. This will speed up the drying time and help prevent the coat from becoming overly dry. Cage dry the dog until the hair is damp. Then finish drying on the table using a blow dryer and a pin brush to separate all the hair and remove all of the loose coat.

9. It is especially important that feathering on the legs, tail, and ears be blown dry to straighten it and give it a long-styled look. Use the fine side of a steel comb as you are drying to separate all hair and give a luxurious blown-dry look.

10. Excess hair on the face can be removed with a #10 blade. Go with the hair grain because the jaw should have a clean outline.

11. With a #7F blade, clip under the chin and down to the throat, to about 2 inches (5 cm) above the breastbone. Lift the clipper slightly as you near the end of your clipped area to blend the clipped area into the nonclipped area of the chest. To accomplish this, it takes a slight twist of the wrist as if you were using the end of the clipper as a shovel. You must work to blend the clipped area into the fringe area, leaving no uneven lines or ridges. How far down you clip depends on how long you wish the neck to appear. Always cut with the lie of the hair, never against or across the grain. Work gradually to ensure that too much coat is not removed.

continued

TOOLS AND EQUIPMENT

- Cotton balls
- Ear cleaner
- High-velocity dryer
- Medicated ear powder
- Molting comb, long hair
- Nail clipper (extra large)
- Oster A-5 clipper/#7F, #10 blades
- Pin brush (large)
- Protein coat conditioner
- Pure boar bristle brush
- Scissors
- Slicker brush
- Steel comb (medium/fine)
- Stripping knife
- Tearless protein shampoo
- Thinning shears

#10

12. Clean out the hair around and under the ears. Blend the sides of the neck, where the shaved area stops, with a twist-of-the-wrist action. Keep the shaved area under the ears and neck. Do not use clippers on the top side of the neck. The neck should look long and lean, without throatiness. Use thinning shears to blend the shaved area into the long area. Always use thinning shears in combination with a comb. Hold thinning shears pointed in the direction the hair grows. Thin and comb to achieve the desired look. Never cut across the grain.

13. The head should be clean, and straggly hair can be removed with a stripping knife. Do not use clippers on the head.

14. Holding the ear leather near the bottom, stretch it and clip the ears with a #10 blade. To give the appearance of a low-set ear, clip one-third of the way down in the direction of hair growth. Do not trim the fold along the front edge of the ear. Trim into the underside of the fold only. Shave the underside of the ear one-third of the way down, also including the burr at the front. You may go against the grain in this area to remove as much hair as possible. The shaved area inside the ear must come down as far as the shaved area on the outside of the ear. Trim the front edge of the upper ear with scissors, blending the short hair into the longer hair. If feathering on the inside of the ear is profuse, blend it down to give the appearance of the ears being carried close to the head. Ears are to be long, and bottoms should be scissored only if uneven or straggly.

15. If the shoulders have profuse hair, use thinning shears to create a smooth line, with the neck gradually widening into the shoulders.

16. The chest hair should be as long as possible and should only be shortened if it is uneven or straggly.

17. Side hair and hair under the body should also be long and natural. Trim and shorten these areas only if they are straggly or if you want to achieve a natural contour from chest to tuckup.

18. Feathering on the back legs and under the tail should be combed down, and only straggly hair should be removed. The hind feet should be trimmed so that they are rounded and catlike in shape, with plenty of hair between the toes. Use thinning shears to trim off excess rough hair or protruding hair between the toes that does not conform to the desired round shape. The back of the hock can be thinned to eliminate any bushiness, but it should not look scissored.

19. Tail feathering should be long and combed down. For hygienic reasons, be sure that any profuse hair on the underside of the tail (hair that hangs over the anus) is removed. Straggly hair on the top side of the tail should be removed with thinning shears. Taper the tail so that it is wide at the base and narrows at the tip. Remove excess hair from the tail tip if it touches the ground; this will give the tail the length to balance the rest of the dog.

20. Trim the front feet as you did the rear feet, but comb the feathering out and trim it to achieve a natural straight line that blends into the pastern.

21. Lightly spray the coat with protein coat conditioner to add brilliance and fragrance, and brush with a pure boar bristle brush.

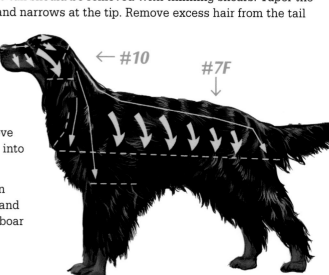

← *#10*

#7F
↓

GROOMING PROCEDURE

1. Brush the coat briskly with a sisal brush.

2. Clean the ears using medicated ear powder.

3. Clean the eyes by wiping them with a cotton ball that has been moistened with eye drops. This will also help to remove any stains around or under the eyes.

4. Cut the tips of the nails with a nail clipper, being careful not to cut the quick.

5. With a damp cotton ball, gently wipe the insides of the lips, being certain to remove any trapped food particles.

6. With scissors, clip the whiskers from the muzzle, under the chin, the sides of the face, and above the eyes. [Note: Clipping the whiskers is a decision to be left to the dog's owner.]

7. Place a cotton ball in each ear (this prevents water from entering the ear canal), and bathe the dog, paying special attention to the white areas (if the dog is a harlequin). Cage dry him.

8. Put a few drops of lanolin coat conditioner into the palms of your hands, rub them together lightly, and gently massage into the coat. Use more as needed.

9. Lightly brush the coat with a sisal brush to distribute the conditioner, and then rub over the coat with a chamois cloth to give it a nice sheen.

10. These large dogs tend to have bald, sometimes sore, patches on their elbows, pasterns, and hock joints. In this case, massage these patches with vitamin E oil to heal them.

The Great Dane rarely needs bathing (every 3 or 4 months), but regular brushing by the owner with a sisal brush, along with a monthly application of lanolin coat conditioner, will help maintain a healthy, shiny coat. The ears should be checked weekly, and the nails should be checked monthly. Clip the nails if necessary.

Great Dane

TOOLS AND EQUIPMENT

- Chamois cloth
- Cotton balls
- Eye drops (eye stain remover)
- Lanolin coat conditioner
- Medicated ear powder
- Nail clipper (large)
- Scissors
- Sisal (natural bristle) brush
- Vitamin E oil

Great Pyrenees

TOOLS AND EQUIPMENT

- Cotton balls
- Ear cleaner
- Eye stain cleaner
- High-velocity dryer
- Long-hair molting comb (#565)
- Medicated ear powder
- Nail clipper (extra large)
- Oster A-5 clipper/#10 blade
- Pin brush
- Protein coat conditioner
- Pure boar bristle brush
- Rubber curry brush
- Scissors
- Slicker brush
- Steel comb (fine/medium)
- Tearless protein shampoo
- Thinning shears
- Undercoat rake
- Wood utility comb

GROOMING PROCEDURE

1. Spray the entire coat with protein coat conditioner. This adds body to the coat and helps repair split ends. Brush through the entire coat with an undercoat rake. This will loosen up the coat and remove dead undercoat. Start at the rear of the dog, at the bottom of the skirt area. Work in sections, using your other hand to lift the hair ahead of the section you are working on. Work through the entire dog, from the back to the neck area. Then brush through the coat with a slicker brush to remove the dead topcoat. If the dog is shedding heavily, finish with a molting comb followed by a rubber curry brush. Work vigorously. The more hair you remove now, the less hair you need to wash and dry.

2. Swab the ears with a cotton ball that has been moistened with ear cleaner. This will remove dirt and control ear odor. Follow this with a dry cotton ball, and dust the ears with medicated ear powder.

3. Cut the nails with a guillotine-type nail clipper. Nails should be cut monthly.

4. Wipe the inside corners of the eyes with a water-moistened cotton ball. Remove any eye stains under and around the eyes with eye stain remover on a cotton ball.

5. Bathe the dog with a tearless protein shampoo that is pH-alkaline to enhance the whiteness of the coat.

6. Use a high-velocity dryer to blow excess water off the dog while he is still in the tub. This will speed up the drying time and help prevent the coat from becoming overly dry. Cage dry the dog until the hair is damp. Then finish drying on the table using a blow dryer and a pin brush to separate all the hair and remove all of the loose coat. Finish with a steel comb through the entire coat, paying special attention to the fine hair behind the ears. Use the fine side of the comb for this area.

7. Scissor any long hair under the tail that hangs over the anus. Be sure the anus is clear, and then use a #10 blade to blend down under the tail area so that it does not collect fecal matter.

8. The hair at the base of the tail can be thinned with thinning shears to shorten the back. Always use thinning shears in combination with a comb. Hold the thinning shears pointed in the direction the hair grows. Never cut across the grain of the hair. Thin and comb the hair to achieve the desired look.

9. Use thinning shears to thin out the rump hair, if profuse, and to level out the topline.

10. Brush up the hair on the legs, and comb straight the feathering and hock hair.

11. Check between the foot pads and under the feet for burrs, tar, etc. Scissor the hair under the foot even with the pads. Trim any hair around the paw that touches the ground, and neaten the entire foot. With thinning shears, trim the hair growing out between the toes.

12. Lightly mist the coat with protein coat conditioner to add brilliance and fragrance.

Greyhound

TOOLS AND EQUIPMENT

- Cotton balls
- Ear cleaner
- Medicated ear powder
- Mink oil spray
- Nail clipper (extra large)
- Pure boar bristle brush
- Scissors
- Sisal hound glove
- Skin cream
- Tearless shampoo or whitening shampoo
- Thinning shears

GROOMING PROCEDURE

1. Brush the coat with a pure bristle brush. Follow with a thorough brushing using the hound glove.

2. Swab the ears with a cotton ball that has been moistened with ear cleaner. This will remove dirt and control ear odor. Follow with a dry cotton ball, and dust the ears with medicated ear powder.

3. Cut the nails with a guillotine-type nail clipper. Nails should be cut monthly.

4. Check between the foot pads and under the feet for burrs, tar, etc.

5. Bathe the dog with a tearless shampoo that is balanced pH-alkaline. Use a tearless whitening shampoo for Greyhounds who are white or partially white.

6. Cage dry until damp. Finish drying on the table using a blow dryer and a pure bristle brush.

7. The whiskers may be removed with scissors to improve expression (optional).

8. With thinning shears, remove any straggly hair on the brisket, the sides of the neck, the backs of the thighs, in the rear tuckup, or on the face.

9. Calluses on the elbows can be rubbed with skin cream to soften and heal them.

10. Finish with a mist of mink oil to create a brilliant shine, and brush this in with a pure boar bristle brush.

GROOMING PROCEDURE

1. Brush the entire coat with a sisal brush, using long, deep strokes for a thorough massage.

2. Clean the ears using medicated ear powder.

3. Clean the eyes by wiping them with a cotton ball that has been moistened with eye drops.

4. Cut the tips of the nails with a nail clipper, being careful not to cut the quick.

5. Using scissors, snip the whiskers from the muzzle, under the chin, the sides of the face, and above the eyes. [Note: Clipping the whiskers is a decision to be left to the owner, if the dog is not a show or hunting dog.]

6. Place a cotton ball in each ear (this prevents water from entering the ear canal), and bathe the dog. Cage dry him, paying special attention to the white areas.

7. Put a few drops of lanolin coat conditioner into the palms of your hands, rub them together lightly, and massage into the coat.

8. Brush the coat with a sisal brush to distribute the conditioner, and lightly rub over the coat with a chamois cloth to give it a nice sheen.

The Hamiltonstovare should be groomed every 10 to 12 weeks if he is kept in a home environment. Hunting dogs need to be groomed less often. Regular brushing by the owner will help maintain a healthy, shiny coat. The ears should be checked weekly and cleaned if necessary, and the nails should be checked monthly and cut if necessary.

Hamiltonstovare

TOOLS AND EQUIPMENT

- Chamois cloth
- Cotton balls
- Eye drops (eye stain remover)
- Lanolin coat conditioner
- Medicated ear powder
- Nail clipper
- Scissors
- Sisal (natural bristle) brush

Harrier

TOOLS AND EQUIPMENT

- Cotton balls
- Ear cleaner
- Medicated ear powder
- Mink oil spray
- Nail clipper (extra large)
- Pure boar bristle brush
- Scissors
- Sisal hound glove
- Skin cream
- Tearless protein shampoo
- Thinning shears

GROOMING PROCEDURE

1. Brush the coat with a pure bristle brush. Follow with a thorough brushing using a hound glove.

2. Swab the ears with a cotton ball that has been moistened with ear cleaner. This will remove dirt and control ear odor. Follow with a dry cotton ball, and dust the ears with medicated ear powder.

3. Cut the nails with a guillotine-type nail clipper. Nails should be cut monthly.

4. Check between the foot pads and under the feet for burrs, tar, etc.

5. Wipe inside the corners of the eyes with a water-moistened cotton ball. Remove any eye stains under and around the eyes with a cotton ball moistened with eye drops.

6. To enhance the white areas of the coat, bathe the dog with a tearless protein shampoo that is balanced pH-alkaline.

7. Cage dry the dog until damp. Finish drying on the table using a blow dryer and a pure bristle brush.

8. The whiskers may be removed with scissors to improve expression, but this is optional.

9. With thinning shears, remove any long hair on the face and any straggly hair on the back of the thighs or on the rump.

10. Calluses on the elbows can be rubbed with skin cream to soften and heal them.

11. Finish with a mist of mink oil to create a brilliant shine, and brush this in with a pure bristle brush.

GROOMING PROCEDURE

1. Brush the entire coat and tail with a slicker brush, paying special attention to the neck, thighs, and tail. Any tangles in these areas can be removed with a metal rake. Comb through the coat, removing all loosened hair.

2. Clean the ears using medicated ear powder, and lightly pluck any stray hair from the insides.

3. Clean the eyes by wiping them with a cotton ball that has been moistened with eye drops.

4. Cut the tips of the nails with a nail clipper, being careful not to cut the quick.

5. With scissors, clip the whiskers from the muzzle, under the chin, the sides of the face, and above the eyes. [Note: Clipping the whiskers is a decision to be left to the dog's owner.]

6. Place a cotton ball in each ear to prevent water from entering the ear canal, and bathe the dog. Cage dry him.

7. Brush the entire coat and tail.

8. With scissors, snip the hair between the pads and toes of the feet and around the edges for a neat appearance.

9. With scissors or thinning shears, remove any straggly hair on the hind legs from the hock joint to the feet and on the front legs from around the ankles.

10. With thinning shears, remove any straggly hair from the tops of the ears and head.

11. Brush and comb through the entire coat.

The Hovawart, if kept in a home environment, should be groomed every 10 to 12 weeks. Regular brushing by the owner will help maintain a healthy, shiny coat. The ears should be checked weekly and cleaned if necessary, and the nails should be checked monthly and cut if needed.

TOOLS AND EQUIPMENT

- Cotton balls
- Eye drops (eye stain remover)
- Medicated ear powder
- Metal comb (wide-toothed)
- Metal rake
- Nail clipper
- Scissors
- Slicker brush
- Thinning shears

Ibizan Hound

TOOLS AND EQUIPMENT

- Cotton balls
- Ear cleaner
- Medicated ear powder
- Mink oil spray
- Nail clipper (extra large)
- Pure boar bristle brush
- Scissors
- Sisal hound glove
- Skin cream
- Tearless protein shampoo

GROOMING PROCEDURE

1. Brush the coat with a pure bristle brush. Follow with a thorough brushing using a hound glove.

2. Swab the ears with a cotton ball that has been moistened with ear cleaner. This will remove dirt and control ear odor. Follow with a dry cotton ball, and dust the ears with medicated ear powder.

3. Cut the nails with a guillotine-type nail clipper. Nails should be cut monthly.

4. Check between the foot pads and under the feet for burrs, tar, etc.

5. Bathe the dog with a tearless protein shampoo that is pH-alkaline.

6. Cage dry until damp. Finish drying on the table using a blow dryer and a pure bristle brush.

7. The whiskers may be removed with scissors to improve expression, although this is optional.

8. Remove any long hair on the face.

9. To soften and heal calluses on the elbows, rub them with skin cream.

10. Finish with a mist of mink oil to create a brilliant shine; brush this in with a hound glove.

GROOMING PROCEDURE

1. Brush through the coat with a slicker brush, paying special attention to the neck, chest, thighs, tail, and leg fringes.

2. Comb through the coat to remove any tangles and loosened hair.

3. Clean the ears using medicated ear powder, and lightly pluck any stray hair from the insides.

4. Clean the eyes by wiping them with a cotton ball that has been moistened with eye drops.

5. Cut the tips of the nails with a nail clipper, being careful not to cut the quick.

6. With scissors, snip the whiskers from the muzzle, under the chin, the sides of the face, and above the eyes. [Note: Clipping the whiskers is a decision to be left to the owner if the dog is not a show dog.]

7. With a #10 blade on an Oster A-5 clipper, shave the stomach from groin to navel and down the insides of the thighs.

8. Shave the anal area, being certain not to put the blade in direct contact with the skin (½ inch [1 cm] each side).

9. Bathe the dog, but first put a cotton ball in each ear to prevent water from entering the ear canal. Cage dry him.

10. Fluff dry (with a slicker brush) all feathering on the ears, tail, and legs.

11. With scissors, snip hair from between the pads and toes of the feet and around the edges.

12. With scissors or thinning shears, trim straggly hairs from around the ankles on the front feet and from the hocks down to the feet on the hind legs.

13. Holding the tail straight out, comb the hair down and trim the lower edge with scissors, keeping the hair wide at the base and tapering it to the tip.

14. With scissors, trim the edges of the leg, chest, and belly fringes.

15. With thinning shears, trim any straggly hairs from the top of the head and the tops of the ears.

16. Comb through the entire coat to remove all loosened hair.

The Irish Red and White Setter should be groomed every 8 to 10 weeks. The ears should be checked weekly and cleaned if necessary, and the nails should be checked monthly and cut if they have become too long.

Irish Red and White Setter

TOOLS AND EQUIPMENT

- Cotton balls
- Eye drops (eye stain remover)
- Medicated ear powder
- Metal comb (medium)
- Nail clipper
- Oster A-5 clipper/#10 blade
- Scissors
- Slicker brush
- Thinning shears

Irish Setter

TOOLS AND EQUIPMENT

- Cotton balls
- Ear cleaner
- High-velocity dryer
- Matting comb for long hair
- Medicated ear powder
- Nail clipper (extra-large)
- Oster A-5 clipper/#7F, #10 blades
- Pin brush (large)
- Protein coat conditioner
- Pure boar bristle brush
- Scissors
- Slicker brush
- Steel comb (medium/fine)
- Stripping knife
- Tearless protein shampoo
- Thinning shears

GROOMING PROCEDURE

1. Spray the entire coat with protein coat conditioner. This adds body to the coat and helps repair split ends. Brush through the entire coat with a pin brush. Then, comb with a molting comb to take out loose, dead undercoat. Use a slicker brush to loosen up matted areas.

2. Swab the ears with a cotton ball that has been moistened with ear cleaner. This will remove dirt and control ear odor. Follow this with a dry cotton ball, and dust the ears with medicated ear powder.

3. Cut the nails with a guillotine-type nail clipper. Nails should be cut monthly.

4. Check between the foot pads and under the feet for burrs, tar, etc. Scissor the hair under the feet to prevent debris from adhering. Trim any hair around the paw that touches the ground. Do not take out any hair between the toes.

5. Scissor any long hair under the tail that hangs over the anus. Be sure the anus is clear, and then trim down under the tail area so it does not become soiled.

6. The whiskers may be removed with scissors to improve the expression (optional).

7. Bathe the dog with a tearless protein shampoo that is pH-alkaline. This will add fullness and body to the coat and restructure damaged hair.

8. Use a high-velocity dryer to blow excess water off the dog while he is still in the tub. This will speed up the drying time and help prevent the coat from becoming overly dry. Cage dry the dog until the hair is damp. Then finish drying on the table using a blow dryer and a pin brush to separate all the hair and remove all of the loose coat

9. It is especially important that feathering on the legs, tail, and ears be blown dry to straighten and give a long-styled look. As you are drying, use the fine side of a steel comb to separate all the hair and give a luxurious blown-dry look.

10. Excess hair on the face can be removed with a #10 blade, going with the grain because the jaw should have a clean outline.

11. With a #7F blade, clip under the chin and down the throat to about 2 inches (5 cm) above the breastbone. As you near the end of your clipped area, lift the clipper slightly to blend the clipped into the nonclipped area of the chest. This takes a slight twist of the wrist, as if you were using the end of the clipper as a shovel. You must work to blend the clipped area into the fringe area, leaving no uneven lines or ridges. How far down you clip depends on how long you wish the neck to appear. Always cut with the lie of the hair, never against or across the grain. Work gradually to ensure that you don't remove too much coat.

12. Clean out the hair around and under the ears. With a twist of the wrist action, blend the sides of the neck where the shaved area stops. Keep this shaved area under the ears and under the

neck. Do not use clippers on the topside of the neck. The neck is to look long and lean, without throatiness. Use thinning shears to blend the shaved area into the long area. Always use thinning shears in combination with a comb. Hold thinning shears pointed in the direction the hair grows; thin and comb to achieve the desired look. Never cut across the grain.

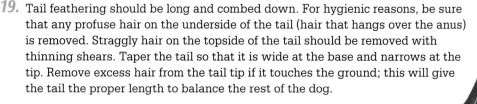

13. The Irish Setter should have a clean appearance, so straggly hair can be removed with a stripping knife. Do not use clippers on the head.

14. Holding the ear leather near the bottom, stretch it; and with a #10 blade, clip the ear one-third of the way down in the direction of hair growth to give the appearance of a low-set ear. Do not trim the fold along the front edge of the ear. Trim into the underside of the fold only. Shave the underside of the ear one-third of the way down, also including the burr at the front to remove as much hair as possible; you may go against the grain in this area. The shaved area inside the ear must be down as far as the shaved area on the outside of the ear. Trim the front edge of the upper ear with scissors, blending the short hair into the longer hair. If the feathering on the inside of the ear is profuse, blend it down to give the appearance of the ears being carried close to the head. Ears are to be long, and bottoms should be scissored only if they are uneven or straggly.

15. If the shoulders have profuse hair, use thinning shears to create a smooth line with the neck, gradually widening into the shoulders.

16. The chest hair should be as long as possible and should only be shortened if it is uneven or straggly.

17. Side hair and underbody hair should also be long and natural. Trim and shorten only if straggly or to achieve a natural contour from chest to tuckup.

18. Feathering on the back legs and under the tail should be combed down; only straggly hair should be removed. The back feet should be trimmed to achieve a rounded foot, catlike in shape, with plenty of hair between the toes. Use thinning shears to trim off excess rough hair or protruding hair between the toes that does not conform to the desired round shape. The back of the hock can be thinned to eliminate any bushiness, but it should not look scissored.

19. Tail feathering should be long and combed down. For hygienic reasons, be sure that any profuse hair on the underside of the tail (hair that hangs over the anus) is removed. Straggly hair on the topside of the tail should be removed with thinning shears. Taper the tail so that it is wide at the base and narrows at the tip. Remove excess hair from the tail tip if it touches the ground; this will give the tail the proper length to balance the rest of the dog.

20. Trim the front feet as you did the rear feet, but comb out the feathering and trim it to achieve a natural straight line that blends into the pastern.

21. Lightly spray the coat with protein coat conditioner to add brilliance and fragrance; brush with a pure bristle brush.

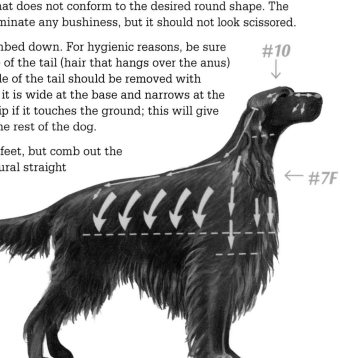

Irish Terrier

TOOLS AND EQUIPMENT

- Coat gloss
- Comb (fine/medium)
- Cotton balls
- Ear cleaner
- Ear forceps
- High-velocity dryer
- Long-hair molting comb (#565)
- Medicated ear powder
- Nail clipper (extra large)
- Oster A-5 clipper/#5, #5F, #7, #7F, #10 blades
- Pin brush
- Protein coat conditioner
- Pure boar bristle brush
- Scissors
- Slicker brush
- Tearless protein shampoo
- Thinning shears

GROOMING PROCEDURE

1. Spray the entire coat with protein coat conditioner. This adds body to the coat and helps repair split ends. Brush through the entire coat with a slicker brush. Then comb thoroughly with the molting comb to remove dead undercoat Start at the rear of the dog, at the bottom of the skirt area. Work in sections through the entire dog, from the back to the neck area, Work vigorously. The more hair you remove now, the less hair you need to wash and dry.

2. Swab the ears with a cotton ball that has been moistened with ear cleaner. This will remove dirt and control ear odor. Follow with a dry cotton ball, and dust the ears with medicated ear powder. With your fingers or ear forceps, pluck the hair inside the ears.

3. Cut the nails with a guillotine-type nail clipper. Nails should be cut monthly.

4. Check between the foot pads and under the feet for burrs, tar, etc. With a #10 blade, clip the hair under the feet and between the pads.

5. Bathe the dog with a tearless protein shampoo that is pH-alkaline. This will add fullness and body to the coat and restructure damaged hair.

6. Use a high-velocity dryer to blow excess water off the dog while he is still in the tub. This will speed up the drying time and help prevent the coat from becoming overly dry. Cage dry the dog until the hair is damp. Mist with coat gloss. Finish drying on the table using a blow dryer and a pin brush to separate all the hair and remove all of the loose coat.

7. To separate all of the hair, comb the entire coat to the skin. Use the medium part of the comb.

8. Use a #10 blade to clip the hair around the anus. Just clear the area and do not use heavy pressure.

9. Shave the abdomen with a #10 blade, going with the lay of the hair.

10. Shave the ear on both sides with a #10 blade. Shave from base to tip. Trim the outside edge, using the thumb as a protective guide to prevent nicks.

11. Clip the top of the skull with a #10 blade, starting behind the eye socket and continuing back to the base of the skull. Leave plenty of eyebrow. Clip the side of the face, making a line from the outside corner of the eye to the mouth. Do not trim between the eyebrows or trim any part of the muzzle or under the eyes.

12. Lifting the beard, clip under the jaw with a #10 blade. Clean out this area, but leave the beard heavy.

13. Clip the throat with a #10 blade, forming a "U" from ear to ear, and shave down to 1 or 2 inches (2.5 or 5 cm) above the breastbone.

14. Clip the body with a #7F blade. Body blades change, depending on the dog's type of coat and skin sensitivity. Clip from the base of the skull to the end of the tail (depending on coat texture, a #7F may be changed to a #7, #5, or #5F). Clip both sides of the body, from the sides of the neck to where the legs join the body in the front, and down to the thighs on the rear legs. In profile, there should be an even incline from elbow to hip. Follow the contour of the body, moving the clipper in the direction the hair grows. Do not go against the grain or across the grain. Lift the clipper slightly as you near the end of the clipped area, to blend the clipped area into the nonclipped area of the skirt and leg. This takes a slight twist of the wrist to accomplish, as if you were using the end of the clipper as a shovel. You must work to blend the clipped area into the fringe area, leaving no uneven lines or ridges.

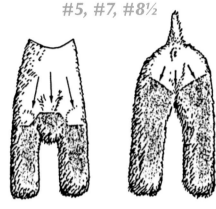

#5, #7, #8½

15. Clip the tail with a #7F blade. Always clip with the grain—the way the hair grows—and never against the growth. To prevent irritation, use very light pressure on the underside of the tail. Closely blend the area under the tail.

16. With a #7F blade, clip the front of the dog's chest straight down to the brisket. Leave a fringe between the front legs to define chest depth.

17. Brush the hair on the front legs up and then down with a slicker brush. Comb through with the medium side of the comb. Lift the foot and shake the leg to allow the hair to fall naturally. Scissor the leg into a cylindrical shape. Use thinning shears to blend in any uneven line that you may have between the shaved area and unshaved area. Blend into the shoulder to create a straight line from shoulder to foot. Shape the foot so that it appears round and compact, but don't expose the nails.

18. Scissor evenly the furnishings on the sides of the body, making them fuller underneath the ribs and chest. Trim evenly the line from brisket to groin, striving for a natural tuckup.

19. Brush the rear leg up and then down, comb, and shake free. With scissors, blend the hip area into the rear leg. The rear leg should show good angulation and should be trimmed evenly to the middle of the thigh. From thigh to hock, remove straggly hair only. Trim evenly the backline of the hock. Round the foot, and blend it into the leg. The inside of the back legs should form an arch.

20. Comb the eyebrows forward, and with scissors pointing toward the nose, trim the hair beside the eyes to make them visible. Scissor the hair between the eyes (at the stop). Recomb. Cut on an angle, from the outside corner of the eye to the opposite corner of the nose.

21. Comb the beard forward and trim any straggly or extra-long whiskers to give a neat appearance.

22. Topbrush the coat with a pure bristle brush that has been sprayed with protein coat conditioner. This will add brilliance and fragrance.

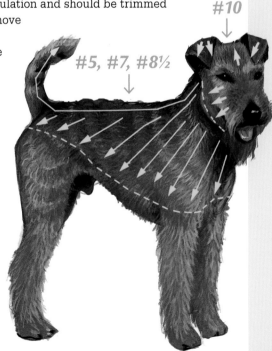

#10

#5, #7, #8½

Irish Water Spaniel

TOOLS AND EQUIPMENT

- Blending shears
- Oster A-5 clipper/#10, #15 blades
- Comb
- Cotton balls
- Ear cleaner
- Nail clipper (guillotine or scissor)
- Shampoo (all-purpose or texturizing)
- Slicker brush
- Straight shears
- Styptic powder

GROOMING PROCEDURE

1. Cut the nails by removing only the tips; avoid cutting the quick. If the nail bleeds, apply styptic powder to stop the bleeding. Any rough nail edges may be smoothed with a file.

2. Clean the ears with a liquid cleaner. Apply the cleaner to a cotton ball and wipe accumulated wax and dirt from all the crevices in both ears.

3. Brush out the entire dog with a slicker brush to remove any matting and dead coat.

4. With a clipper and a #10 blade, clip the face with the growth of the hair, from the nose over the muzzle and cheeks to the front of the ear opening. Do not clip higher than the line from the corner of the eye to the top of the ear opening. Leave the peak of hair that grows into the stop, as this is a breed characteristic. Another characteristic is the beard that this breed sports. It may be left in place. The hair on the throat below the beard should be short, as the face is, and may be clipped into a "V," with the point ending at the breastbone. Clip with blending shears, if desired.

5. Before the bath, the body may be scissored to remove excess hair and to encourage the coat to curl. Comb the coat so that it stands away from the body and sticks straight out. With straight shears, scissor the entire body coat to a length of about 2 inches (5 cm). Leave more on the ribcage to accent the spring of the ribs. Take a little more off on the neck to accentuate length, and a little more under the ears (on the neck) to help the ears lie closer to the head.

6. Bathe the dog in a shampoo of your choice, and rinse thoroughly.

7. Pat dry with a towel so as not to muss the curls.

8. The legs, from the elbows down (in front) and from the hocks down (in rear) should be blown dry while brushing gently with a slicker brush. The ears may be blown dry, too. Do not blow dry the body coat. This should be encouraged to curl by air drying only.

9. To scissor the legs, take a comb and pull the hair so that it stands away from the leg. Scissor evenly into a full column. Remove excess hair from the underside of the foot, and scissor the hair between the pads or clip it with a #15 blade. Round the foot to blend in with the rest of the leg. The rear legs, from the hocks down, should be scissored to remove excess hair. Remove hair from the underside of the foot. Round the foot and cut the hair on the outer edge of the foot close to help the rear look straight. The hair on the inside of the hock should be cut shorter, as well, to help the rear look straight. When the legs have been scissored, they may be sprayed with a mist of water to encourage the coat to recurl.

10. The hair on the tail may be smoothed out with blending shears. The base of the tail should be covered with curls that extend out from the body approximately 3 inches (8 cm). The rest of the tail should be covered with short, smooth hair, as if the tail had been clipped. This so-called "rat tail" is a striking characteristic of the breed.

11. The topknot should be shaped to form a well-defined peak that extends to a point between the eyes. The hair at the top of the ears should be shortened to accentuate a low ear set.

12. The skirt should be straight, but it should gently slope up to the rear—not enough to create a tuckup.

13. The topline should be straight or slightly higher in the rear, so any hair that sticks out and disrupts the line should be removed.

14. The hair on the back of the back leg, just above the hock, should be scissored short to accentuate the angulation.

The Irish Water Spaniel should give the appearance of a smart, strongly-built (but not leggy) dog with tight curls all over his body. This breed should be groomed every 4 to 8 weeks.

Irish Wolfhound

TOOLS AND EQUIPMENT

- Cotton balls
- Ear cleaner
- Ear forceps
- Eye stain remover
- Medicated ear powder
- Nail clipper
- Protein coat conditioner
- Pure boar bristle brush
- Scissors
- Short-hair molting comb (#564)
- Slicker brush
- Steel comb (medium/fine)
- Stripping knife
- Tearless protein shampoo
- Thinning shears

GROOMING PROCEDURE

1. Spray the entire coat with protein coat conditioner. This adds body to the coat and helps repair split ends. Brush through the entire coat with a slicker brush to remove loose hair. Then, to take out loose undercoat, comb with a molting comb made for shorthaired breeds (#564).

2. Swab the ears with a cotton ball that has been moistened with ear cleaner. This will remove dirt and control ear odor. Follow this with a dry cotton ball, and dust the ears with medicated ear powder. With your fingers or ear forceps, pull out any dead hair inside the ears.

3. Cut the nails with a guillotine-type nail clipper. Nails should be cut monthly.

4. Bathe the dog with a tearless protein shampoo that is pH-alkaline. This will add fullness and body to the coat and restructure damaged hair.

5. Use a high-velocity dryer to blow excess water off the dog while he is still in the tub. This will speed up the drying time and help prevent the coat from becoming overly dry. Cage dry the dog until the hair is damp. Then finish drying on the table using a blow dryer and a pin brush to separate all the hair and remove all of the loose coat. Finish with a steel comb through the entire coat, paying special attention to the fine hair behind the ears. Use the fine side of the comb for this area.

6. Check between the foot pads and under the feet for burrs, tar, etc. Scissor the hair under the feet even with the pads. Trim around the paw and neaten the entire foot. Use thinning shears to trim the hair growing out between the toes. Be sure to neaten the hair on the back of the rear pasterns.

7. The whiskers may be removed with scissors to improve expression, although this is optional.

8. Using the thumb and forefinger, strip the dead hair on the outside of the ear.

9. Use a stripping knife or thinning shears to remove any unruly hair on top of the head.

10. Thin excess ruff on both sides of the neck.

11. Use thinning shears to remove any excess tufts on the elbows.

12. Neaten the beard and whiskers, leaving them square and full.

13. Remove any straggly hair from the body, and neaten the leg featherings and tail with thinning shears.

14. Spray the coat with protein coat conditioner to add brilliance and fragrance, and brush this in with a pure bristle brush.

GROOMING PROCEDURE

1. Brush the coat with a pure boar bristle brush, followed by a rubber curry brush.

2. Swab the ears with a cotton ball that has been moistened with ear cleaner. This will remove dirt and control ear odor. Follow with a dry cotton ball, and dust the ears with medicated ear powder.

3. Cut the nails with a guillotine-type nail clipper. Nails should be cut monthly.

4. Check between the foot pads and under the feet for burrs, tar, etc.

5. Bathe the dog with a tearless protein shampoo that is pH-alkaline. This will add body to the coat and restructure damaged hair.

6. Cage dry until damp. Finish drying on the table using a blow dryer and a pure bristle brush.

7. The whiskers may be removed with scissors to improve expression, although this is optional.

8. Trim any stray hair on or in the ears with scissors.

9. Smooth any hair that detracts from an overall sleek look. Use a fine stripping knife to remove any long hair on the underside of the tail.

10. Use thinning shears to trim any hair between the toes that looks long. The foot should be compact and neat.

11. Finish with a mist of mink oil to create a brilliant shine, and brush this in with a pure bristle brush.

Italian Greyhound

TOOLS AND EQUIPMENT

- Cotton balls
- Ear cleaner
- Medicated ear powder
- Mink oil spray
- Nail clipper
- Pure boar bristle brush
- Rubber curry brush
- Scissors
- Stripping knife, fine
- Tearless protein shampoo
- Thinning shears

Italian Spinone

TOOLS AND EQUIPMENT

- Cotton balls
- Eye drops (eye stain remover)
- Medicated ear powder
- Metal comb (fine)
- Nail clipper
- Pin brush
- Scissors
- Thinning shears

GROOMING PROCEDURE

1. Brush the entire coat with a pin brush. Then comb through the coat to remove all loosened hair.

2. Clean the ears using medicated ear powder, and lightly pluck any stray hair from the insides.

3. Clean the eyes by wiping them with a cotton ball that has been moistened with eye drops.

4. Cut the tips of the nails with a nail clipper, being careful not to cut the quick.

5. Place a cotton ball in each ear to prevent water from entering the ear canal, and bathe the dog. Cage dry him.

6. Brush and comb through the coat.

7. With scissors, snip the hair between the pads and toes of the feet and around the edges for a neat appearance.

8. With thinning shears, trim straggly hair from the top of the head and ears and from the back.

9. Comb through the entire coat to remove all loosened hair.

The Italian Spinone should be groomed every 10 to 12 weeks if kept in a home environment. The ears should be checked weekly and cleaned if necessary, and the nails should be checked monthly and cut if necessary.

GROOMING PROCEDURE

1. Starting at the head, brush the entire coat.

2. With a metal rake, gently rake through the coat. In the nonshedding season, do not rake out the undercoat; just untangle it with a rake and/or mat-splitting comb. Comb through the coat to remove all loosened hair.

3. Clean the ears using medicated ear powder.

4. Clean the eyes by wiping them with a cotton ball that has been moistened with eye drops. This will also help in removing any stains around and under the eyes.

5. Cut the tips of the nails with a nail clipper, being careful not to cut the quick.

6. With scissors, cut the whiskers from the muzzle, under the chin, the sides of the face, and above the eyes. [Note: Clipping the whiskers is optional, if the dog will not be shown.]

7. Put a cotton ball in each ear, bathe the dog, and cage dry or fluff dry him. (Fluff drying may be preferable, if the undercoat is excessively heavy.)

8. With scissors, snip the hair between the pads and toes on the feet and around the edges to give a neat appearance.

9. With thinning shears, remove any straggly hair from the hock joint to the feet on the hind legs.

10. Brush and comb through the entire coat.

The Japanese Spitz should be groomed every 8 to 10 weeks. Regular brushing by the owner will help keep the coat healthy and the undercoat free of tangles. The ears should be checked weekly and cleaned if necessary, and the nails should be checked monthly and cut if necessary. It should be noted that the hair on the ears of these dogs is a natural protection and should not be touched; however, hair may be removed from the ear canals for hygienic reasons.

Japanese Spitz

TOOLS AND EQUIPMENT

- Cotton balls
- Eye drops (eye stain remover)
- Mat-splitting comb
- Medicated ear powder
- Metal comb (wide-toothed)
- Metal rake
- Nail clipper
- Scissors
- Slicker brush
- Thinning shears

Japanese Toy Spaniel

TOOLS AND EQUIPMENT

- Cotton balls
- Ear cleaner
- Ear forceps
- Eye stain remover
- Medicated ear powder
- Nail clipper
- Oster A-5 clipper/#10 blade
- Protein coat conditioner
- Pure boar bristle brush
- Scissors
- Slicker brush (gentle)
- Steel comb (medium/fine)
- Tearless protein shampoo
- Thinning shears

GROOMING PROCEDURE

1. Spray the entire coat with protein coat conditioner. This adds body to the coat and helps repair split ends. Brush through the entire coat with a gentle slicker brush.

2. Swab the ears with a cotton ball that has been moistened with ear cleaner. This will remove dirt and control ear odor. Follow with a dry cotton ball, and dust the ears with medicated ear powder. Pluck the hair inside the ears with your fingers or ear forceps.

3. Wipe inside the comers of the eyes with a water-moistened cotton ball. Remove any eye stains under and around the eye with a cotton ball that has been moistened with eye stain remover.

4. Cut the nails with a guillotine-type nail clipper. Nails should be cut monthly.

5. Check between the pads and under the feet for burrs, tar, etc. Scissor the hair under the feet even with the pads to prevent debris from adhering. With a thinning shear, trim any hair around the paw that touches the ground or grows out between the toes.

6. Use a #10 blade to clip the hair around the anus. Just clear the area and do not use heavy pressure. Scissor any long hair under the tail that hangs over the anus and that may become soiled.

7. Shave the stomach area with a #10 blade, going with the lay of the hair.

8. Bathe the dog with a tearless protein shampoo that is pH-alkaline. This will add fullness and body to the coat and restructure damaged hair.

9. Cage dry the dog until the hair is damp. Then finish drying on the table using a blow dryer and a pin brush to separate all the hair and remove all of the loose coat. Comb to the skin with the fine side of a steel comb to separate all the hair.

10. Use thinning shears to thin out any heavy areas, to remove straggly hair, and to give the dog an overall well-sculptured look.

11. The whiskers may be removed with scissors to improve expression (optional).

12. To add brilliance and fragrance, spray a pure bristle brush with protein coat conditioner and topbrush the coat.

GROOMING PROCEDURE

1. Spray the entire coat with protein coat conditioner. This adds body to the coat and helps repair split ends. Brush through the entire coat with a large pin brush, alternating with a slicker brush in matted areas. Start at the rear of the dog, at the bottom of the skirt area. Work in sections, using your other hand to lift the hair ahead of the section you are working on. Work layer by layer, working on thin layers at a time. Brush down and out until all mats and loose hair are removed. Work deep into the coat, but do not brush to the skin or you will cause abrasions. Work through the entire coat until the outer coat is well separated.

2. If there is heavy matting around the reproductive organs or in the armpits on the front legs, use a #10 blade to carefully remove the mats, as brushing these areas can be uncomfortable for the dog. As you use the clipper, lift the coat out of the way so that when it is put back in place the "shaved-out" areas will not be visible.

3. Then comb through the entire coat with a long-hair molting comb. Work vigorously. The more hair you remove now, the less hair you will need to wash and dry.

4. Comb the finer hair behind the ears with a fine steel comb.

5. Swab the ears with a cotton ball that has been moistened with ear cleaner. This will remove dirt and control ear odor. Follow this with a dry cotton ball, and dust the ears with medicated ear powder.

6. Cut the nails with a guillotine-type nail clipper. Nails should be cut monthly.

7. Bathe the dog with a tearless protein shampoo that is pH-alkaline. This will add fullness and body to the coat and restructure damaged hair.

8. Use a high-velocity dryer to blow excess water off the dog while he is still in the tub. This will speed up the drying time and help prevent the coat from becoming overly dry. Cage dry the dog until the hair is damp. Then finish drying on the table using a blow dryer and a pin brush to separate all the hair and remove all of the loose coat.

9. Follow by combing through the entire coat with a steel comb, paying special attention to the fine hair behind the ears. Use the fine side of the comb for this area.

10. Scissor any long hair under the tail that hangs over the anus. Be sure the anus is clear. Use a #10 blade down under the tail so it does not collect feces.

11. Check between the foot pads and under the feet for burrs, tar, etc. Scissor the hair under the foot even with the pads. With thinning shears, trim the hair growing out between the toes.

continued

TOOLS AND EQUIPMENT

- Cotton balls
- Ear cleaner
- High-velocity dryer
- Long-hair molting comb (#565)
- Medicated ear powder
- Nail clipper (extra large)
- Oster A-5 clipper/#10 blade
- Pin brush (large)
- Protein coat conditioner
- Scissors
- Slicker brush (large)
- Steel comb (fine/medium)
- Tearless protein shampoo
- Thinning shears

12. Comb out the leg feathering and neaten. The hind legs should be smooth below the hock joint and perpendicular from hock to ground. Leave full the feathering on the forelegs, but trim it so that it meets the pastern naturally and does not touch the ground.

13. Back brush the entire coat with a pin brush so the coat stands out and away from the body.

14. The whiskers may be removed with scissors to improve expression, but this is optional.

15. Lightly mist the coat with protein coat conditioner to add brilliance and fragrance.

GROOMING PROCEDURE

1. Spray the entire coat with protein coat conditioner. This adds body to the coat and helps repair split ends. Brush through the entire coat with a slicker brush. Then comb thoroughly with a molting comb to remove dead undercoat. Start at the rear of the dog, at the bottom of the skirt area. Work in sections through the entire dog, from the back to the neck area. Work vigorously. The more hair you remove now, the less hair you need to wash and dry.

2. Swab the ears with a cotton ball that has been moistened with ear cleaner. This will remove dirt and control ear odor. Follow with a dry cotton ball, and dust the ears with medicated ear powder. With your fingers or ear forceps, pluck hair inside the ears.

3. Cut the nails with a guillotine-type nail clipper. Nails should be cut monthly.

4. Check between the foot pads and under the feet for burrs, tar, etc. Clip the hair under the feet and between the pads with a #10 blade.

5. Bathe the dog in a tearless protein shampoo that is pH-alkaline. This will add fullness and body to the coat and restructure damaged hair.

6. Use a high-velocity dryer to blow excess water off the dog while he is still in the tub. This will speed up the drying time and help prevent the coat from becoming overly dry. Cage dry the dog until the hair is damp. Mist with coat gloss. Then finish drying on the table using a blow dryer and a pin brush to separate all the hair and remove all of the loose coat.

7. Comb the entire coat to the skin, using the medium part of the comb to separate all hair.

8. Use a #10 blade to clip the hair around the anus. Just clear the area and do not use heavy pressure.

9. Shave the abdomen with a #10 blade, going with the lay of the hair.

10. Shave the ear with a #10 blade on both sides. Shave from the base to the tip. Then trim the outside edge of the ear, using your thumb as a protective guide to prevent nicks.

11. Clip the top of the skull with a #10 blade, starting behind the eye socket and continuing back to the base of the skull. Leave plenty of eyebrow. Clip the side of the face, making a line from the outside corner of the eye to the mouth. Do not trim between the eyebrows or trim any part of the muzzle or under the eyes.

12. Picking up the beard, clip under the jaw with a #10 blade. Leave a heavy beard, but clean out under the beard.

13. Clip the throat with a #10 blade, forming a "U" from ear to ear, and shave down to 1 or 2 inches (2.5 or 5 cm) above the breastbone.

continued

TOOLS AND EQUIPMENT

- Coat gloss
- Comb (fine/medium)
- Cotton balls
- Ear cleaner
- Ear forceps
- High-velocity dryer
- Long-hair molting comb, #565
- Medicated ear powder
- Nail clipper (extra large)
- Oster A-5 clipper/#7F, #10 blades
- Pin brush
- Protein coat conditioner
- Pure boar bristle brush
- Scissors
- Slicker brush
- Tearless protein shampoo
- Thinning shears

14. Clip the body with a #7F blade. Body blades change, depending on the dog's type of coat and skin sensitivity. Clip from the base of the skull to the end of the tail (depending on coat texture, the #7F may be changed to a #7, #5, or #5F). Clip both sides of the body, from the sides of the neck to where the legs join the body in the front. Clip down to the thighs on the rear legs. In profile, there should be an even incline from elbow to hip. Follow the contour of the body, directing your clipper in the direction the hair grows. Do not go against the grain or across the grain. Lift the clipper slightly as you near the end of the skirt and leg. To accomplish this, it takes a slight twist of the wrist, as if you were using the end of the clipper as a shovel. You must work to blend the clipped area into the fringe area, leaving no uneven lines or ridges.

15. Clip the tail with a #7F blade. Always clip with the grain— the way the hair grows—and never against the growth. To prevent irritation, use very light pressure on the underside of the tail. Blend the area under the tail quite close.

16. With a #7F blade, clip the front of the dog's chest straight down the brisket, leaving a fringe between the front legs to define chest depth.

#5, #7

17. With a slicker, brush the hair on the front legs up and then down. Comb through with the medium side of a comb. Lift the foot and shake the leg to allow the hair to fall naturally. Scissor the leg into a cylindrical shape. Use thinning shears to blend in any uneven line that you may have between the shaved area and unshaved area. Blend into the shoulder to create a straight line from shoulder to foot. Shape the foot so that it appears round and compact, but don't expose the nails.

18. Scissor evenly the furnishings on the sides of the body, making them fuller underneath the ribs and chest. Trim evenly the line from brisket to groin, striving for a natural tuckup.

19. Brush the rear leg up and then down, comb, and shake free. Blend the hip area into the rear leg using scissors. The rear leg should show good angulation and should be trimmed evenly to the middle of the thigh. From thigh to hock, remove straggly hair only. Trim evenly the backline of the hock. Round the foot and blend it into the leg. The inside of the back legs should form an arch.

20. Comb the eyebrows forward, and with scissors pointing toward the nose, trim the hair beside the eyes to make them visible. Leave the fall (a fringe or shock of hair on top of the head) full between the eyebrows.

21. Comb the beard forward and trim any straggly or extra-long whiskers to give a neat appearance.

22. Topbrush the coat with a pure bristle brush that has been sprayed with protein coat conditioner. This adds brilliance and fragrance.

← #10

#7F →

GROOMING PROCEDURE

1. Clean the ears using medicated ear powder, and lightly pluck any stray hair from the insides.

2. Clean the eyes by wiping them with a cotton ball that has been moistened with eye drops. This will also help to remove any stains around the eyes.

3. Cut the nails with a nail clipper, being careful not to cut the quick.

4. With a #10 blade on the Oster A-5 clipper, shave the anal area, being certain not to put the blade in direct contact with the skin (½ inch [1 cm] each side).

5. Shave the abdomen from groin to navel and down the insides of the thighs.

6. Place a cotton ball in each ear (this prevents water from entering the ear canals), and place the dog in a half-full tub of warm water.

7. With a soft cloth and/or sponge, work the water through all the cords, making sure the entire dog is thoroughly soaked.

8. Empty the dirty water from the tub.

9. Apply diluted whitening shampoo to the cords with a sponge, making sure all cords have been penetrated to the skin.

10. Starting at the head, hose down the dog with clean water, using the sponge to squeeze through the cords until the water runs clear.

11. With warm towels, squeeze the cords to rid them of excess water. Cage dry the dog.

12. With scissors, trim all cords to a length of 4 to 5 inches (10 to 13 cm). This length should ensure that the cords clear the floor.

TOOLS AND EQUIPMENT

- Eye drops (eye stain remover)
- Hair-styling gel
- Mat-splitting comb
- Medicated ear powder
- Metal comb (wide-tooth)
- Nail clipper
- Oster A-5 clipper/#10 blade
- Scissors
- Soft cloth/sponge
- Whitening shampoo

The coat of the Komondor starts to cord when the dog is 1½ to 2 years of age. If mats start to form in the coat before cording, these must be removed with a mat-splitting comb and re-corded by hand. This is done with a metal comb, parting the coat into square sections approximately ¾ inch (2 cm) in diameter. Apply hair-styling gel (one section at a time) and twist the hair around a finger, thus making a cord. During the first 1½ years, the Komondor should be groomed about every 3 to 4 weeks. This will ensure that the cords are forming and the coat is not matting. Once the cords have formed, grooming should occur every 6 to 8 weeks. The ears should be checked weekly and cleaned if necessary, and the nails should be checked monthly and cut if necessary.

Kuvasz

GROOMING PROCEDURE

1. Spray the entire coat with protein coat conditioner. This adds body to the coat and helps repair split ends. Comb through the entire coat with a molting comb. This will loosen up the coat and remove dead undercoat. Start at the rear of the dog, at the bottom of the skirt area. Work in sections, using your other hand to lift the hair ahead of the section you are working on. Work through the entire dog, from the back to the neck area. Then brush through the coat with a slicker brush to remove the top dead coat. Work vigorously. The more hair you remove now, the less you need to wash and dry.

2. Swab the ears with a cotton ball that has been moistened with ear cleaner. This will remove dirt and control ear odor. Follow this with a dry cotton ball, and dust the ears with medicated ear powder.

3. Cut the nails with a guillotine-type nail clipper. Nails should be cut monthly.

4. Wipe the inside corners of the eyes with a water-moistened cotton ball. Remove any stains under and around the eyes with a cotton ball that has been moistened with eye stain remover.

5. To enhance the whiteness of the coat, bathe the dog with a tearless whitening shampoo that is pH-alkaline.

6. Use a high-velocity dryer to blow excess water off the dog while he is still in the tub. This will speed up the drying time and help prevent the coat from becoming overly dry. Cage dry the dog until the hair is damp. Then finish drying on the table using a blow dryer and a pin brush to separate all the hair and remove all of the loose coat. Finish with a steel comb through the entire coat, paying special attention to the fine hair behind the ears. Use the fine side of a comb for this area.

GROOMING PROCEDURE

1. Nails should be cut by removing only the tips; avoid cutting the quick. If the nail bleeds, apply styptic powder to stop the bleeding. Any rough nail edges may be smoothed with a file.

2. Clean the ears with a liquid cleaner. Apply the cleaner to a cotton ball and wipe accumulated wax and dirt from all crevices in both ears.

3. Brush out the entire coat to remove any dead hair.

4. Bathe the dog in a shampoo of your choice. Rinse thoroughly.

5. Towel dry the dog until damp, and finish drying him in a cage dryer.

6. This breed needs little finishing, if any at all. The tail may be trimmed to a blunt point to accentuate the "otter-like" tail that this breed sports.

7. A light misting with a coat conditioner or coat gloss may be applied and buffed until shiny. This is especially useful on black or chocolate Labs.

8. The whiskers may be removed if desired.

Labrador Retrievers should be groomed every 8 to 12 weeks.

Labrador Retriever

TOOLS AND EQUIPMENT

- Blending shears
- Cotton balls
- Ear cleaner
- Nail clipper
- Shampoo
- Slicker brush
- Spray coat gloss
- Styptic powder

Lakeland Terrier

TOOLS AND EQUIPMENT

- Coat gloss
- Comb (fine/medium)
- Cotton balls
- Ear cleaner
- Ear forceps
- High-velocity dryer
- Long-hair molting comb, #565
- Medicated ear powder
- Nail clipper (extra large)
- Oster A-5 clipper/#5F, #7, #7F, #8½, #10 blades
- Pin brush
- Protein coat conditioner
- Pure boar bristle brush
- Scissors
- Slicker brush
- Tearless protein shampoo
- Thinning shears

GROOMING PROCEDURE

1. Spray the entire coat with protein coat conditioner. This adds body to the coat and helps repair split ends. Brush through the entire coat with a slicker brush. Then comb thoroughly with a molting comb to remove dead undercoat. Start at the rear of the dog, at the bottom of the skirt area. Work in sections through the entire dog, from the back to the neck area. Work vigorously. The more hair you remove now, the less hair you need to wash and dry.

2. Swab the ears with a cotton ball that has been moistened with ear cleaner. This will remove dirt and control ear odor. Follow with a dry cotton ball, and dust the ears with medicated ear powder. With your fingers or ear forceps, pluck stray hair inside the ears.

3. Cut the nails with a guillotine-type nail clipper. Nails should be cut monthly.

4. Check between the foot pads and under the feet for burrs, tar, etc. Clip the hair under the feet and between the pads with a #10 blade.

5. Bathe the dog with a tearless protein shampoo that is pH-alkaline. This will add fullness and body to the coat and restructure damaged hair.

6. Use a high-velocity dryer to blow excess water off the dog while he is still in the tub. This will speed up the drying time and help prevent the coat from becoming overly dry. Cage dry the dog until the hair is damp. Mist with coat gloss. Finish drying on the table using a blow dryer and a pin brush to separate all the hair and remove all of the loose coat.

7. Comb through the entire coat to the skin, using the medium part of the comb to separate all of the hair.

8. Use a #10 blade to clip the hair around the anus. Just clear the area and be careful not to use heavy pressure.

9. Shave the abdomen with a #10 blade, going with the lay of the hair.

10. Shave the ears on both sides with a #10 blade. Shave from the base to the tip. Trim the outside edge, using the thumb as a protective guide to prevent nicks.

11. Clip the top of the skull with a #10 blade, starting behind the eye socket and continuing back to the base of the skull. Leave plenty of eyebrow. Clip the side of the face, making a line from the outside corner of the eye to the mouth. Do not trim between the eyebrows or trim any part of the muzzle or under the eyes.

12. Lifting the beard, clip under the jaw with a #8½ blade. Clean out this area, but leave the beard heavy.

13. Clip the throat with a #8½ blade, forming a "U" from ear to ear, and shave down to 1 or 2 inches (2.5 or 5 cm) above the breastbone.

14. Clip the body with a #7F blade. Blades for clipping the body vary, depending on coat type and skin sensitivity. Clip from the base of the skull to the end of the tail (depending on coat texture, a #7F may be changed to #7, #5, or #5F). Clip both sides of the body, from the sides of the neck to where the legs join the body in the front, and down to the thighs on the rear legs. In profile, there should be an even incline from elbow to hip. Follow the contour of the body, directing your clipper in the direction the hair grows. Do not go against the grain or across the grain. Lift the clipper slightly as you near the end of the clipped area to blend the clipped area into the nonclipped area of the skirt and leg. This takes a slight twist of the wrist to accomplish, as if you were using the end of the clipper as a shovel. You must work to blend the clipped area into the fringe area, leaving no uneven lines or ridges.

15. Clip the tail with a #7F blade. Always clip with the grain—the way the hair grows—and never against the growth. To prevent irritation, use a very light pressure on the underside of the tail. Blend close the area under the tail.

16. With the #7F blade, clip the front of the dog's chest straight down to the brisket. Leave a fringe between the front legs to define chest depth.

17. Brush the hair on the front legs up and then down with a slicker brush. Comb through with the medium side of the comb. Lift the foot and shake the leg to allow the hair to fall naturally. Scissor the leg into a cylindrical shape. Use thinning shears to blend in any uneven line that you may have between the shaved area and the unshaved area. Blend into the shoulder to create a straight line from shoulder to foot. Shape the foot so that it appears round and compact, but don't expose the nails.

18. Scissor evenly the furnishings on the sides of the body, making them fuller underneath the ribs and chest. Trim evenly the line from brisket to groin, striving for a natural tuckup.

19. Brush the rear leg up and then down, comb, and shake free. With scissors, blend the hip area into the rear leg. The rear leg should show good angulation and should be trimmed evenly to the middle of the thigh. From thigh to hock, remove straggly hair only. Trim evenly the backline of the hock. Round the foot and blend it into the leg. The inside of the back legs should form an arch.

20. Comb the eyebrows forward, and with scissors pointing toward the nose, trim the hair beside the eyes to make them visible. Leave the fall (a fringe or shock of hair on the top of the head) full between the eyebrows, but remove any uneven tufts.

21. Comb the beard forward and trim any straggly or extra-long whiskers to give a neat appearance.

22. Topbrush the coat with a pure bristle brush that has been sprayed with protein coat conditioner to add brilliance and fragrance.

#5, #7, #8½, #10

#10 →

← #7F
#8½
#10

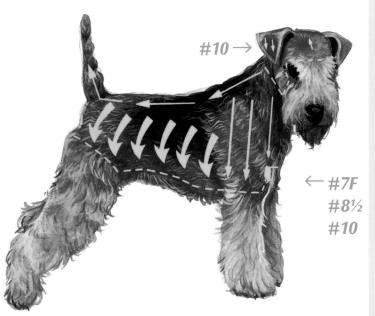

Lancashire Heeler

TOOLS AND EQUIPMENT

- Cotton balls
- Eye drops (eye stain remover)
- Medicated ear powder
- Nail clipper
- Pin brush
- Scissors
- Sisal (natural bristle) brush

GROOMING PROCEDURE

1. Brush the coat thoroughly with a sisal brush (use a pin brush during the shedding season).

2. Clean the ears using medicated ear powder.

3. Clean the eyes by wiping them with a cotton ball that has been moistened with eye drops.

4. Cut the tips of the nails with a nail clipper, being careful not to cut the quick.

5. With scissors, snip the whiskers from the muzzle, under the chin, the sides of the face, and above the eyes. [Note: This is optional if the dog is not a show dog.]

6. Place a cotton ball in each ear to prevent water from entering the ear canal, and bathe the dog. Cage dry him.

7. Brush the coat with a sisal brush, using firm strokes to obtain a nice sheen.

The Lancashire Heeler should be groomed every 8 to 10 weeks. The ears should be checked weekly and cleaned if necessary, and the nails should be checked monthly and cut if necessary.

GROOMING PROCEDURE

1. Brush the entire coat with a slicker brush. Then comb through the coat and remove all tangles and loosened hair. Pay special attention to the neck, chest, thighs, and tail.

2. Clean the ears using medicated ear powder, and lightly pluck any stray hair from the insides.

3. Clean the eyes by wiping them with a cotton ball that has been moistened with eye drops.

4. Cut the tips of the nails with a nail clipper, being careful not to cut the quick.

5. With scissors, snip the whiskers from the muzzle, under the chin, the sides of the face, and above the eyes. [Note: Clipping the whiskers is a decision to be left to the owner if the dog is not a show dog.]

6. With a #10 blade on the Oster A-5 clipper, shave the abdomen from groin to navel and down the insides of the thighs.

7. Shave the anal area, being certain not to put the blade in direct contact with the skin (½ inch [1 cm] on either side).

8. Put a cotton ball in each ear to prevent water from entering the ear canal as you bathe the dog. Cage dry or fluff dry him.

9. With scissors, snip hair from between the pads and toes of the feet and around the edges.

10. With scissors or thinning shears, trim straggly hairs from around the ankles on the front feet and from the hocks down to the feet on the hind legs.

11. With thinning shears, trim any straggly hairs from the top of the head and the tops of the ears.

12. Comb through the entire coat to remove all loosened hair.

Large Munsterlander

TOOLS AND EQUIPMENT

- Cotton balls
- Eye drops (eye stain remover)
- Medicated ear powder
- Metal comb (medium)
- Nail clipper
- Oster A-5 clipper/#10 blade
- Scissors
- Slicker brush
- Thinning shears

Leonberger

TOOLS AND EQUIPMENT

- Cotton balls
- Eye drops (eye stain remover)
- Mat-splitting comb
- Medicated ear powder
- Metal comb (wide-toothed)
- Metal rake
- Nail clipper
- Scissors
- Slicker brush
- Thinning shears

GROOMING PROCEDURE

1. Brush the entire coat with a slicker brush.

2. With a metal rake, gently rake through the coat. During the nonshedding season, do not rake out the undercoat. Just untangle it with a mat-splitting comb and/or metal rake, especially on the neck, thighs, and tail. Comb through the coat to remove all loosened hair.

3. Clean the ears using medicated ear powder, and lightly pluck any stray hair from the insides.

4. Clean the eyes by wiping them with a cotton ball that has been moistened with eye drops.

5. Cut the tips of the nails with a nail clipper, being careful not to cut the quick.

6. With scissors, snip the whiskers from the muzzle, under the chin, the sides of the face, and above the eyes. [Note: Clipping the whiskers is a decision to be left to the owner if the dog is not a show dog.]

7. Place a cotton ball in each ear to prevent water from entering the ear canal, and bathe the dog. Cage dry him.

8. With scissors, snip the hair between the pads and toes of the feet to give a neat appearance.

9. With thinning shears, remove any straggly hair from the hock joints to the feet on the hind legs.

10. Brush and comb through the entire coat.

The Leonberger should be groomed every 10 to 12 weeks and brushed regularly by the owner to help maintain a healthy coat. The ears should be checked weekly and cleaned if necessary, and the nails should be checked monthly and cut if necessary.

GROOMING PROCEDURE

1. Brush the entire coat and tail with a slicker brush, removing any mats with the matting comb. Comb through the coat, using the medium-toothed metal comb.

2. Clean the ears using medicated ear powder, and lightly pluck stray hair from the insides of the ears.

3. Cut the tips of the nails with a nail clipper, being careful not to cut the quick.

4. Clean the eyes by wiping them with a damp cotton ball. If the eyes are excessively watery and sticky, snip the stained hair from the corners with scissors.

5. Using a #10 blade, shave the anal area, being certain not to put the blade in direct contact with the skin.

6. Using a #10 blade, shave the abdomen from groin to navel and down the insides of the thighs.

7. Put a cotton ball in each ear to prevent water from entering the ear canals. Once this is done, bathe the dog and fluff dry him.

8. Using a medium metal comb, part the coat down the center of the back from the top of the head to the base of the tail. Next, part the hair from the top of the head to the tip of the nose.

9. Comb through the entire coat, first with a medium-toothed and then a fine-toothed metal comb.

10. Comb the tail thoroughly.

11. Scissor the hair between the pads of the feet. Comb the hair on the legs downward, and while the dog is standing, scissor around the edges of the feet to give a round effect

12. Some owners prefer the topknot tied in a ponytail fashion. To do this, part the hair on the head from the corner of each eye to the front corner of each ear, and across the head from ear to ear. Gather this hair, comb through evenly and slightly to the back, and secure it with a rubber band. An alternative is to make a braid and secure the end with a rubber band. Attach a bow to either of the rubber bands.

13. Comb the entire coat and tail with a fine-toothed metal comb.

continued

Lhasa Apso

TOOLS AND EQUIPMENT

- Cotton balls
- Matting comb
- Medicated ear powder
- Metal combs (medium/fine)
- Nail clipper
- Oster A-5 clipper/#10 blade
- Rubber bands
- Scissors
- Slicker brush

Lhasa Apso *continued*

Some dog owners use conditioning rinse and similar products on these dogs, but I have found, through experience, that these products cause the coats to become more matted in the long run. A good protein-enriched shampoo is entirely adequate. The long-coated Lhasa Apso should be groomed every 2 or 3 weeks. The ears should be checked weekly and cleaned if necessary, and the nails should be checked at the grooming sessions.

For owners who prefer a short, cuddly look, refer to the Teddy Bear Clip in the General Information section. For owners who like the long-haired look, even during the heat of summer, the entire undercoat can be thinned out so that the dog will be more comfortable. The same instructions apply for grooming, bathing, and fluff drying the Lhasa Apso (i.e., steps 1 through 7). Then part the coat, using the medium-toothed metal comb, about 1½ to 2 inches (4 to 5 cm) from the center of the back, down one side. Comb the top hair to the other side (so you do not touch the outer coat), and with thinning shears, thin out the remaining undercoat about 1 inch (2.5 cm) at a time. Repeat on the opposite side and across the chest and thighs. Part the coat down the center of the back and thoroughly comb through it, first with the medium-toothed and then with the fine-toothed metal comb. Tie the topknot and scissor the feet, as mentioned before in the grooming instructions for Lhasa Apsos.

GROOMING PROCEDURE

1. Brush the entire coat with a slicker brush, removing any mats or tangles with a metal rake. Comb through the coat to remove all loosened hair.

2. Clean the ears using medicated ear powder, and lightly pluck any stray hair from the insides.

3. Clean the eyes by wiping them with a cotton ball that has been moistened with eye drops. This will also help to remove stains around the eyes. If the eyes are excessively watery and sticky, snip the stained hair from the corners with scissors.

4. Cut the tips of the nails with a nail clipper, being careful not to cut the quick.

5. With a #10 blade on the Oster A-5 clipper, shave the abdomen from groin to navel and down the insides of the thighs.

6. Shave the anal area, being certain not to put the blade in direct contact with the skin (½ inch [1 cm] on either side).

7. With a #15 blade on the Oster A-5 clipper, shave the feet. Start by shaving between the pads. Then shave up just clear of the largest pad; this will be the shave line for the whole foot. Make sure there are no hairs left on or between the toes.

8. With a #15 blade, shave the front legs from the elbows to just above the knees.

9. Shave the pattern by making a line just in front of the rear legs (about ¾ inch [2 cm]), and shave up the flanks and over the back, down the other side.

10. Shave the entire rear end, down the hips and down the rear legs to the hock joints.

11. Shave the tail almost half the length from the base. Leave a tuft of hair, which resembles a plume, at the tip.

12. Comb through the coat to remove all excess hair.

13. Place a cotton ball in each ear (this prevents water from entering the ear canal), and bathe the dog. Fluff dry, using a slicker brush in an upward motion.

14. Using the same blade as before (the #15), repeat the process for the pattern, this time shaving against the lay of the coat for a clean, sharp finish.

15. Comb the hair on the ankles downward, and scissor straight around, using thinning shears to blend the hair down from the pattern (i.e., from the knees on the front legs and from the hocks on the rear legs).

16. Comb the plume on the tail, and trim the ends with scissors or thinning shears.

17. With scissors, trim straggly hairs from the pattern edges.

continued

TOOLS AND EQUIPMENT

- Cotton balls
- Eye drops (eye stain remover)
- Medicated ear powder
- Metal comb (medium)
- Metal rake
- Nail clipper
- Oster A-5 clipper/#10, #15 blades
- Scissors
- Slicker brush
- Thinning shears

18. Fluff up the body hair, and trim all straggly hairs with thinning shears.

19. Comb the chest and belly fringes downward, and with thinning shears or scissors, trim the lower edges.

20. With thinning shears, trim any straggly hairs on the head, ears, face, and chest.

21. Comb through the coat and pom-poms to remove excess hair, and trim where necessary, especially around the ankles.

The Lowchen, also known as the Little Lion Dog, should be groomed every 6 to 8 weeks. The ears should be checked weekly and cleaned if necessary, and the nails should be checked and cut at the grooming session. [Note: The pattern is shaved with the lay of the coat prior to bathing and against the lay of the coat afterward.]

GROOMING PROCEDURE

1. Starting with the head, brush the entire coat and tail with a slicker brush, removing any mats with a matting comb. Comb through the coat, using the medium-toothed metal comb.

2. Clean the ears using medicated ear powder, and lightly pluck stray hair from the inside of the ears.

3. Cut the tips of the nails with the nail clipper, being careful not to cut the quick.

4. Clean the eyes by wiping them with a cotton ball that has been moistened with eye drops. If the eyes are excessively watery and sticky, snip the stained hair from the corners with scissors.

5. Using a #10 blade, shave the anal area, being certain not to put the blade in direct contact with the skin (½ inch [1 cm] on either side).

6. Using a #10 blade, shave the abdomen from groin to navel and down the insides of the thighs.

7. Place a cotton ball in each ear (this prevents water from entering the ear canal), and bathe the dog. Fluff dry him.

8. Using a medium-toothed metal comb, part the coat down the center of the back, from the top of the head to the base of the tail. Then part the hair from the top of the head to the tip of the nose. Comb all hair downward from the part. An alternative is to make a part on the head from the outer corner of each eye to the front corner of each ear, and across the head from ear to ear. Comb this hair evenly, slightly to the back, and secure it with a rubber band. Attach a bow.

9. Scissor the hair between the pads of the feet. Comb the hair on the legs downward, and while the dog is standing, scissor the edges of the feet to give a round effect.

10. Comb the entire coat downward with a fine-toothed metal comb.

Some dog groomers use conditioning rinse and similar products on these dogs, but I have found, through experience, that these products cause the coat to become more matted in the long run. A good protein-enriched shampoo is entirely adequate. The longhaired Maltese should be groomed every 4 weeks. The owner should brush and comb the dog on a regular basis, thus preventing the coat from becoming matted. The ears should be checked weekly and cleaned if necessary, and the nails should be checked at the grooming session.

For Maltese owners who prefer a short, easy to keep, cuddly look, refer to the Teddy Bear Clip in the General Information section.

TOOLS AND EQUIPMENT

- Cotton balls
- Eye drops (eye stain remover)
- Matting comb
- Medicated ear powder
- Metal combs (medium/fine)
- Nail clipper
- Oster A-5 clipper/#10 blade
- Rubber bands
- Scissors
- Slicker brush

Manchester Terrier, Standard

TOOLS AND EQUIPMENT

- Cotton balls
- Ear cleaner
- Medicated ear powder
- Mink oil spray
- Nail clipper
- Pure boar bristle brush
- Rubber dog brush
- Scissors
- Tearless protein shampoo

GROOMING PROCEDURE

1. Brush the coat with a rubber dog brush. Follow with a thorough brushing using a pure bristle brush.

2. Swab the ears with a cotton ball that has been moistened with ear cleaner. This will remove dirt and control ear odor. Follow with a dry cotton ball, and dust the ears with medicated ear powder.

3. Cut the nails with a guillotine-type nail clipper. Nails should be cut monthly.

4. Check between the foot pads and under the feet for burrs, tar, etc.

5. Bathe the dog with a tearless protein shampoo that is balanced pH-alkaline.

6. Cage dry until damp. Finish drying the dog on the table using a blow dryer and a pure bristle brush.

7. The whiskers may be removed with scissors to improve expression, but this is optional.

8. Finish with a mist of mink oil to create a brilliant shine; brush this in with a pure bristle brush.

GROOMING PROCEDURE

1. Brush the coat with a rubber dog brush. Follow with a thorough brushing using a pure bristle brush.

2. Swab the ears with a cotton ball that has been moistened with ear cleaner. This will remove dirt and control ear odor. Follow with a dry cotton ball, and dust the ears with medicated ear powder.

3. Cut the nails with a guillotine-type nail clipper. Nails should be cut monthly.

4. Check between the foot pads and under the feet for burrs, tar, etc.

5. Bathe the dog in a tearless protein shampoo that is balanced pH-alkaline.

6. Cage dry until damp. Finish drying on the table using a blow dryer and a pure bristle brush.

7. The whiskers may be removed with scissors to improve expression, although this is optional.

8. Finish with a mist of mink oil to create a brilliant shine, and brush this in with a pure bristle brush.

Manchester Terrier, Toy

TOOLS AND EQUIPMENT

- Cotton balls
- Ear cleaner
- Medicated ear powder
- Mink oil spray
- Nail clipper
- Pure boar bristle brush
- Rubber dog brush
- Scissors
- Tearless protein shampoo

Maremma Sheepdog

TOOLS AND EQUIPMENT

- Cotton balls
- Eye drops (eye stain remover)
- Mat-splitting comb
- Medicated ear powder
- Metal comb (wide-toothed)
- Metal rake
- Nail clipper
- Scissors
- Shampoo (whitening)
- Slicker brush
- Thinning shears

GROOMING PROCEDURE

1. Brush the entire coat and tail with a slicker brush, paying special attention to the neck, thigh, and tail areas.

2. With a metal rake, gently rake through the coat. During the nonshedding season do not rake out the undercoat; just untangle it with a metal rake and/or a mat-splitting comb. Comb through the coat to remove all loosened hair and make sure it is free of tangles.

3. Clean the ears using medicated ear powder.

4. Clean the eyes by wiping them with a cotton ball that has been moistened with eye drops. This will also help to remove stains around the eyes.

5. Cut the tips of the nails with a nail clipper, being careful not to cut the quick.

6. With scissors, cut the whiskers from the muzzle, under the chin, the sides of the face, and above the eyes. [Note: Clipping the whiskers is optional, unless the dog is a show dog.]

7. Place a cotton ball in each ear to prevent water from entering the ear canal, and bathe the dog using whitening shampoo. Cage dry or fluff dry the dog.

8. With scissors, snip the hair between the pads and toes of the feet and around the edges to give a neat appearance.

9. With thinning shears, remove any straggly hair from the hock joints to the feet on the hind legs and from around the ankles on the front legs.

10. Brush and comb the coat thoroughly.

The Maremma Sheepdog should be groomed every 10 to 12 weeks. Regular brushing by the owner will help to keep the coat healthy and the undercoat free of tangles. The ears should be checked weekly and cleaned if necessary, and the nails should be checked monthly and cut if needed.

GROOMING PROCEDURE

1. Brush the coat well with a rubber dog brush. Follow with a thorough brushing using a pure bristle brush.

2. Swab the ears with a cotton ball that has been moistened with ear cleaner. This will remove dirt and control ear odor. Follow with a dry cotton ball, and dust the ears with medicated ear powder.

3. Cut the nails with a guillotine-type nail clipper. Nails should be cut monthly.

4. Check between the foot pads and under the feel for burrs, tar, etc.

5. Wipe the inside comers of the eyes with a water-moistened cotton ball. Remove any stains under and around the eyes with a cotton ball that has been moistened with eye stain remover.

6. Wrinkles on the face should be cleaned with a water-moistened cotton ball. Dry and powder.

7. Bathe the Mastiff with a tearless protein shampoo that is pH-alkaline. This will add body to the coat and restructure damaged hair.

8. Cage dry until damp. Finish drying on the table using a blow dryer and a pure bristle brush.

9. The whiskers may be removed with scissors to improve expression (optional).

10. Finish with a mist of mink oil to create a brilliant shine, and brush this in with a pure bristle brush.

TOOLS AND EQUIPMENT

- Baby powder or talcum powder
- Cotton balls
- Ear cleaner
- Eye stain cleaner
- Medicated ear powder
- Mink oil spray
- Nail clipper (extra large)
- Pure boar bristle brush
- Rubber brush
- Scissors
- Tearless protein shampoo
- Thinning shears

Miniature Pinscher

TOOLS AND EQUIPMENT

- Cotton balls
- Ear cleaner
- Medicated ear powder
- Mink oil spray
- Nail clipper
- Pure boar bristle brush
- Rubber brush
- Scissors
- Tearless protein shampoo
- Thinning shears

GROOMING PROCEDURE

1. Brush the coat well with a rubber dog brush. Follow with a thorough brushing using a pure bristle brush.

2. Swab the ears with a cotton ball that has been moistened with ear cleaner. This will remove dirt and control ear odor. Follow with a dry cotton ball, and dust the ears with medicated ear powder.

3. Nails should be cut monthly with a guillotine-type nail clipper.

4. Check between the foot pads and under the feet for burrs, tar, etc.

5. Bathe the dog with a tearless protein shampoo that is pH-alkaline. This adds body to the coat and restructures damaged hair.

6. Cage dry until damp. Finish drying on the table using a blow dryer and a pure bristle brush.

7. This step is optional, but the whiskers may be removed with scissors to improve expression.

8. With fine thinning shears, tidy up the long hair on the back of the front and rear legs, as well as any long hair on the side of the neck. Use regular scissors to remove any stray hair in the ears.

9. Finish with a mist of mink oil to create a brilliant shine, and brush this in with a pure bristle brush.

GROOMING PROCEDURE

Miniature Schnauzer

1. Begin with a rough clip outline before bathing. Start with the body, using either a #8 ½ or #10 blade. Run the clipper from occiput (top of skull) down the sides of the neck. Clip down the body to the elbow, on the shoulders, and on the chest. Always follow the lay of the hair. Continue clipping down the sides of the body to the underbelly. Leave "fringe" for later scissoring.

2. Finish clipping the body, tail, and rear legs in an even pattern with the same blade. Stay about 2 inches (5 cm) above the rear hocks. Leave leg furnishings on the stifle. Clip around and under the tail. Move the blade downward to clean the vent area. Use caution and a light touch so as not to cause clipper burn. Never leave an "apron" on the chest or rear.

3. Clip the head from the top of the eyebrows to the top of the skull. Clip the cheeks and throat with the body blade. Clip the ears inside and out with a #15 blade. Again, use caution to avoid clipper burn on these sensitive areas.

4. Lift the dog by his front legs. With a #15 blade, clean the belly to the navel, the hindquarters, and one-third the way down the inner thighs. Leave outer fringe on the belly edge and on the stifle.

5. Bathe the dog. Towel dry him by squeezing water out of the legs and beard. Comb through the legs and beard while wet, using a detangling solution if necessary. Cut nails now, while they are soft from bathing.

6. Fluff dry, using a pin brush up and out on the legs. Pin brush down on the eyebrows and beard. Drying can be completed in a cage.

7. The Miniature Schnauzer is now ready for scissoring. Start with the head. Comb the eyebrows and beard down and forward. Scissor the brows by slanting your scissor points toward the base of the ear. Scissor between the brows in a diamond shape. Clean out hair from the inner ear with blunt scissors, a hemostat, and liquid ear cleaner. Scissor off the edges of the ears. The Miniature Schnauzer head should appear rectangular, never round. Scissor the lower chest, between the legs, as flat and smooth as possible.

continued

TOOLS AND EQUIPMENT

- Detangling solution
- Liquid ear cleaner
- Metal comb
- Nail clipper
- Oster A-5 clipper/# 8½, #10, #15, blades
- Pin brush
- Scissors, regular straight edge
- Scissors, small blunt tip

8. Fluff and comb up the hair on the legs. Scissor the elbows close to the body. Scissor down the front legs to achieve a barber pole effect. The rear legs are scissored to give an arc-like shape to the stifle, and the hocks are scissored evenly. Scissor around the toes and under the foot pads. Never cut hair from between the toes. Strive for straight legs.

9. Underbelly fringe should be scissored to the shape of the body, never leaving more than 1 or 2 inches (2.5 or 5 cm) in depth.

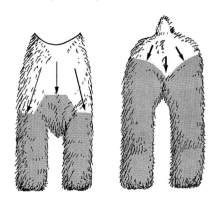

#7, #8½, #10

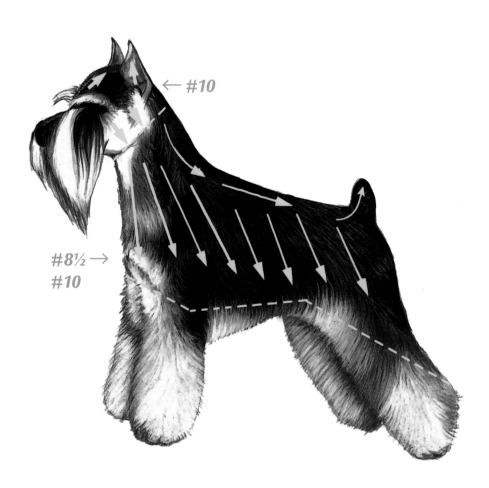

← #10

#8½ →
#10

GROOMING PROCEDURE

1. Brush the coat vigorously with a sisal brush.

2. Clean the ears using medicated ear powder.

3. Clean the eyes by wiping them with a cotton ball that has been moistened with eye drops. This will also help to remove any stains from the corners of the eyes.

4. Cut the tips of the nails with a nail clipper, being careful not to cut the quick.

5. Using a damp cotton ball, clean the insides of the lips, being certain to remove any trapped food particles.

6. With scissors, clip the whiskers from the muzzle, under the chin, the sides of the face, and above the eyes. [Note: Clipping the whiskers is a decision to be left up to the owner if the dog is not a show dog.]

7. Place a cotton ball in each ear (this prevents water from entering the ear canal), and bathe the dog. Cage dry him.

8. Clean the furrows on the face and head thoroughly with a cotton ball that has been moistened with eye drops. Dry and then dust them with medicated talcum powder. Stress to the dog's owner that if this is done on a daily basis, it will help keep the furrows clean and help prevent soreness or infection.

9. Put a few drops of lanolin coat conditioner in the palms of your hands, rub them together lightly, and gently massage into the coat.

10. Brush the coat with a sisal brush to distribute the conditioner, and then lightly rub with a chamois cloth to give it a nice sheen.

The Neapolitan Mastiff rarely needs bathing if he is brushed by his owner on a regular basis. To maintain a healthy, shiny coat, use lanolin coat conditioner monthly, or more often as needed. The ears should be checked weekly and cleaned if necessary, and the nails should be checked monthly and cut if necessary.

Neapolitan Mastiff

TOOLS AND EQUIPMENT

- Chamois cloth
- Cotton balls
- Eye drops (eye stain remover)
- Lanolin coat conditioner
- Medicated ear powder
- Medicated talcum powder
- Nail clipper
- Scissors
- Sisal (natural bristle) brush

Newfoundland

TOOLS AND EQUIPMENT

- Cotton balls
- Ear cleaner
- High-velocity dryer
- Long-hair molting comb (#565)
- Medicated ear powder
- Nail clipper (extra large)
- Oster A-5 clipper/#10 blade
- Pin brush
- Protein coat conditioner
- Scissors
- Slicker brush
- Steel comb (fine/medium)
- Tearless protein shampoo
- Thinning shears

GROOMING PROCEDURE

1. Spray the entire coat with protein coat conditioner. This adds body to the coat and helps repair split ends. Brush through the entire coat with a pin brush. This will loosen up the coat and remove dead undercoat. Start at the rear of the dog, at the bottom of the skirt area. Work in sections, using your other hand to lift the hair ahead of the section you are working on. Work through the entire dog from the back to the neck area. Then brush through the coat with a slicker brush to remove the top dead coat. Work vigorously. The more hair you remove now, the less hair you need to wash and dry.

2. Swab the ears with a cotton ball that has been moistened with ear cleaner. This will remove dirt and control ear odor. Follow this with a dry cotton ball, and dust the ears with medicated ear powder.

3. Cut the nails with a guillotine-type nail clipper. Nails should be cut monthly.

4. Bathe the dog with a tearless protein shampoo that is pH-alkaline. This adds body to the coat and restructures damaged hair.

5. Use a high-velocity dryer to blow excess water off the dog while he is still in the tub. This will speed up the drying time and help prevent the coat from becoming overly dry. Cage dry the dog until the hair is damp. Then finish drying him on the table using a blow dryer and a pin brush to separate all the hair and remove all of the loose coat. Finish with a steel comb through the entire coat, paying special attention to the fine hair behind the ears. Use the fine side of the comb for this area.

6. Scissor any long hair under the tail that hangs over the anus. Be sure the anus is clear, and then use a #10 blade to blend down under the tail area so it does not collect fecal matter.

7. Check between the foot pads and under the feet for burrs, tar, etc. Scissor the hair under the feet even with the pads. Trim any hair around the paw that touches the ground and neaten the entire foot. With thinning shears, trim the hair growing between the toes.

8. The whiskers may be removed with scissors to improve expression; however, this is optional.

9. Lightly mist the coat with protein coat conditioner to add brilliance and fragrance.

GROOMING PROCEDURE

1. Brush with a pure boar bristle brush, and then comb thoroughly.

2. Swab the ears with a cotton ball that has been moistened with ear cleaner. This will remove dirt and control ear odor. Follow this with a dry cotton ball, and dust the ears with medicated ear powder.

3. Cut the nails with a guillotine-type nail clipper. Nails should be cut monthly.

4. Check between the foot pads and under the feet for burrs, tar, etc. With thinning shears, scissor the hair around the paw that touches the ground or that grows between the foot pads.

5. Bathe the dog with a tearless terrier shampoo that adds body and texture to the coat

6. Cage dry until damp. Finish drying on the table using a blow dryer and a pure bristle brush.

7. Comb with a steel comb.

8. With your thumb and forefinger, pluck any dead hair on the outside of the ears.

9. Use a fine stripping knife to remove any unruly hair on the head.

10. Comb the eyebrows forward and the whiskers down.

11. With a coarse stripping knife, strip or trim any unruly hair on the tail.

12. Trim the hair around the anus.

13. Spray a pure bristle brush with protein coat conditioner and topbrush the coat to add brilliance and fragrance.

Norfolk Terrier

TOOLS AND EQUIPMENT

- Coarse and fine stripping combs
- Cotton balls
- Ear cleaner
- Medicated ear powder
- Nail clipper
- Protein coat conditioner
- Pure boar bristle brush
- Scissors
- Steel comb (medium/fine)
- Tearless terrier shampoo
- Thinning shears

Norwegian Buhund

TOOLS AND EQUIPMENT

- Cotton balls
- Eye drops (eye stain remover)
- Medicated ear powder
- Metal comb (wide-toothed)
- Metal rake
- Nail clipper
- Scissors
- Slicker brush
- Thinning shears

GROOMING PROCEDURE

1. Brush the entire coat and tail with a slicker brush.

2. With a metal rake, gently rake through the coat. During the nonshedding season, do not rake out the undercoat; simply untangle it with a metal rake, especially on the neck, thighs, and tail areas. Comb through the coat to remove all loosened hair and make sure it is free of tangles.

3. Clean the ears using medicated ear powder, and lightly pluck any stray hair from the inside.

4. Clean the eyes by wiping them with a cotton ball that has been moistened with eye drops. This will also help to remove any stains.

5. Cut the tips of the nails with a nail clipper, being careful not to cut the quick.

6. With scissors, snip the whiskers from the muzzle, under the chin, the sides of the face, and above the eyes. [Note: Clipping the whiskers is optional if the dog is not a show dog.]

7. Place a cotton ball in each ear (this prevents water from entering the ear canal), and bathe the dog. Cage dry him.

8. With scissors, snip the hair between the pads and toes of the feet and around the edges to give a neat appearance.

9. With thinning shears, remove any straggly hair from the hock joints to the feet on the hind legs and from around the ankles on the front legs.

10. Brush and comb the coat thoroughly.

The Norwegian Buhund should be groomed every 10 to 12 weeks. Regular brushing by the owner will help to keep the coat healthy. The ears should be checked weekly and cleaned if necessary, and the nails should be checked monthly and cut if needed.

GROOMING PROCEDURE

1. Spray the entire coat with protein coat conditioner. This adds body to the coat and helps repair split ends. Brush through the entire coat with an undercoat rake. This will loosen up the coat and remove dead undercoat. Start at the rear of the dog, at the bottom of the skirt area. Work in sections, using your other hand to lift the hair ahead of the section you are working on. Work through the entire dog, from the back to the neck area. Then brush through the coat with a slicker brush to remove the top dead coat. Work vigorously. The more hair you remove now, the less hair you need to wash and dry.

2. Swab the ears with a cotton ball that has been moistened with ear cleaner. This will remove dirt and control ear odor. Follow with a dry cotton ball, and dust the ears with medicated ear powder.

3. Cut the nails with a guillotine-type nail clipper. Nails should be cut monthly.

4. Check between the foot pads and under the feet for burrs, tar, etc. Scissor the hair under the feet to prevent debris from adhering. With thinning shears, trim any hair around the paw that touches the ground or grows out between the paws.

5. Bathe the dog with a tearless protein shampoo that is pH-alkaline. This will add fullness and body to the coat and restructure damaged hair.

6. Use a high-velocity dryer to blow excess water off the dog while he is still in the tub. This will speed up the drying time and help prevent the coat from becoming overly dry. Cage dry the dog until the hair is damp. Then finish drying on the table using a blow dryer and a pin brush to separate all the hair and remove all of the loose coat.

7. Brush the entire coat, using the dryer to style and separate the hair. Be sure to brush to the skin. Follow by combing the entire coat with the medium-toothed comb. Use the fine part of the comb on the soft hair behind the ears.

Norwegian Elkhound

TOOLS AND EQUIPMENT

- Comb (fine/medium)
- Cotton balls
- Ear cleaner
- High-velocity dryer
- Medicated ear powder
- Nail clipper
- Pin brush
- Protein coat conditioner
- Pure boar bristle brush
- Scissors
- Slicker brush
- Tearless protein shampoo
- Thinning shears
- Undercoat rake

Norwich Terrier

TOOLS AND EQUIPMENT

- Cotton balls
- Eye drops (eye stain remover)
- Medicated ear powder
- Metal comb (medium)
- Nail clipper
- Oster A-5 clipper/#10, #15 blades
- Scissors
- Sisal (natural bristle) brush
- Thinning shears

GROOMING PROCEDURE

1. Briskly brush through the coat with a sisal brush. Comb through and remove all tangles and any loosened hair.

2. Clean the ears using medicated ear powder, and lightly pluck any stray hair from the insides.

3. Clean the eyes by wiping them with a cotton ball that has been moistened with eye drops. This will also help to remove stains around and under the eyes.

4. Cut the tips of the nails with a nail clipper, being careful not to cut the quick.

5. With a #10 blade on the Oster A-5 clipper, shave the anal area, being certain not to put the blade in direct contact with the skin (½ inch [1 cm] on each side).

6. Shave the abdomen from groin to navel and down the insides of the thighs.

7. With a #15 blade, shave both sides of the ears from base to tip.

8. Place a cotton ball in each ear to prevent water from entering the ear canal, and bathe the dog. Cage dry him.

9. Brush the coat with a sisal brush.

10. Scissor around the edges of the ears.

11. With scissors, snip the hair between the dog's foot pads; while he is standing, snip around the edges of the feet to make a neat appearance.

12. With thinning shears, trim straggly hair from the shoulders and body for a neat appearance. The chest should be full.

13. Using thinning shears, make the rump appear nice and round, sloping into the rear end.

14. With scissors, trim the tail so that it is wide at the base and tapers to the tip.

15. Brush and comb through the entire coat.

The Norwich Terrier should be groomed every 6 to 8 weeks. The ears should be checked weekly and cleaned if necessary, and the nails should be checked monthly and cut if necessary.

GROOMING PROCEDURE

1. Starting at the head, thoroughly brush the entire coat with a slicker brush. Remove any mats with a mat-splitting comb. Comb through the coat to remove all loosened hair. If the dog is excessively matted, start at the feet and brush the legs upward in sections. On the body, work from rear to front in the same manner.

2. Clean the ears using medicated ear powder, and lightly pluck any stray hair from the insides.

3. Clean the eyes by wiping them with a cotton ball that has been moistened with eye drops. This will also help to remove stains under or around the eyes.

4. Cut the tips of the nails with a nail clipper, being careful not to cut to the quick.

5. With a #10 blade, shave the anal area being certain not to put the blade in direct contact with the skin (½ inch [1 cm] each side).

6. Shave the abdomen from groin to navel and down the insides of the thighs.

7. Put a cotton ball in each ear to prevent water from entering the ear canal. Now you're ready to bathe the dog. Cage dry him to remove excess water.

8. Lift the dog onto a grooming table and complete drying with a blow dryer and a slicker brush.

9. Scissor the hair between the pads of the feet; while the dog is standing, lightly scissor around the edges of the feet to make a neat appearance.

10. Using thinning shears on the rump, make it appear nice and round. The rump should slope into the rear end.

11. Brush the body hair to make it full and fluffy, and brush the leg hair downward.

The Old English Sheepdog should be groomed every 3 or 4 weeks, although regular brushing by the owner will help maintain a healthy coat and keep it free of tangles. The ears should be checked weekly and cleaned if necessary, and the nails should be checked and cut at the grooming session.

Old English Sheepdog

TOOLS AND EQUIPMENT

- Cotton balls
- Eye drops (eye stain remover)
- Mat-splitting comb
- Metal comb (medium)
- Nail clipper
- Oster A-5 clipper/#10 blade
- Scissors
- Slicker brush
- Thinning shears

Otterhound

TOOLS AND EQUIPMENT

- Cotton balls
- Eye drops (eye stain remover)
- Mat-splitting comb
- Medicated ear powder
- Metal comb (wide-toothed)
- Nail clipper
- Oster A-5 clipper/#10 blade
- Scissors
- Slicker brush
- Thinning shears

GROOMING PROCEDURE

1. Starting at the head, brush through the entire coat and tail with a slicker brush. Remove any mats or tangles with a mat-splitting comb. Comb through the coat to remove all loosened hair.

2. Clean the ears using medicated ear powder, and lightly pluck any stray hair from the insides.

3. Clean the eyes by wiping them with a cotton ball that has been moistened with eye drops. This also helps to remove any stains.

4. Cut the tips of the nails, being careful not to cut the quick.

5. With a #10 blade, shave the anal area, being certain not to put the blade in direct contact with the skin (½ inch [1 cm] each side).

6. With a #10 blade, shave the abdomen from groin to navel and down the insides of the thighs.

7. Place a cotton ball in each ear (this prevents water from entering the ear canal) and bathe the dog. Cage dry or fluff dry him.

8. Brush and comb through the coat.

9. Using thinning shears, trim any straggly hair from the head; the eyebrows should be left full.

10. Using thinning shears, trim any straggly hair from the top of the back so that the coat appears even.

11. Using scissors, trim around the edges of the ears to make the fringe even.

12. Scissor the edges of the beard to make a square effect.

13. Scissor the hair between the pads of the feet; while the dog is standing, scissor around the edges of the feet for a neat appearance.

14. Comb through the entire coat and tail to remove all loosened hair.

The Otterhound should be groomed every 6 to 8 weeks. Regular brushing by the owner will help to keep the coat healthy and free of tangles. The ears should be checked weekly and cleaned if necessary, and the nails should be checked monthly and cut if necessary.

GROOMING PROCEDURE

1. Nails should be cut by removing only the tips; avoid cutting the quick. If the nail bleeds, apply styptic powder to stop the bleeding. Any rough nail edges may be removed with a file.

2. Clean the ears with a liquid cleaner. Apply the cleaner to a cotton ball and wipe accumulated wax and dirt from all the crevices in both ears.

3. Brush through the coat with a slicker brush to remove all mats and dirt.

4. Bathe the dog with a shampoo of your choice. Rinse thoroughly. A conditioner may be used to cut down on static electricity and to help the coat lie smoothly.

5. Towel dry the dog until damp, then finish drying with a blow dryer. While drying the coat, brush in the direction of growth to get the hair to lie smoothly.

6. With straight scissors, remove the hair between the pads and underside of the foot. If desired, the hair that grows between the toes on top of the foot may be removed if the dog is not showing.

7. Comb through the dog's coat to make sure all knots and tangles have been removed. A conditioner may be lightly sprayed on the coat to help cut down on "flyaway" hair.

The Papillon should be groomed every 6 to 8 weeks.

TOOLS AND EQUIPMENT

- Comb
- Cotton balls
- Ear cleaner
- Nail clipper (guillotine or scissor)
- Shampoo (conditioning or whitening)
- Slicker brush
- Straight scissors
- Styptic powder

Pekingese

TOOLS AND EQUIPMENT

- Cotton balls
- Eye drops (eye stain remover)
- Matting comb (medium)
- Medicated ear powder
- Medicated talcum powder
- Nail clipper
- Oster A-5 clipper/#10 blade
- Scissors
- Slicker brush

GROOMING PROCEDURE

1. Brush the entire coat and tail with a slicker brush, starting at the head and working down the back. Remove any mats with a matting comb. When brushing the legs, start at the feet and work up. Comb through the coat with a metal comb.

2. Clean the ears using medicated ear powder, and lightly pluck any stray hair from the insides of the ears.

3. Cut the tips of the nails with a nail clipper, being careful not to cut the quick.

4. Clean the eyes by wiping them with a cotton ball that has been moistened with eye drops. If the eyes are excessively watery and sticky, snip stained hair from the corners with scissors.

5. Clean the furrows on the face with a moistened cotton ball. Daily use of eye drops or medicated talcum powder on the furrows will keep them dry and help prevent soreness or infection.

6. Using a #10 blade, shave the anal area, being certain not to put the blade in direct contact with the skin (½ inch [1 cm] on either side).

7. Using a #10 blade, shave the abdomen from groin to navel and down the insides of the thighs.

8. Place a cotton ball in each ear (this prevents water from entering the ear canal), and bathe the dog. Towel dry him.

9. Place the dog on the grooming table and fluff dry with a slicker brush, brushing the coat in an upward motion for a fuller, thicker look.

10. With scissors, snip the hair between the pads of the feet and the toes. Snip around the edges of the feet for a neat effect.

11. Comb through the tail using a metal comb. Make a part down the center and allow it to fall naturally across the dog's back.

The Pekingese should be groomed every 6 or 8 weeks, depending on the fullness of the coat. The owner should brush the dog on a regular basis.

GROOMING PROCEDURE

1. Spray the entire coat with protein coat conditioner. This adds body to the coat and helps repair split ends. Brush through the entire coat with a gentle slicker to remove loose hair. Then comb with a molting comb made for shorthaired breeds (#564) to take out loose undercoat.

2. Swab the ears with a cotton ball that has been moistened with ear cleaner. This will remove dirt and control ear odor. Follow this with a dry cotton ball, and dust the ears with medicated ear powder.

3. Cut the nails with a guillotine-type nail clipper. Nails should be cut monthly.

4. Bathe the dog with a tearless protein shampoo that is pH-alkaline. This will add fullness and body to the coat and restructure damaged hair.

5. Cage dry the dog until damp. Finish drying on the table using a blow dryer and a pure bristle brush. Thoroughly comb through the entire dog.

6. Check between the foot pads and under the feet for burrs, tar, etc. Scissor the hair under the feet even with the pads. Trim any hair around the paw that touches the ground and neaten the entire foot. Use thinning shears to trim the hair growing between the toes. Be sure to neaten the hair on the back of the rear pasterns.

7. The whiskers may be removed with scissors to improve the expression (optional).

8. Topbrush with a pure bristle brush that has been sprayed with protein coat conditioner. This adds brilliance and fragrance to the coat.

Pembroke Welsh Corgi

TOOLS AND EQUIPMENT

- Cotton balls
- Ear cleaner
- Eye stain remover
- Medicated ear powder
- Nail clipper
- Protein coat conditioner
- Pure boar bristle brush
- Scissors
- Short-hair molting comb (#564)
- Steel comb (medium/fine)
- Slicker brush (gentle)
- Tearless protein shampoo

Petit Basset Griffon Vendeen

TOOLS AND EQUIPMENT

- Cotton balls
- Eye drops (eye stain remover)
- Medicated ear powder
- Metal comb (medium)
- Nail clipper
- Oster A-5 clipper/#10 blade
- Scissors
- Slicker brush
- Thinning shears

GROOMING PROCEDURE

1. Brush the coat thoroughly with a slicker brush.

2. Comb through the coat to remove all loosened hair.

3. Clean the ears using medicated ear powder, and lightly pluck any stray hair from the insides.

4. Clean the eyes by wiping them with a cotton ball that has been moistened with eye drops.

5. Cut the tips of the nails with a nail clipper, being careful not to cut the quick.

6. With a #10 blade, shave the abdomen from groin to navel and down the insides of the thighs.

7. Shave the anal area, being certain not to put the blade in direct contact with the skin (½ inch [1 cm] on either side).

8. Put a cotton ball in each ear (this prevents water from entering the ear canal), and bathe the dog. Cage dry him.

9. With scissors or thinning shears, trim straggly hairs from around the ankles on the front feet and from the hocks down to the feet on the hind legs.

10. With scissors, snip hair from between the pads and toes of the feet and around the edges for a neat effect.

11. Comb through the entire coat to remove all loosened hair.

The Petit Basset Griffon Vendeen should be groomed every 8 to 10 weeks. The ears should be checked weekly and cleaned if necessary, and the nails should be checked monthly and cut if necessary.

GROOMING PROCEDURE

1. Brush the coat briskly with a sisal brush.

2. Clean the ears using medicated ear powder.

3. Clean the eyes by wiping them with a cotton ball that has been moistened with eye drops. This will also help in removing any stains.

4. Cut the tips of the nails with a nail clipper, being careful not to cut the quick.

5. Using scissors, clip the whiskers from the muzzle, from the chin, from the sides of the face, and from above the eyes. [Note: Clipping the whiskers is a decision to be left to the owner if the dog is not a show dog.]

6. Put a cotton ball in each ear to prevent water from entering the ear canal. Bathe and then cage dry the dog.

7. Put a few drops of lanolin coat conditioner into the palms of your hands, rub them together lightly, and gently massage into the coat.

8. Brush the coat with a sisal brush to distribute the conditioner; then lightly rub over the coat with a chamois cloth to give it a nice sheen.

The Pointer should be bathed every 8 or 10 weeks. Regular brushing by the owner between baths helps maintain a healthy, shiny coat. The ears should be checked weekly and cleaned if necessary, and the nails should be checked monthly and cut if necessary.

Pointer

TOOLS AND EQUIPMENT

- Chamois cloth
- Cotton balls
- Eye drops (eye stain remover)
- Lanolin coat conditioner
- Nail clipper
- Scissors
- Sisal (natural bristle) brush

Polish Lowland Sheepdog

TOOLS AND EQUIPMENT

- Cotton balls
- Eye drops (eye stain remover)
- Mat-splitting comb
- Metal comb (medium)
- Metal rake
- Nail clipper
- Oster A-5 clipper/#10 blade
- Scissors
- Slicker brush

GROOMING PROCEDURE

1. Starting at the head, thoroughly brush the entire coat with a slicker brush. Remove any mats with a mat-splitting comb and/or metal rake. Comb through the coat to remove all loosened hair.

2. Clean the ears using medicated ear powder, and lightly pluck any stray hair from the insides.

3. Clean the eyes by wiping them with a cotton ball that has been moistened with eye drops. This will also help in removing any stains around the eyes.

4. Cut the tips of the nails with a nail clipper, being careful not to cut the quick.

5. With a #10 blade, shave the abdomen from groin to navel and down the insides of the thighs.

6. Shave the anal area, being certain not to put the blade in direct contact with the skin (½ inch [1 cm] on either side).

7. Place a cotton ball in each ear (this prevents water from entering the ear canal), and bathe the dog. Cage dry to remove excess water.

8. Place the dog on a grooming table and complete the drying with a blow dryer and slicker brush to fluff dry.

9. Scissor the hair between the pads of the feet; while the dog is standing, lightly scissor around the edges of the feet to give a neat appearance.

10. Comb through the entire coat to remove all excess hair.

The Polish Lowland Sheepdog, also known as the Polski Owczarek Nizinny, should be groomed every 6 to 8 weeks. Regular brushing by the owner will help maintain a healthy coat and keep the undercoat free of tangles. The ears should be checked weekly and cleaned if necessary, and the nails should be checked and cut at the grooming session.

GROOMING PROCEDURE

1. Nails should be cut by removing the tips only; avoid cutting the quick. If the nail bleeds, apply styptic powder to stop the bleeding. Any rough nail edges may be smoothed with a file.

2. Clean the ears with a liquid cleaner by applying the liquid to a cotton ball and wiping all accumulated wax and dirt from the crevices in both ears.

3. Brush through the entire dog to remove mats and dead hair.

4. Bathe the dog in a shampoo of your choice. Rinse thoroughly. A conditioning rinse may be used to help remove dead hair and cut down on static electricity.

5. Towel dry the dog until he is just damp. A blow dryer will have to be used to finish drying him. While blowing the coat dry, brush through the coat. The hair may be brushed against the growth to give added fullness to the coat.

6. With scissors, remove excess hair between the foot pads and on the bottom of the feet. The hair that grows between the toes on the top of the foot may be removed to tighten up the foot. Excess hair on the back of the hock may be removed, as well as stray hairs in the ears.

7. The hair around the anal area should be trimmed close.

8. Comb through the entire dog to make sure all knots and tangles have been removed.

The completed Pomeranian should resemble a "powder puff," and he should be groomed every 6 to 8 weeks.

TOOLS AND EQUIPMENT

- Comb
- Cotton balls
- Ear cleaner
- Nail clipper (guillotine or scissor)
- Shampoo (all-purpose or conditioning)
- Slicker brush
- Straight scissors
- Styptic powder

Poodle, Dutch Clip

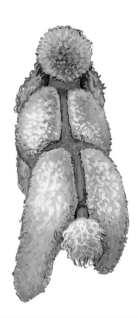

TOOLS AND EQUIPMENT

- Cotton balls
- Eye drops (eye stain remover)
- Mat-splitting comb
- Medicated ear powder
- Metal combs (medium/wide)
- Metal rake
- Nail clipper
- Oster A-5 clipper/#⅝, #⅞, #7, #10, #15 blades
- Scissors
- Slicker brush

GROOMING PROCEDURE

1. Brush the coat thoroughly with a slicker brush, using upward strokes. Remove any mats or tangles with a mat-splitting comb and/or metal rake. Comb through the coat with a medium comb, removing all loosened hair.

2. Clean the ears using medicated ear powder, and lightly pluck any stray hair from the insides.

3. Clean the eyes by wiping them with a cotton ball that has been moistened with eye drops. This will also help to remove any stains under or around the eyes.

4. Cut the tips of the nails with a nail clipper, being careful not to cut the quick.

5. With a #15 blade, shave the feet. Start by shaving between the pads, and then shave up just clear of the largest pad—this will be the shave line for the whole foot. Make sure there are no hairs left on or between the toes.

6. Shave the face, selecting a style from "Poodle Heads and Faces."

7. Shave the tail one-third of the length from the base.

8. With a #10 blade, shave the abdomen from groin to navel and down the insides of the thighs.

9. Shave the anal area with a #10 blade, being certain not to put the blade in direct contact with the skin (½ inch [1 cm] each side).

10. With a #15 blade, shave around the neck one blade width from the base of the ears, base of the skull, and under the jaw. This pattern line should reach a point at just above the shoulder on a small dog. (Increase the blade width with the size of the dog, so that the pattern line reaches that point.)

11. With the #⅝ blade (for toys), #⅞ blade (for miniatures), or #15 blade (for standards), shave the pattern line straight down the center of the back, from the neck pattern to the base of the tail.

12. Using the same blade, shave from the center back pattern down the sides at the flanks (this line should be just in front of the rear legs).

13. Comb through the coat with a medium comb to remove excess hair.

14. Place a cotton ball in each ear (this prevents water from entering the ear canal), and bathe the dog. Fluff dry using a slicker brush in an upward motion.

15. Brush through the coat and fluff up, with a wide-toothed comb, all areas to be scissored.

16. Using the same blades as before, repeat the process for the pattern, this time shaving against the lay of the coat for a clean sharp look.

17. With a #15 blade, shaving against the lay of the coat, round off all pattern corners.

18. With a #7 blade on the Oster A-5 clipper, lightly blend the hair down from the pattern. Scissor all straggly hairs from the edges.

19. With a wide-toothed comb, fluff up the hair on the body and scissor evenly into a full, round barrel shape.

20. Scissor the chest, between the front legs and underneath, even with the body.

21. Comb downward the hair on the front legs by the ankles and scissor straight around.

22. With a wide-toothed comb, fluff up the hair on the front legs and scissor into straight tubular shapes, blending into the body.

23. Comb the hair on the rear legs by the ankles downward and scissor straight around.

24. With a wide-toothed comb, fluff up the hair on the rear legs and scissor into straight, full shapes to make them appear roundish on the hips.

25. Scissor the tail into a full, round pom-pom.

26. Comb the hair on the head straight up and scissor around the edges. Fluff up the hair with a wide-toothed comb and scissor it round on top, tapering it into the ears and neck.

27. With a comb, fluff up the hair on the legs and body; trim any straggly hairs, especially around the ankles, with scissors.

The Poodle should be groomed every 4 to 6 weeks, depending on the thickness of the coat and how fast it grows. Regular brushing and combing by the owner between groomings will help keep the coat healthy and free of tangles. The ears should be checked weekly and cleaned if necessary, and the nails should be checked and cut at the grooming session. It should be noted that all shaved areas should be shaved against the lay of the coat, except on a dog with sensitive skin. In this case, use a #10 blade and shave with the lay of the coat. The pattern should be shaved with the lay of the coat prior to the bath and against the lay of the coat afterward.

Poodle, Kennel Clip

TOOLS AND EQUIPMENT

- Cotton balls
- Eye drops (eye stain remover)
- Mat-splitting comb
- Medicated ear powder
- Metal combs (medium/wide)
- Metal rake
- Nail clipper
- Oster A-5 clipper/#4, #5, #7, #10, #15 blades
- Scissors
- Slicker brush

GROOMING PROCEDURE

1. Brush the coat thoroughly with a slicker brush, using upward strokes. Remove any mats or tangles with a mat-splitting comb and/or metal rake. Comb through the coat with a medium comb, removing all loosened hair.

2. Clean the ears using medicated ear powder, and lightly pluck any stray hair from the insides.

3. Clean the eyes by wiping them with a cotton ball that has been moistened with eye drops. This will also help to remove any stains.

4. Cut the tips of the nails with a nail clipper, being careful not to cut the quick.

5. With a #15 blade, shave the feet. Start by shaving between the pads; then shave up just clear of the largest pad. This becomes the shave line for the whole foot. Make sure there are no hairs left on or between the toes.

6. Shave the face, selecting a style from "Poodle Heads and Faces."

7. Shave the tail one-third of the length from the base.

8. With a #10 blade, shave the abdomen from groin to navel and down the insides of the thighs.

9. Shave the anal area (#10 blade), being certain not to put the blade in direct contact with the skin (½ inch [1 cm] each side).

10. With the #7, #5, or #4 blade (depending on the length of coat desired), clip down the back from the base of the skull to the base of the tail.

11. From the base of the ears, clip down the shoulders to the tops of the front legs.

12. Clip down the front and between the front legs.

13. From the first clip down the back, clip down the sides of the abdomen and underneath it.

14. Clip down the hips to the tops of the rear legs.

15. Comb through the coat with a wide-toothed comb to remove excess hair.

16. Place a cotton ball in each ear (this prevents water from entering the ear canal), and bathe the dog. Fluff dry, using a slicker brush in an upward motion.

17. Brush the clipped area on the body and comb the legs upward with a wide-toothed comb.

18. Using the same blade as before, repeat the process for the pattern, blending the hair into the tops of the legs.

19. Comb the hair on the front legs by the ankles downward and scissor straight around.

20. With a wide-toothed comb, fluff up the hair on the front legs and scissor it into short, straight tubular shapes that taper at the tops and blend into the body.

21. Comb downward the hair on the rear legs by the ankles and scissor straight around.

22. With a wide-toothed comb, fluff up the hair on the rear legs and scissor them short, following the natural contours and blending into the hips.

23. Fluff up the hair on the legs and trim any straggly hairs, especially around the ankles.

24. Scissor the tail into a full, round pom-pom.

25. Comb the hair on the head straight up and scissor around the edges. Fluff up the hair with a wide-toothed comb and scissor it round on top, tapering it into the ears and the neck.

The Poodle should be groomed every 4 to 6 weeks, depending on the thickness of the coat and how fast it grows. Regular brushing and combing by the owner between groomings will help keep the coat healthy and free of tangles. The ears should be checked weekly and cleaned if necessary, and the nails should be checked and cut at the grooming session. It should be noted that all shaved areas should be shaved against the lay of the coat, except on a dog with sensitive skin. In this case, use a #10 blade and shave with the lay of the coat. It is also acceptable to use a #4 blade lightly on the legs. Then fluff the hair up with a wide-toothed comb and scissor any straggly hairs.

#4, #5, #7
↓

← #15

↑
#10

Poodle, Lamb Clip

TOOLS AND EQUIPMENT

- Cotton balls
- Eye drops (eye stain remover)
- Mat-splitting comb
- Medicated ear powder
- Metal combs (medium/wide)
- Metal rake
- Nail clipper
- Oster A-5 clipper/#4, #5, #7, #10, #15 blades
- Scissors
- Slicker brush

GROOMING PROCEDURE

1. Brush the coat thoroughly with a slicker brush, using upward strokes. Remove any mats or tangles with a mat-splitting comb and/or metal rake. Comb through the coat with a medium comb, removing all loosened hair.

2. Clean the ears using medicated ear powder, and lightly pluck any stray hair from the insides.

3. Clean the eyes by wiping them with a cotton ball that has been moistened with eye drops. This helps to remove any stains around the eyes.

4. Cut the tips of the nails with a nail clipper, being careful not to cut the quick.

5. With a #15 blade, shave the feet. Start by shaving between the pads; then shave up just clear of the largest pad. This becomes the shave line for the whole foot. Make sure there are no hairs left on or between the toes.

6. Shave the face. Select a style from "Poodle Heads and Faces."

7. Shave the tail one-third of the length from the base.

8. With a #10 blade, shave the abdomen from groin to navel and down the insides of the thighs.

9. Shave the anal area (#10 blade), being certain not to put the blade in direct contact with the skin (½ inch [1 cm] each side).

10. With the #7, #5, or #4 blade (depending on the length of coat desired), clip down the back from the base of the skull to the base of the tail.

11. From the base of the ears, clip down to the shoulders and down the front to the breastbone.

12. From the first clip down the back, clip down the sides of the abdomen and over the hips.

13. Comb through the coat with a medium comb to remove excess hair.

14. Put a cotton ball in each ear (this prevents water from entering the ear canal), and bathe the dog. Fluff dry, using a slicker brush in an upward motion.

15. Brush up the clipped area on the body, and fluff up the legs with a wide-toothed comb.

16. Using the same blades as before, repeat the process for the pattern, blending the hair into the chest, lower stomach, and tops of the legs.

17. Scissor evenly the chest, between the front legs and under the abdomen, and blend this area into the body. [Note: It is acceptable to use the same body blade on these areas.]

18. Comb the hair on the front legs by the ankles downward and scissor straight around.

19. With a wide-toothed comb, fluff up the hair on the front legs and scissor into straight tubular shapes, tapering them slightly at the tops and blending into the body and shoulders.

20. Comb downward the hair on the rear legs by the ankles and scissor straight around.

21. With a wide-toothed comb, fluff up the hair on the rear legs and scissor it into straight full shapes, blending into the body at the hips.

22. Scissor the tail into a full, round pom-pom.

23. Comb the hair on the head straight up and scissor around the edges. Fluff up the hair with a wide-toothed comb and scissor it round on top, tapering it into the ears and neck.

24. With the comb, fluff up all the hair on the legs and trim any straggly hairs, especially around the ankles, with scissors.

The Poodle should be groomed every 4 to 6 weeks, depending on the thickness of the coat and how fast it grows. Regular brushing and combing by the owner between groomings will help keep the coat healthy and free of tangles. The ears should be checked weekly and cleaned if necessary, and the nails should be checked and cut at the grooming session. It should be noted that all shaved areas should be shaved against the lay of the coat, except on a dog with sensitive skin. In this case, use a #10 blade and shave with the lay of the coat.

← #15

← #4
#5
#7

Poodle, Puppy Clip

TOOLS AND EQUIPMENT

- Cotton balls
- Eye drops (eye stain remover)
- Mat-splitting comb
- Medicated ear powder
- Metal combs (medium/wide)
- Metal rake
- Nail clipper
- Oster A-5 clipper/#8½, #10, #15 blades
- Scissors
- Slicker brush

GROOMING PROCEDURE

1. Brush the coat thoroughly with upward strokes using a slicker brush. Remove any mats or tangles with a mat-splitting comb and/or metal rake. Comb through the coat with a medium comb, removing all excess hair.

2. Clean the ears using medicated ear powder, and lightly pluck any stray hair from the insides.

3. Clean the eyes by wiping them with a cotton ball that has been moistened with eye drops. This will also help in removing any stains around the eyes.

4. Cut the tips of the nails with a nail clipper, being careful not to cut the quick.

5. With a #15 blade, shave the feet. Start by shaving between the pads; then shave up just clear of the largest pad. This becomes the shave line for the whole foot. Make sure there are no hairs left on or between the toes.

6. With a #10 blade, shave the face. Select a style from "Poodle Heads and Faces."

7. With a #10 blade, shave the tail one-third of the length from the base.

8. With a #8½ blade, shave the abdomen from groin to navel and down the insides of the thighs.

9. Shave the anal area (#8½ blade), being certain not to put the blade in direct contact with the skin (½ inch [1 cm] each side).

10. Comb through the coat with a wide-toothed comb to remove excess hair.

11. Place a cotton ball in each ear (this prevents water from entering the ear canal), and bathe the dog. Fluff dry, using a slicker brush in an upward motion.

12. Brush the entire coat upward and fluff it up with a wide-toothed comb.

13. Scissor the entire body to an even length (1 to 2 inches [2.5 to 5 cm] or whatever length is desired by the owner).

14. Comb the hair on the front legs by the ankles downward and scissor straight around.

15. Fluff up the hair on the front legs with a wide-toothed comb and scissor into straight tubular shapes, blending them into the body.

16. Comb downward the hair on the rear legs by the ankles and scissor straight around.

17. With a wide-toothed comb, fluff up the hair on the rear legs and scissor them straight and full. Blend these areas into the body.

18. Scissor the tail into a full, round pom-pom.

19. Comb back the hair on the head and scissor around the front edge, across the eyes to the ears. Fluff up the remaining hair with a comb, and scissor it round on the top. Blend this into the body, around the neck, and into the ears.

20. With the comb, fluff up all hair and trim any straggly hairs with scissors, especially around the ankles.

The Poodle should be groomed every 4 to 6 weeks, depending on the thickness of the coat and how fast it grows. Regular brushing and combing by the owner between groomings will help keep the coat healthy and free of tangles. By the time the puppy reaches 6 to 8 months, the owner may consider one of the other Poodle clips. The ears should be checked weekly and cleaned if necessary, and the nails should be checked and cut at the grooming session. It should be noted that a Poodle puppy's skin is usually sensitive, so use a #10 blade on the face and tail, shaving with the lay of the coat. Use the #8½ blade on the abdomen and anal areas as specified. For adult Poodles whose owners prefer to see them in a Puppy clip, use a #15 blade on the face, feet, and tail and a #10 blade on the abdomen and anal areas.

#10 →

← #10

↑
#8½

#15→

Poodle, Royal Dutch Clip

GROOMING PROCEDURE

1. Brush the coat thoroughly with a slicker brush, using upward strokes. Remove any mats or tangles with a mat-splitting comb and/or metal rake. Comb through the coat with a medium comb, removing all loosened hair.

2. Clean the ears using medicated ear powder, and lightly pluck any stray hair from the insides.

3. Clean the eyes by wiping them with a cotton ball that has been moistened with eye drops. This will also help in removing any stains around the eyes.

4. Cut the tips of the nails, being careful not to cut the quick.

5. With a #15 blade, shave the feet. Start by shaving between the pads; then shave up just clear of the largest pad. This becomes the shave line for the whole foot. Make sure there are no hairs left on or between the toes.

6. Shave the face, selecting a style from "Poodle Heads and Faces."

7. Shave the tail one-third of the length from the base.

8. With a #10 blade, shave the abdomen from groin to navel and down the insides of the thighs.

9. Shave the anal area (#10 blade), being certain not to put the blade in direct contact with the skin (½ inch [1 cm] each side).

10. With a #15 blade, shave around the neck, one blade width from the base of the ears, base of the skull, and under the jaw. This pattern line should reach to a point just above the shoulder on a small dog. (Increase the blade width with the size of the dog so that the pattern line reaches that point).

11. With a #7/8 blade (for toys/small miniatures) or #15 blade (for miniatures/standards), shave a pattern line straight down the center of the back, from the neck pattern to the base of the tail.

12. Using the same blade, shave from the center back pattern down the sides at the flanks. (This line should fall just in front of the rear legs).

13. Comb through the coat with a medium comb to remove excess hair.

14. Place a cotton ball in each ear (this prevents water from entering the ear canal), and bathe the dog. Fluff dry, using a slicker brush in an upward motion.

15. Brush through the coat, and fluff up with a wide-toothed comb, all areas to be scissored.

16. Using the same blades as before, repeat the process for the pattern, this time shaving against the lay of the coat for a clean sharp look.

17. With a #15 blade, and shaving against the lay of the coat, round off all pattern corners.

TOOLS AND EQUIPMENT

- Cotton balls
- Eye drops (eye stain remover)
- Mat-splitting comb
- Medicated ear powder
- Metal combs (medium/wide)
- Metal rake
- Nail clipper
- Oster A-5 clipper/#7/8, #7, #10, #15 blades
- Scissors
- Slicker brush

18. With a #7 blade, lightly blend the hair down from the pattern. Scissor all straggly hairs from the edges.

19. With a wide-toothed comb, fluff up the hair on the body and scissor it evenly into a full, round barrel shape.

20. Scissor the chest, between the front legs and underneath, even with the body.

21. Comb downward the hair on the front legs by the ankle and scissor straight around.

22. With a wide-toothed comb, fluff up the hair on the front legs and scissor it into straight, tubular shapes. Blend these areas into the body.

23. Comb the hair on the rear legs by the ankles downward and scissor straight around.

24. With a wide-toothed comb, fluff up the hair on the rear legs and scissor it into straight, full shapes that appear roundish on the hips.

25. Scissor the tail into a full, round pom-pom.

26. Comb the hair on the head straight up and scissor around the edges. Fluff up the hair with a wide-toothed comb and scissor it round on top, tapering it into the ears and neck.

27. With the comb, fluff up all the hair on the legs and body and trim any straggly hairs, especially around the ankles, with scissors.

The Poodle should be groomed every 4 to 6 weeks, depending on the thickness of the coat and how fast it grows. Regular brushing and combing by the owner between groomings will help keep the coat healthy and free of tangles. The ears should be checked weekly and cleaned if necessary, and the nails should be checked and cut at the grooming session. It should be noted that all shaved areas should be shaved against the lay of the coat, except on a dog with sensitive skin. In this case, use a #10 blade and shave with the lay of the coat. The pattern should be shaved with the lay of the coat prior to bathing and against the lay of the coat afterward.

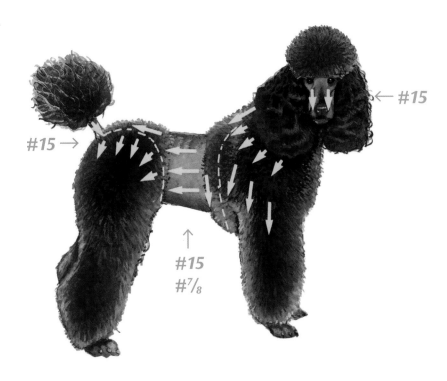

#15 →

← #15

↑
#15
#⁷/₈

Poodle, Royal Dutch Clip

Poodle, Summer Clip

1. Brush the coat thoroughly with upward strokes using a slicker brush. Remove any mats or tangles with a mat-splitting comb and/or metal rake. Comb through the coat with a medium comb, removing all loosened hair.

2. Clean the ears using medicated ear powder, and lightly pluck any stray hair from the insides.

3. Clean the eyes by wiping them with a cotton ball that has been moistened with eye drops. This will also help remove any stains around the eyes.

4. Cut the tips of the nails with a nail clipper, being careful not to cut the quick.

5. With a #15 blade, shave the feet. Start by shaving between the pads; then shave up just clear of the largest pad. This becomes the shave line for the whole foot. Make sure there are no hairs left on or between the toes.

6. Shave the face, selecting a style from "Poodle Heads and Faces."

7. Shave the tail one-third of the length from the base.

8. With a #10 blade, shave the abdomen from groin to navel and down the insides of the thighs.

9. Shave the anal area (#10 blade), being certain not to put the blade in direct contact with the skin (½ inch [1 cm] each side).

10. With the #10 or #7 blade, clip the entire body from the base of the skull (neck area) to the base of the tail, down the chest, between the front legs, and around and under the stomach.

11. Continue clipping down the legs to a point just above the elbows on the front legs and to the hock joints on the rear legs.

12. To remove excess hair, comb through the remaining hair on the head, ears, tail, and ankles.

13. Place a cotton ball in each ear (this prevents water from entering the ear canal), and bathe the dog. Fluff dry, using a slicker brush in an upward motion.

14. Lightly brush up the clipped area on the body and legs, and using the same blade as before, repeat the process for the pattern.

15. With a wide-toothed comb, fluff up the hair on the head, ankles, and tail.

TOOLS AND EQUIPMENT

- Cotton balls
- Eye drops (eye stain remover)
- Mat-splitting comb
- Medicated ear powder
- Metal combs (medium/wide)
- Metal rake
- Nail clipper
- Oster A-5 clipper/#7, #10, #15 blades
- Scissors
- Slicker brush

16. Comb downward the hair on the ankles and scissor it straight around; then comb this hair upward and again scissor straight around. Now fluff the hair out with the comb and scissor into round pom-poms.

17. Scissor the tail into a full, round pom-pom.

18. Comb the hair on the head straight up and scissor around the edges. Fluff up the hair with a wide-toothed comb and scissor it round on top, tapering into the ears and neck.

The Poodle should be groomed every 4 to 6 weeks, depending on the thickness of the coat and how fast it grows. Regular brushing and combing by the owner between groomings will help keep the coat healthy and free of tangles. The ears should be checked weekly and cleaned if necessary, and the nails should be checked and cut at the grooming session. It should be noted that all shaved areas should be shaved against the lay of the coat, except on a dog with sensitive skin. Then use a #10 blade and shave with the lay of the coat. In this clip, also known as the Clown clip, the body and legs are also shaved with the lay of the coat.

#7, #10
↓

← #10
#15

← #15

Poodle, Town and Country Clip

TOOLS AND EQUIPMENT

- Cotton balls
- Eye drops (eye stain remover)
- Mat-splitting comb
- Medicated ear powder
- Metal combs (medium/wide)
- Metal rake
- Nail clipper
- Oster A-5 clipper/#⅝, #7, #10, #15 blades
- Scissors
- Slicker brush

GROOMING PROCEDURE

1. Brush the coat thoroughly with a slicker brush, using upward strokes. Remove any mats or tangles with a mat-splitting comb and/or metal rake. Comb through the coat with a medium comb, removing all loosened hair.

2. Clean the ears using medicated ear powder, and lightly pluck any stray hair from the insides.

3. Clean the eyes by wiping them with a cotton ball that has been moistened with eye drops. This will also help to remove any stains under or around the eyes.

4. Cut the tips of the nails with a nail clipper, being careful not to cut the quick.

5. With a #15 blade, shave the feet. Start by shaving between the pads; then shave up just clear of the largest pad. This serves as the shave line for the whole foot. Make sure there are no hairs left on or between the toes.

6. Shave the face, selecting a style from "Poodle Heads and Faces."

7. Shave the tail one-third of the length from the base.

8. With a #10 blade, shave the abdomen from groin to navel and down the insides of the thighs.

9. Shave the anal area (#10 blade), being certain not to put the blade in direct contact with the skin (½ inch [1 cm] each side).

10. With a #10 blade, shave around the neck, one blade width from the base of the ears, base of the skull, and under the jaw. This pattern line should reach to the top of the shoulder on a small dog. (Increase the blade width with the size of the dog so that the pattern line reaches the top of the shoulder.)

11. With a #⅝ blade (for toys/small miniatures) or #10 blade (miniatures/standards), shave a pattern line straight down the center of the back, from the neck pattern to the base of the tail.

12. Using a #10 blade (for all sizes of Poodle), shave from the center back pattern down the sides of the abdomen. (This pattern should fall just in front of the rear legs and about 1 inch [2.5 cm] behind the front legs.) Continue this pattern around and underneath the abdomen, even with the front pattern line.

13. Comb through the coat with a medium comb to remove excess hair.

14. Place a cotton ball in each ear (this prevents water from entering the ear canal), and bathe the dog. Fluff dry, using a slicker brush in an upward motion.

15. Brush the coat and fluff up, with a wide-toothed comb, all areas to be scissored.

16. Using the same blades as before, repeat the process for the pattern, still shaving with the lay of the coat and rounding off all pattern corners.

17. With a #7 blade, lightly blend down the hair from the pattern. Scissor all straggly hairs from the edges.

18. With a wide-toothed comb, fluff up the hair on the chest, between the front legs and underneath, and scissor evenly. (It is acceptable to use a #10 blade on these areas also.)

19. Comb the hair on the front legs by the ankles downward and scissor straight around.

20. With a wide-toothed comb, fluff up the hair on the front legs and scissor it into straight, tubular shapes. Blend these areas into the body. Scissor evenly the outsides of the legs; continue up and over the shoulders and round off on the tops.

21. Comb downward the hair on the rear legs by the ankles and scissor straight around.

22. With a wide-toothed comb, fluff up the hair on the rear legs and scissor it into straight, full shapes that appear roundish on the hips.

23. Scissor the tail into a full, round pom-pom.

24. Comb the hair on the head straight up and scissor around the edges. Fluff up the hair with a wide-toothed comb and scissor it round on top, tapering it into the ears and neck.

25. With the comb, fluff up all of the hair on the legs and front of the body (if a #10 blade was not used) and trim any straggly hairs, especially around the ankles, with scissors.

The Poodle should be groomed every 4 to 6 weeks, depending on the thickness of the coat and how fast it grows. Regular brushing and combing by the owner between groomings will help keep the coat healthy and free of tangles. The ears should be checked weekly and cleaned if necessary, and the nails should be checked and cut at the grooming session. It should be noted that all shaved areas should be shaved against the lay of the coat, except on a dog with sensitive skin. In this case, use a #10 blade and shave with the lay of the coat. The pattern on the Town and Country clip is shaved with the lay of the coat. Do not shave this pattern against the hair grain.

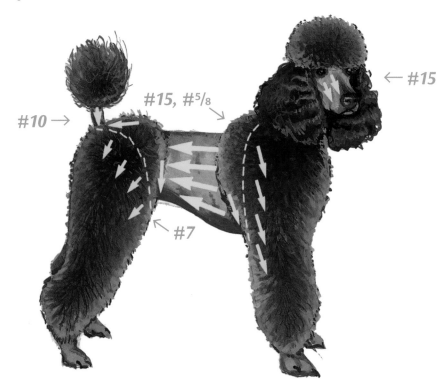

Poodle, Town and Country Clip

Poodle, Heads and Faces

GROOMING PROCEDURE

1. With a #15 blade, fold one ear back and shave from the center of the ear base to the outer corner of the eye. From the center of the ear base, shave forward to within ¾ inch (2 cm) of the corner of the mouth and under the eye to the inner corner. This should create a line from the corner of the mouth to the top of the nose. From between the eyes, shave down the top of the nose to the tip. From the lower ear base, shave down to a point at the base of the throat; from the line just made, shave up and under the lower jaw, pulling the lips back to shave the edges clean.

2. Repeat the process on the other side of the face.

3. Comb the moustache straight down and scissor the lower edge evenly.

On a dog with sensitive skin, use a #10 blade on the clipper and shave with the lay of the coat, except on the edge of the lips; otherwise, shave against the lay of the coat to achieve a clean, sharp look.

Poodle, French Moustache

TOOLS AND EQUIPMENT

- Metal comb (medium)
- Oster A-5 clipper/#10, #15 blades
- Scissors

Poodle, Moustache

GROOMING PROCEDURE

1. With a #15 blade, fold one ear back and shave from the center of the ear base to the outer corner of the eye. From the center of the ear base, shave forward to within ¾ inch (2 cm) of the corner of the mouth and under the eye to the inner corner. This should create a line from the corner of the mouth to the top of the nose, across and under the chin. From between the eyes, shave down the top of the nose to the tip. From the lower ear base, shave down to a point at the base of the throat; from the line just made, shave up toward the line on the lower jaw.

2. Repeat the process on the other side of the face.

3. Comb the moustache outward from the nose and chin and scissor the edges evenly.

On a dog with sensitive skin, use a #10 blade on the clipper and shave with the lay of the coat.

TOOLS AND EQUIPMENT

- Metal comb (medium)
- Oster A-5 clipper/#10, #15 blades
- Scissors

GROOMING PROCEDURE

1. With a #15 blade, fold one ear back and shave from the center of the ear base to the outer corner of the eye. From the outer corner of the eye, shave under the eye to the inner corner and from between the eyes to the tip of the nose. From the lower ear base, shave down to a point at the base of the throat; from the line just made, shave up toward the nose tip and under the lower jaw, pulling the lips back to shave the edges clean.

2. Repeat the process on the other side of the face.

On a dog with sensitive skin, use a #10 blade on the clipper and shave with the lay of the coat, except on the edges of the lips. Otherwise, shave against the lay of the coat to achieve a clean, sharp look.

Poodle, Clean Face

TOOLS AND EQUIPMENT

- Oster A-5 clipper
  #10, #15 blades

Portuguese Water Dog

TOOLS AND EQUIPMENT

- Comb (fine/medium)
- Cotton balls
- Ear cleaner
- Ear forceps
- High-velocity dryer
- Medicated ear powder
- Nail clipper (extra large)
- Oster A-5 clipper/#4, #5, #10 blades/1½ inch (4 cm) guard
- Pin brush
- Protein coat conditioner
- Pure boar bristle brush
- Scissors
- Slicker brush
- Tearless protein color shampoo

GROOMING PROCEDURE

1. Spray the entire coat with protein coat conditioner. This adds body to the coat and helps repair split ends. Brush through the entire coat with a slicker brush, using brisk upward strokes to lift the hair. Then comb the coat thoroughly to be sure all tangles have been removed. Start at the rear of the dog, at the bottom of the skirt area. Work in sections through the entire dog, from the back to the neck area. If the coat is badly matted, or has excessive growth, rough clip the dog with a #5 blade before the bath.

2. Swab the ears with a cotton ball that has been moistened with ear cleaner. This will remove dirt and control ear odor. Follow with a dry cotton ball, and dust the ears with medicated ear powder. With your fingers or ear forceps, pluck stray hair inside the ears.

3. Cut the nails with a guillotine-type nail clipper. Nails should be cut monthly.

4. Check between the foot pads and under the feet for burrs, tar, etc. With a #10 blade, clip the hair under the feet and between the pads.

5. Bathe the dog with a tearless protein shampoo formulated for black or brown hair. This will add fullness and body to the coat, restructure damaged hair, and enhance coat color.

6. Use a high-velocity dryer to blow excess water off the dog while he is still in the tub. This will speed up the drying time and help prevent the coat from becoming overly dry. Cage dry the dog until the hair is damp. Finish drying on the table, using a blow dryer, a pin brush, and a comb to separate all of the hair and to achieve a fluff-dried look.

7. Use a #10 blade to clip the hair around the anus. Just clear the area and do not use heavy pressure.

8. Shave the abdomen with a #10 blade, going with the lay of the hair.

9. Clip the back and sides of the neck with a #5 blade.

10. Clip the body with a #5 blade. Body blades change depending on coat type and skin sensitivity. Depending on coat texture, a #5 may be changed to a #7, #5F, or for a plushier look, a #10 blade with a #1 guard. Clip from the base of the skull to the base of the tail. Clip both sides of the body, from the sides of the neck to where the leg joins the body in the front and down to the thigh on the rear leg. Follow the contour of the body, directing your clipper in the direction the hair grows. Do not go against the grain or across the grain. Lift your clipper slightly as you near the end of the clipped area to blend the clipped area into the nonclipped area of the leg. This takes a slight twist of the wrist to accomplish, as if you were using the end of the clipper as a shovel. You must work to blend the clipped area into the fringe area, leaving no uneven lines or ridges.

11. With a #5 blade, clip the front chest of the dog straight down from the throat. Forelegs and hindlegs should not be touched with the clipper.

12. Clip the tail with a #5 blade, but leave a 5 to 6 inch (13 to 15 cm) plume on the end of the tail. Always clip with the grain—the way the hair grows—and never against the growth. To prevent irritation, use a very light pressure on the underside of the tail. Neaten any uneven hairs of the plume.

13. With a slicker, brush up the hair on the front legs. Comb through the hair with the medium side of the comb. Lift the foot and shake the leg to allow the hair to fall naturally. Scissor to shape cylindrically. Blend in any uneven line you may have between the shaved area and unshaved area. Blend into the shoulder to create a straight line from shoulder to foot. Shape the foot so that it is round and compact, but don't expose the nails.

14. Brush the rear leg up, comb, and shake the hair free. With scissors, blend the hip area into the rear leg. The rear leg should show strong angulation and should be trimmed evenly. Trim evenly the back line of the hock. Shape the foot round and blend it into the leg.

15. The head should be styled into a wedge, like that of the Bichon Frise. Scissor short or clip the muzzle with a #4 blade, forming a wedge into the cheeks. Clip or scissor under the jaw. The face should be uniformly short—wedge-shaped—longer in back and blending into the topknot. There should be no ear separation, and it is preferred that the face be scissored rather than clipped.

16. Comb the topknot back and up from the eyes. Scissor it short and blend into the ears, leaving no separation.

17. Scissor the bottoms of the ears to the jaw line. With scissors, top scissor down to make the ears neat and to remove bulk.

18. Top brush the coat with a pure bristle brush that has been sprayed with protein coat conditioner. This adds brilliance and fragrance.

Pug

TOOLS AND EQUIPMENT

- After-shampoo skin and coat conditioner
- Bristle brush
- Cotton balls
- Eye drops
- Fine-toothed flea comb
- Hound glove
- Medicated ear powder
- Mink oil spray
- Nail clipper
- Oster A-5 clipper/#10 blade
- Petroleum jelly
- Rubber curry brush
- Scissors
- Shampoo
- Styptic powder

GROOMING PROCEDURE

1. Spray the coat with mink oil and let it remain for 10 to 15 minutes.

2. Brush out the coat with a bristle brush or rubber curry brush to loosen any dead hair.

3. Comb through the coat with a fine-toothed flea comb.

4. Clean under the roll (over the nose) with a damp cotton ball and dry thoroughly.

5. Check inside the ears for accumulation of wax or any odor. Clean out the wax with a cotton ball and apply ear powder.

6. Check the eyes for anything unusual; Pugs are very susceptible to eye injuries. Clean the eyes with a few eye drops.

7. Teeth should be checked for any accumulation of tartar, which should be removed by a veterinarian.

8. Remove whiskers on the muzzle with a #10 blade for a nice clean look. (This is usually done on show Pugs.)

9. Bathe the dog with a good shampoo. Lightly scrub him, using either your fingers or a curry brush, and pay special attention to the legs and under the curl of the tail. With your fingers, clean between the pads of the feet. Rinse and repeat.

10. Apply a good skin and coat conditioner and leave it on for 5 minutes. Rinse.

11. Either cage or blow dry the dog.

12. While the dog is on the grooming table, brush the coat with a bristle brush and comb it with a fine-toothed comb.

13. Scissor, in an even line, the hair on the "pants." Scissor stray hairs on the tail while in its curled position. Scissor any stray hairs on the stomach. When you have finished scissoring, your Pug should have a nice, clean outline.

14. Clip the nails very carefully. Pug nails are usually black, so the quick will not be visible; just clip the tips. Have styptic powder on hand just in case you clip a nail too short.

15. Apply a small amount of petroleum jelly to the nose.

16. Spray the coat with a light mist of coat dressing.

17. Finish off by polishing the coat with a hound glove.

Periodically check under the facial roll, particularly if it is a heavy roll. Check the nails every few weeks and do not allow them to grow too long. Check the ears every two weeks.

GROOMING PROCEDURE

1. Spray the entire coat with protein coat conditioner. This adds body to the coat and helps repair split ends. Brush through the entire coat with a slicker to remove loose hair and break up mats. Then, alternate with a molting comb and pin brush. Start at the rear of the dog, at the bottom of the skirt area. Work in sections, lifting the hair and brushing it layer by layer. Mist each section with coat gloss as you work. Never brush the dog dry-coated. Work through the entire coat from the back to the neck area. Never bathe this breed with mats in the coat because water will tighten them and make them harder to remove.

2. Swab the ears with a cotton ball that has been moistened with ear cleaner. This will remove dirt and control ear odor. Follow this with a dry cotton ball, and dust the ears with medicated ear powder. With your fingers or ear forceps, pull out any dead hair inside the ears.

3. Cut the nails with a guillotine-type nail clipper. Nails should be cut monthly.

4. Check between the foot pads and under the feet for burrs, tar, etc. Scissor the hair under the feet even with the pads to prevent debris from adhering. Trim any hair around the paw that touches the ground.

5. Scissor any long hair under the tail that hangs over the anus and that may become soiled with fecal matter. Scissor the hair around the anus to be sure it is clear. Trim or blend down the hair under the tail area if it is profuse.

6. Bathe the dog with a tearless protein shampoo that is pH-alkaline. This will add fullness and body to the coat and restructure damaged hair.

7. Comb the face around the eyes and muzzle with a fine-toothed comb.

8. Comb the hair on the head to follow the natural shape of the skull. Make a short part (about 2 inches [5 cm] long) in the center of the head and comb down each side toward the cheek.

9. Comb the front part (in front of the previous part) down over the brow and eyes. Don't cut the hair over the eyes. Comb the hair behind the part toward the back.

continued

TOOLS AND EQUIPMENT

- Cotton balls
- Ear cleaner
- Fine-toothed comb
- Large pin brush
- Long-hair molting comb (#565)
- Medicated ear powder
- Nail clipper (extra large)
- Protein coat conditioner
- Pure boar bristle brush
- Scissors
- Slicker brush
- Steel comb (coarse)
- Tearless protein shampoo

Puli *continued*

10. The hair under the chin should be combed out toward the muzzle. The rest of the face and the hair on the ears should be combed down.

11. The body hair should be combed down in a natural lay. There should be no part on the back. A natural part is fine, but do not create a part.

12. Scissor the outside edges of the feet to make them neat and round.

13. Lightly spray mink oil from above and allow it to mist over the coat. Brush the coat with a pure bristle brush to add a beautiful gloss and aroma.

GROOMING PROCEDURE

1. Briskly brush the entire coat with a sisal brush.

2. Clean the ears using medicated ear powder.

3. Clean the eyes by wiping them with a cotton ball that has been moistened with eye drops.

4. Cut the tips of the nails with a nail clipper, being careful not to cut the quick.

5. With scissors, snip the whiskers from the muzzle, under the chin, the sides of the face, and above the eyes. [Note: Clipping the whiskers is a decision to be left to the owner, if the dog is not a show dog.]

6. Place a cotton ball in each ear (this prevents water from entering the ear canals), and bathe the dog. Cage dry him.

7. Put a few drops of lanolin coat conditioner into the palms of your hands, rub them together lightly, and massage into the coat.

8. Brush the entire coat with a sisal brush to distribute the conditioner, and then lightly rub over the coat with a chamois cloth to give it a nice sheen.

The Rhodesian Ridgeback should be groomed every 12 to 14 weeks. The ears should be checked weekly and cleaned if necessary, and the nails should be checked monthly and cut if necessary.

Rhodesian Ridgeback

TOOLS AND EQUIPMENT

- Chamois cloth
- Cotton balls
- Eye drops (eye stain remover)
- Lanolin coat conditioner
- Medicated ear powder
- Nail clipper
- Scissors
- Sisal (natural bristle) brush

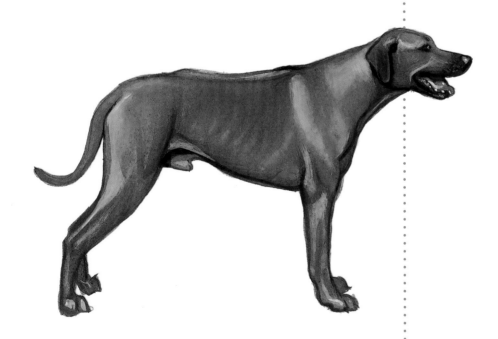

Rottweiler

GROOMING PROCEDURE

1. Nails should be cut by removing the tips only; avoid cutting the quick. If the nail bleeds, apply styptic powder to stop the bleeding. Any rough nail edges may be smoothed with a file.

2. Clean the ears with a liquid cleaner. Apply cleaner to a cotton ball and wipe accumulated dirt and wax from all crevices in both ears.

3. With a slicker brush, brush out the entire dog to remove dead coat.

4. Bathe the dog in a shampoo of your choice and rinse well. A conditioning rinse may be used to help control dandruff. A rubber brush may be used to lather the dog and to remove excess dead coat.

5. Towel dry the dog and place him in a cage with a dryer until he is completely dry.

6. With blending shears, even up any stray hairs on the back of the thighs, back of the front legs, and the ruff on the neck. Keep trimming to a minimum so as not to be detectable.

7. As a final touch, spray a light mist of spray conditioner or coat gloss over the entire dog. With a clean cloth, buff the coat until it shines.

The completed Rottweiler should present a strong, clean outline, with a shiny, smooth coat. Grooming should be done every 8 to 10 weeks.

GROOMING PROCEDURE

1. Thoroughly brush the entire coat with a slicker brush, paying special attention to the neck, chest, thighs, and tail. Remove any mats from these areas with a mat-splitting comb and/or metal rake. Comb through the coat to remove all loosened hair.

2. Clean the ears using medicated ear powder.

3. Clean the eyes by wiping them with a cotton ball that has been moistened with eye drops. This will also help to remove any stains around the eyes.

4. Cut the tips of the nails with a nail clipper, being careful not to cut the quick.

5. Using a damp cotton ball, clean the insides of the lips; make certain that you remove any trapped food particles.

6. With scissors, snip the whiskers from the muzzle, under the chin, the sides of the face, and above the eyes. [Note: Clipping the whiskers is a decision to be left to the owner, if the dog is not a show dog.]

7. Put a cotton ball in each ear to prevent water from entering the ear canal. Now you are ready to bathe the dog. Cage dry him or fluff dry him.

8. With thinning shears, remove any straggly hair on the hind legs from the hock joint to the feet and from around the ankles on the front legs.

9. Brush and comb through the coat.

St. Bernard, Rough Coat

TOOLS AND EQUIPMENT

- Cotton balls
- Eye drops (eye stain remover)
- Mat-splitting comb
- Medicated ear powder
- Metal comb (medium)
- Metal rake
- Nail clipper
- Scissors
- Slicker brush

St. Bernard, Smooth Coat

TOOLS AND EQUIPMENT

- Cotton balls
- Eye drops (eye stain remover)
- Medicated ear powder
- Metal comb
- Nail clipper
- Scissors
- Shedding blade
- Slicker brush

GROOMING PROCEDURE

1. Thoroughly brush the entire coat with a slicker brush. (During the shedding season, use a shedding blade. Start from the rear and continue to the front, paying special attention to the neck, chest, thighs, and tail.) Comb through the coat to remove all loosened hair.

2. Clean the ears using medicated ear powder.

3. Clean the eyes by wiping them with a cotton ball that has been moistened with eye drops. This will also help to remove any stains under or around the eyes.

4. Cut the tips of the nails with a nail clipper, being careful not to cut the quick.

5. Using a damp cotton ball, clean the insides of the lips; be certain to remove any trapped food particles.

6. With scissors, snip the whiskers from the muzzle, under the chin, the sides of the face, and above the eyes. [Note: Clipping the whiskers is a decision to be left to the owner, if the dog is not a show dog.]

7. Place a cotton ball in each ear (this prevents water from entering the ear canals), and bathe the dog. Cage dry him.

8. Brush and comb through the coat.

The smooth-coated St. Bernard should be groomed every 8 or 10 weeks. The ears should be checked weekly and cleaned if necessary, and the nails should be checked and clipped at the grooming session.

GROOMING PROCEDURE

1. Brush the body with a sisal brush, using firm, long strokes. Brush the ears, tail, and all feathering with a pin brush. Comb through the entire coat and tail, removing any tangles and all loosened hair.

2. Clean the ears using medicated ear powder, and lightly pluck any stray hair from the insides.

3. Clean the eyes by wiping them with a cotton ball that has been moistened with eye drops.

4. Cut the tips of the nails with a nail clipper, being careful not to cut the quick.

5. With scissors, snip the whiskers from the muzzle, under the chin, the sides of the face, and above the eyes. [Note: Clipping the whiskers is a decision to be left to the owner, if the dog is not a show dog.]

6. Place a cotton ball in each ear (this prevents water from entering the ear canal), and bathe the dog. Cage dry him.

7. Fluff dry all feathering on the ears, tail, and legs with a pin brush.

8. With scissors, clip hair between the pads and toes on the feet and around the edges to give a neat appearance.

9. Trim evenly the front leg fringes.

10. With scissors or thinning shears, trim any straggly hair from the hocks down to the feet on the hind legs.

11. Holding the tail straight out, comb the hair down and trim the lower edge, keeping it wide at the base and tapering it toward the tip.

12. Put a few drops of lanolin coat conditioner into the palms of your hands, rub them together lightly, and massage into the body.

13. Brush through the entire coat with a sisal brush.

The Saluki should be groomed every 8 to 10 weeks. The ears should be checked weekly and cleaned if necessary, and the nails should be checked monthly and cut if necessary.

TOOLS AND EQUIPMENT

- Cotton balls
- Eye drops (eye stain remover)
- Lanolin coat conditioner
- Medicated ear powder
- Metal comb (medium)
- Nail clipper
- Pin brush
- Scissors
- Sisal (natural bristle) brush
- Thinning shears

Samoyed

TOOLS AND EQUIPMENT

- Cotton balls
- Eye drops (eye stain remover)
- Mat-splitting comb
- Medicated ear powder
- Metal comb (wide-toothed)
- Metal rake
- Nail clipper
- Scissors
- Shampoo (whitening)
- Slicker brush

GROOMING PROCEDURE

1. Starting at the head, brush the entire coat with a slicker brush.

2. With a metal rake, gently rake through the coat. During the nonshedding season, do not rake out the undercoat; simply untangle it with a mat-splitting comb and/or metal rake. Comb through the coat to remove any loosened hair.

3. Clean the ears with medicated ear powder.

4. Clean the eyes by wiping them with a cotton ball that has been moistened with eye drops. This helps to remove any stains under or around the eyes.

5. Cut the tips of the nails with a nail clipper, being careful not to cut the quick.

6. With scissors, snip the whiskers from the muzzle, under the chin, the sides of the face, and above the eyes. [Note: Clipping the whiskers is a decision to be left to the owner, if the dog is not a show dog.]

7. Place a cotton ball in each ear (this prevents water from entering the ear canal), and bathe the dog. Cage or fluff dry him.

8. With scissors, clip the hair between the pads and toes on the feet and around the edges of the feet to give a neat appearance.

9. Brush and comb through the entire coat.

The Samoyed, because of his white coloring and home environment, should be groomed every 10 to 12 weeks. Regular brushing with a slicker brush by the owner will help to keep the coat healthy and the undercoat free of tangles. The ears should be checked weekly and cleaned if necessary, and the nails should be checked monthly and cut if necessary.

GROOMING PROCEDURE

1. Brush the entire coat with a slicker brush. Comb through with a metal comb, removing all loosened hair.

2. Clean the ears with medicated ear powder, and lightly pluck any stray hair from the insides.

3. Cut the tips of the nails with a nail clipper, being careful not to cut the quick.

4. With scissors, snip the whiskers from the muzzle, under the chin, the sides of the face, and above the eyes. [Note: Clipping the whiskers is a decision to be left to the owner if the dog is not a show dog.]

5. Place a cotton ball in each ear (this prevents water from entering the ear canal), and bathe the dog. Cage dry him. If the undercoat is still damp, place the dog on the grooming table and finish by fluff drying with a slicker brush.

6. With scissors, clip the hair between the pads and toes of the feet and around the edges to give a neat appearance.

7. Scissor evenly the lower edge of the chest and the edge of the belly fringe to the flanks.

8. Scissor evenly any stray hair on the legs.

9. With thinning shears, thin out the rump area to give it a round, sloping appearance.

10. Brush and comb through the entire coat.

The Schipperke should be groomed about every 6 to 8 weeks. The ears should be checked weekly and cleaned if necessary, and the nails should be checked and cut at the grooming session.

TOOLS AND EQUIPMENT

- Cotton balls
- Medicated ear powder
- Metal comb
- Nail clipper
- Scissors
- Shampoo
- Slicker brush
- Thinning shears

Scottish Deerhound

TOOLS AND EQUIPMENT

- Cotton balls
- Eye drops (eye stain remover)
- Medicated ear powder
- Metal comb (fine)
- Nail clipper
- Scissors
- Sisal (natural bristle) brush
- Stripping knife
- Thinning shears

GROOMING PROCEDURE

1. Brush through the coat.

2. Clean inside the ears.

3. Clean the eyes by wiping them with a cotton ball that has been moistened with eye drops.

4. Cut the nails with a nail clipper, being careful not to cut the quick.

5. Put a cotton ball in each ear to prevent water from entering the ear canal. After you have done this, bathe the dog and cage dry him.

6. Lightly brush through the coat with a sisal brush.

7. With thinning shears or a stripping knife, trim any straggly hair from the top of the head and ears.

8. With thinning shears, trim any straggly hair from the sides of the face, neck, and chest.

9. Lightly scissor around the whiskers and the beard, making this hair square and full.

10. With scissors, snip hair from between the pads and toes of the feet and around the edges. This gives a neat appearance to the feet.

11. Trim the front leg fringes to make them even.

12. With scissors or thinning shears, trim any straggly hair from the hocks down to the feet on the hind legs.

13. Holding the tail straight out, comb the hair down and trim the lower edge, making it wide at the base and tapering toward the tip.

14. Brush through the entire coat with a sisal brush.

GROOMING PROCEDURE

1. Brush the entire coat and tail with a slicker brush. Comb through with a metal comb, paying attention to any tangles.

2. Clean the ears using medicated ear powder, and lightly pluck any stray hair from the insides.

3. Clean the eyes by wiping them with a cotton ball that has been moistened with eye drops.

4. Cut the tips of the nails with a nail clipper, being careful not to cut the quick.

5. With a #10 blade on the Oster clipper, shave the anal area, being certain not to put the blade in direct contact with the skin (½ inch [1 cm] on either side).

6. Shave the abdomen from groin to navel and down the insides of the thighs.

7. With a #10 blade, shave the head, starting at the center of the eyebrows and continuing back to the base of the skull. Again, from the center, shave to the outer corners of the eyes. This line should be about ¾ inch (2 cm) above the inner corner of the eye, tapering into the outer corner, thus making a triangle. Next, shave down from the outer corners of the eyes to within ¾ inch (2 cm) of the corners of the mouth; continue this line across, under the chin.

8. Shave down diagonally from the back edges of the ears to a point at the base of the throat, thus forming a "V" shape.

9. There will be a triangular-shaped "tuft" left on the front edge of the ear from halfway along the base on the outside, tapering up to about ¾ inch (2 cm) from the tip. Now shave the rest of the ears inside and out.

10. With a #8½, #7, or #5 blade (according to the coat length desired), start at the base of the skull and clip down the back to the base of the tail.

11. Clip the top half of the tail and blend down either side of the bottom fringe. Comb the fringe downward and scissor the lower edge, making it wide at the base and tapering it to a point at the tip.

12. With the clipper, clip down the sides of the neck to the tops of the shoulders.

13. Clip down the chest to about 1 inch (2.5 cm) above the breastbone.

14. From the first clip down the back, clip down the flanks and hips. (From the side, the pattern should be a straight line from front to back).

15. Brush and comb through the coat to remove all loosened hair.

16. Place a cotton ball in each ear (this prevents water from entering the ear canal), and bathe the dog. Cage dry him.

continued

TOOLS AND EQUIPMENT

- Cotton balls
- Eye drops (eye stain remover)
- Medicated ear powder
- Metal comb (medium)
- Nail clipper
- Oster A-5 clipper/#5, #7, #8½, #10 blades
- Scissors
- Slicker brush
- Thinning shears

Scottish Terrier *continued*

17. Brush and comb through the coat.

18. Using the same blade as before, repeat the process for the pattern. With the blade, blend the hair down from the pattern.

19. Scissor around the back edges of the ears and the ¾ inch (2 cm) at the tip on the front edge. Comb the tuft outward and scissor the edge, making it wide at the base and tapering it into the top.

20. Comb the eyebrows forward and scissor a "V" in the center for the separation.

21. Comb the hair on the face and eyebrows forward and downward, aligning the base of your scissors at the nose and the tip of the scissors at the outer corner of the eye. Scissor the eyebrows from this angle, thus making a deep triangle.

22. Lightly scissor stray hairs from around the edges and sides of the beard. Use thinning shears to make the beard appear long and straight.

23. With scissors, snip the hair between the pads of the feet; while the dog is standing, scissor around the edges to give a neat effect.

24. Using thinning shears, trim any straggly hairs from the fringes and legs so that they appear even.

25. Comb the chest fringe downward and scissor the lower edge straight and even.

26. Comb the belly fringe downward and scissor the lower edge evenly, following the contour of the body. Make the belly fringe level with the chest fringe in front and then taper it to the flanks at the rear.

27. Lightly comb through the legs, fringes, and face, removing all excess hair.

The Scottish Terrier should be groomed every 6 to 8 weeks. The ears should be checked weekly and cleaned if necessary, and the nails should be checked and cut at the grooming session.

GROOMING PROCEDURE

1. Brush the entire coat and tail with a slicker brush. Comb through with a metal comb and remove any mats or tangles with a mat-splitting comb.

2. Clean the ears using medicated ear powder, and lightly pluck any stray hair from the insides.

3. Clean the eyes by wiping them with a cotton ball that has been moistened with eye drops. This will also help to remove any stains.

4. Cut the tips of the nails with a nail clipper, being careful not to cut the quick.

5. With a #10 blade, shave the head, starting at the center of the eyebrows and continuing back to the base of the skull. Again, shave from the center to the outer corners of the eyes. This line should be about ¾ inch (2 cm) above the inner corner of the eye and should taper into the outer corner, thus forming a triangle. Next shave down from the outer corners of the eyes to within ¾ inch (2 cm) of the corners of the mouth; continue this line across, under the chin.

6. Shave both sides of the ears; from the back edge of the ears, shave down diagonally to a point at the base of the throat, thus forming a "V" shape.

7. Shave the anal area, being certain not to put the blade in direct contact with the skin (½ inch [1 cm] on either side).

8. Shave the abdomen from groin to navel and down the insides of the thighs.

9. With a #8½, #7, or #5 blade (according to the coat length desired), start at the base of the skull and clip down the back to the base of the tail.

10. With the same blade, clip the entire tail.

11. With a clipper, clip down the sides of the neck to the tops of the shoulders.

12. Clip down the chest to about 1 inch (2.5 cm) above the breastbone.

13. From the first clip down the back, clip down the flanks and the hips. (From the side, the pattern should resemble a straight line from front to back.)

14. Brush and comb through the coat to remove all excess hair.

15. Place a cotton ball in each ear (this prevents water from entering the ear canal), and bathe the dog. Cage or fluff dry.

16. Brush and comb through the coat.

continued

Sealyham Terrier

TOOLS AND EQUIPMENT

- Eye drops (eye stain remover)
- Mat-splitting comb
- Medicated ear powder
- Metal comb
- Nail clipper
- Oster A-5 clipper/#5, #7, #8½, #10 blades
- Scissors
- Slicker brush
- Thinning shears

17. Using the same blade on the Oster A-5 clipper as before, repeat the process for the pattern, blending the hair down from the pattern with the blade.

18. Scissor around the edges of the ears.

19. Comb the hair on the eyebrows and face forward and downward, aligning the base of your scissors at the nose and the tip of the scissors at the outer corner of the eye. Scissor the eyebrows from this angle, making a triangle. Make sure that no hair is cut from between the eyebrows or on top of the muzzle.

20. Lightly scissor stray hairs from around the edges and sides of the beard. Use thinning shears to make the beard appear long and straight.

21. With scissors, snip the hair between the pads of the feet; while the dog is standing, scissor around the edges to give a neat effect.

22. Using thinning shears, trim any straggly hairs from the fringes and legs so that they appear even.

23. Comb the chest fringe downward and scissor evenly the ends of the lower edge.

24. Comb the belly fringe downward, and scissor the ends of the lower edge evenly, following the contour of the body. The belly fringe should be level with the chest fringe in front and taper to the flanks at the rear.

25. Lightly comb through the legs, fringes, and face, removing all excess hair.

The Sealyham Terrier should be groomed every 6 to 8 weeks. The ears should be checked weekly, and the nails should be checked and cut at the grooming session.

← #10

#5, #7, #8½
↓

GROOMING PROCEDURE

1. Spray the entire coat with protein coat conditioner. This adds body to the coat and helps repair split ends. Brush through the entire coat with a large pin brush, alternating with a slicker brush in matted areas and a molting comb as needed. Work layer by layer, alternating brush and comb to remove mats and loose undercoat. Lift the coat up with your hand, working on thin layers at a time. Brush down and out until all mats and loose hair are removed. Work deeply into the coat, but do not brush to the skin; otherwise, you will cause abrasion. Start at the rear of the dog, at the bottom of the skirt area. Work through the entire coat until the outer coat is separated well and combs smoothly. Work vigorously. The more hair you remove now, the less hair you need to wash and dry.

2. Comb through the entire coat with a wide-toothed utility comb. Use a fine-toothed steel comb on the soft hair behind the ears. With your fingers, strip out dead hair behind the ears.

3. Swab the ears with a cotton ball that has been moistened with ear cleaner. This will remove dirt and control ear odor. Follow with a dry cotton ball, and dust the ears with medicated ear powder.

4. Cut the nails with a guillotine-type nail clipper. Nails should be cut monthly.

5. Check between the foot pads and under the feet for burrs, tar, etc. Scissor the hair under the feet even with the pads. Trim any hair around the paw that touches the ground and neaten the entire foot. With thinning shears, trim the hair growing between the toes, which should lie close like a cat's foot.

6. Bathe the dog with a tearless protein shampoo that is pH-alkaline. This will add fullness and body to the coat and restructure damaged hair.

7. Use a high-velocity dryer to blow excess water off the dog while he is still in the tub. This will speed up the drying time and help prevent the coat from becoming overly dry. Cage dry him until the hair is damp. Then finish drying on the table using a blow dryer and a pin brush to separate all the hair and remove all of the loose coat.

8. Brush the entire coat and be sure to brush to the skin, using the dryer to style and separate the hair. Follow by combing the entire coat.

9. The whiskers may be removed with scissors to improve the expression, although this is optional.

continued

TOOLS AND EQUIPMENT

- Cotton balls
- Ear cleaner
- High-velocity dryer
- Large pin brush
- Long-hair molting comb (#565)
- Medicated ear powder
- Nail clipper
- Oster A-5 clipper/#10 blade
- Protein coat conditioner
- Pure boar bristle brush
- Scissors
- Slicker brush
- Steel comb (fine/medium)
- Tearless protein shampoo
- Thinning shears
- Wood utility comb

10. Use a fine-toothed comb to finish the head and the ears. Excess hair behind the ears may be thinned with thinning shears.

11. Comb out leg feathering. Trim excess hair on the feet and hocks. The hind legs are to be smooth below the hock joint, with a perpendicular line from hock to ground. Leave full the feathering on the forelegs, but trim it so that it naturally meets the pastern and does not touch the ground.

12. Scissor any long hair under the tail that hangs over the anus. Be sure the anus is clear, and then use a #10 blade to blend down under the tail area so that it does not collect fecal matter.

13. Lightly mist the coat with protein coat conditioner to add brilliance and fragrance. Back brush the coat with a pin brush so that the coat stands out, away from the body.

GROOMING PROCEDURE

1. Brush the entire coat and tail with a slicker brush, removing any mats with the matting comb. Comb through the coat, using the medium-toothed metal comb.

2. Clean the ears using medicated ear powder, and lightly pluck stray hair from the insides of the ears.

3. Cut the tips of the nails with a nail clipper, being careful not to cut the quick.

4. Clean the eyes by wiping them with a cotton ball that has been moistened with eye drops. Using scissors, snip any stained hair from the corners of the eyes.

5. Using a #10 blade, shave the anal area, being certain not to put the blade in direct contact with the skin (½ inch [1 cm] on either side).

6. Using a #10 blade, shave the abdomen from groin to navel and down the insides of the thighs.

7. Place a cotton ball in each ear (this prevents water from entering the ear canal), and bathe the dog. Fluff dry him.

8. Using a medium metal comb, part the coat down the center of the back from the top of the head to the base of the tail. Then make a part from the top of the head to the tip of the nose. An alternate way is to make a part on the head from the outer corner of each eye to the front corner of each ear and across the head from ear to ear. Comb this hair evenly, slightly to the back, and secure it with a rubber band. Attach a bow. Or, you might want to gather the hair, comb it evenly, and make a braid. Secure the end with a rubber band and attach a bow.

9. Scissor the hair between the foot pads. Comb the hair on the legs downward; while the dog is standing, scissor around the edges of the feet to give a round effect.

10. Comb through the entire coat with a fine-toothed metal comb.

Some groomers use conditioning rinse and similar products on the Shih Tzu; however, I have found, through experience, that these products cause the coat to become more matted in the long run and that a good protein-enriched shampoo is adequate.

The longhaired Shih Tzu should be groomed every 2 or 3 weeks. The ears should be checked weekly, and the nails should be checked at the grooming session.

For owners who prefer a short, cuddly look, use the Teddy Bear clip. (See the General Information section.)

continued

TOOLS AND EQUIPMENT

- Cotton balls
- Eye drops (eye stain remover)
- Matting comb
- Medicated ear powder
- Metal combs (medium/fine)
- Nail clipper
- Oster A-5 clipper/#10 blade
- Rubber bands
- Scissors
- Slicker brush

Shih Tzu *continued*

For owners who like the longhaired look, even during the heat of summer, the entire coat can be thinned out so that the dog will be more comfortable. The same instructions apply for grooming, bathing, and fluff drying the Shih Tzu (i.e., steps 1 through 7). Then, part the coat using the medium metal comb, about 1½ to 2 inches (4 to 5 cm) from the center of the back, down one side. Comb the top hair to the other side (so you do not touch the outer coat), and with thinning shears, thin out the remaining undercoat about 1 inch (2.5 cm) at a time. Repeat on the opposite side and across the chest and thighs. Part the coat down the center of the back and thoroughly comb through it, first with the medium- and then with the fine-toothed metal comb. Tie the topknot and scissor the feet as mentioned previously in the grooming instructions for Shih Tzus.

GROOMING PROCEDURE

1. Thoroughly brush the entire coat with a slicker brush. During the shedding season, use the shedding blade (work from the rear to the front). Remove any mats in the undercoat with a mat-splitting comb and a metal rake.

2. Clean the ears using medicated ear powder, and lightly pluck any stray hair from the insides.

3. Clean the eyes by wiping them with a cotton ball that has been moistened with eye drops. This will also help to remove stains around the eyes.

4. Cut the tips of the nails with a nail clipper, being careful not to cut the quick.

5. With scissors, clip the whiskers from the muzzle, chin, sides of the face, and above the eyes. [Note: Clipping the whiskers is a decision to be left to the owner if the dog is not a show dog.]

6. Put a cotton ball in each ear (this prevents water from entering the ear canal), and bathe the dog. Cage dry him.

7. Brush through the coat briskly with a slicker brush, rake through with a metal rake, and then comb through with a metal comb.

8. With scissors, snip the hair between the pads and toes on the feet and around the edges to give a neat appearance.

The Siberian Husky should be groomed every 8 or 10 weeks. Regular brushing by the owner will help to keep the topcoat shiny and the undercoat free of tangles. The ears should be checked weekly and cleaned if necessary, and the nails should be checked and cut at the grooming session.

Siberian Husky

TOOLS AND EQUIPMENT

- Cotton balls
- Eye drops (eye stain remover)
- Mat-splitting comb
- Medicated ear powder
- Metal comb (wide-toothed)
- Metal rake
- Nail clipper
- Scissors
- Shedding blade
- Slicker brush

Silky Terrier

TOOLS AND EQUIPMENT

- Cotton balls
- Eye drops (eye stain remover)
- Medicated ear powder
- Metal combs (medium/fine)
- Nail clipper
- Oster A-5 clipper/#10 blade
- Scissors
- Slicker brush
- Thinning shears

GROOMING PROCEDURE

1. Lightly brush the entire coat and tail with a slicker brush, being sure to remove all mats and tangles. Comb through the coat with a medium-toothed metal comb.

2. Clean the ears using medicated ear powder, and lightly pluck stray hairs from the insides of the ears.

3. Cut the tips of the nails with a nail clipper, being careful not to cut the quick.

4. Clean the eyes by wiping them with a cotton ball that has been moistened with eye drops, especially if they are excessively watery and sticky. With scissors, snip any stained hair from the corners of the eyes.

5. Using a #10 blade, shave the anal area, being certain not to put the blade in direct contact with the skin (½ inch [1 cm] on either side).

6. Using a #10 blade, shave the abdomen from groin to navel and down the insides of the thighs.

7. Put a cotton ball in each ear (this prevents water from entering the ear canal), and bathe the dog. Fluff dry him.

8. Shave the insides of the ears with a #10 blade and, with scissors, snip the long hairs from around the edges of the ears to give a neat appearance.

9. With thinning shears, clip the hair on the back legs from the hock to the foot and to the first joint on the front legs.

10. With scissors, trim any stray hairs on the feet and between the foot pads; while the dog is standing, scissor around the edges of the feet to give a round effect.

11. Holding the tail straight out, comb the hair downward on both sides and trim the edge with scissors to within ½ inch (1 cm) from the tail.

12. Using a medium metal comb, part the coat down the center of the back, from the top of the head to the base of the tail. Then part the hair from the top of the head to the tip of the nose.

13. With a fine-toothed metal comb, comb the entire coat downward.

The Silky Terrier should be groomed about every 6 weeks. The ears should be checked weekly and cleaned if necessary, and the nails should be checked at the grooming session.

GROOMING PROCEDURE

1. Lightly brush the entire coat and tail with a slicker brush, removing any mats with the matting comb. Comb through the coat with a medium metal comb.

2. Clean the ears using medicated ear powder, and lightly pluck stray hairs from the insides of the ears.

3. Cut the tips of the nails with a nail clipper, being careful not to cut the quick.

4. Clean the eyes by wiping them with a cotton ball that has been moistened with eye drops. With scissors, snip any stained hair from the corners of the eyes.

5. Using a #10 blade, shave the anal area, being certain not to put the blade in direct contact with the skin (½ inch [1 cm] on either side).

6. Using a #10 blade, shave the abdomen from groin to navel and down the insides of the thighs.

7. Place a cotton ball in each ear (this prevents water from entering the ear canals), and bathe the dog. Fluff dry him.

8. Lightly brush and thoroughly comb through the entire coat with a fine-toothed metal comb.

9. Using a medium metal comb, part the coat down the center of the back, from the top of the head to the base of the tail. Then make a part from the top of the head to the tip of the nose.

10. From the center part, comb all hair downward.

11. While the dog is standing, scissor around the outside edges of the feet to give a round effect.

12. Holding the tail straight out, comb the hair downward on both sides and scissor the lower edge. Taper the tail to a point. The tail fringe should be as long and full as possible.

Some owners use conditioning rinse and similar products on Skyes; however, I have found, through experience, that these products cause the coat to become more matted in the long run and that a good protein-enriched shampoo is entirely adequate.

The Skye Terrier should be groomed about every 4 weeks. The owner should brush and comb the dog on a regular basis, thus preventing the coat from becoming matted. The ears should be checked weekly, and the nails should be checked at the grooming session.

Skye Terrier

TOOLS AND EQUIPMENT

- Cotton balls
- Matting comb
- Medicated ear powder
- Metal combs (medium/fine)
- Nail clipper
- Oster A-5 clipper/#10 blade
- Scissors
- Slicker brush

Sloughi

TOOLS AND EQUIPMENT

- Chamois cloth
- Cotton balls
- Eye drops (eye stain remover)
- Lanolin coat conditioner
- Medicated ear powder
- Nail clipper
- Scissors
- Sisal (natural bristle) brush

GROOMING PROCEDURE

1. Brush the coat vigorously with a sisal brush, using long deep strokes.

2. Clean the ears using medicated ear powder.

3. Clean the eyes by wiping them with a cotton ball that has been moistened with eye drops. This will also help to remove stains around the eyes.

4. Cut the tips of the nails with a nail clipper, being careful not to cut the quick.

5. With scissors, snip the whiskers from the muzzle, under the chin, the sides of the face, and above the eyes. [Note: Clipping the whiskers is a decision to be left to the owner if the dog is not a show dog.]

6. Put a cotton ball in each ear (this prevents water from entering the ear canal), and bathe the dog. Cage dry him.

7. Put a few drops of lanolin coat conditioner into the palms of your hands, rub them together lightly, and massage into the coat.

8. Brush the coat with a sisal brush to distribute the conditioner, then lightly rub over the coat with a chamois cloth to give it a nice sheen.

The Sloughi should be groomed every 10 to 12 weeks. The ears should be checked weekly and cleaned if necessary, and the nails should be checked monthly and cut if necessary.

GROOMING PROCEDURE

1. Spray the entire coat with protein coat conditioner. This adds body to the coat and helps repair split ends. Brush through the entire coat with a slicker brush. Then comb thoroughly with a molting comb to remove dead undercoat. Start at the rear of the dog, at the bottom of the skirt area. Work in sections through the entire dog, from the back to the neck area. Work vigorously. The more hair you remove now, the less hair you need to wash and dry.

2. Swab the ears with a cotton ball that has been moistened with ear cleaner. This will remove dirt and control ear odor. Follow with a dry cotton ball, and dust the ears with medicated ear powder. With your fingers or ear forceps, pluck the hair inside the ears.

3. Cut the nails with a guillotine-type nail clipper. Nails should be cut monthly.

4. Check between the foot pads and under the feet for burrs, tar, etc. With a #10 blade, clip the hair under the feet and between the foot pads.

5. Bathe the dog with a tearless protein shampoo that is pH-alkaline. This will add fullness and body to the coat and restructure damaged hair.

6. Use a high-velocity dryer to blow excess water off the dog while he is still in the tub. This will speed up the drying time and help prevent the coat from becoming overly dry. Cage dry the dog until the hair is damp. Mist with coat gloss. Finish drying on the table, using a blow dryer and a pin brush to separate all the hair and remove all of the loose coat.

7. Comb the entire coat to the skin, using the medium part of a comb to separate the hair.

8. Use a #10 blade to clip the hair around the anus. Just clear the area and do not use heavy pressure.

9. Shave the abdomen with a #10 blade, going with the lay of the hair.

10. Shave the ear on the inside with a #10 blade. Shave from base to tip. Back comb the outside of the ear flap. Leave hair above the fold line of the ear; this will become part of the topknot. Lay thinning shears against the skin at the ear tip and point them toward the fold. Angle the shears out so that the hair, when cut, will be shorter at the tip than at the fold. The hair at the fold should be the same length as the hair on top of the skull. Trim the outside edge of the ear, using the thumb as a protective guide to prevent nicks.

11. Picking up the beard, clip under the jaw with a #4 blade. Leave a heavy beard.

continued

Soft-Coated Wheaten Terrier

TOOLS AND EQUIPMENT

- Coat gloss
- Comb (fine/medium)
- Cotton balls
- Ear cleaner
- Ear forceps
- High-velocity dryer
- Long-hair molting comb, #565
- Medicated ear powder
- Mink oil spray
- Nail clipper (extra large)
- Oster A-5 clipper/#4, #10 blades, #1 guard
- Pin brush
- Protein coat conditioner
- Pure boar bristle brush
- Scissors
- Slicker brush
- Tearless protein shampoo
- Thinning shears

12. With a #4 blade, clip the throat, forming a "U" from ear to ear.

13. With a #4 blade, clip the body from the base of the skull to the end of the tail. Clip the back and sides of the neck. Body blades change depending on the type of coat you're working with and your preference for a finished look. The #4 may be changed to a #5, or, for a plushier look, to a #10 with a #1 guard. Clip both sides of the body, from the sides of the neck to where the legs join the body in the front, and down to the thigh on the rear leg. In profile, there should be an even incline from the dog's elbow to his hip. Follow the contour of the body, directing your clipper in the direction the hair grows. Do not go against the grain or across the grain. Lift the clipper slightly as you near the end of your clipped area to blend the clipped area into the nonclipped area of the skirt and leg. This takes a slight twist of the wrist, as if you were using the end of the clipper as a shovel. You must work to blend the clipped area into the fringe area, leaving no uneven lines or ridges.

14. Clip the tail with a #4 blade. Always clip with the grain—the way the hair grows—and never against the growth. To prevent irritation, use very light pressure on the underside of the tail. Trim the underside of the tail quite close. The finished tail should resemble an ice cream cone, narrow at the tip and broader at the base.

15. With a #4 blade, clip the dog's front chest straight down the brisket, leaving a fringe between the front legs to define chest depth. With shears pointing down and angled under the dog toward the rear legs, trim under this line of fringe.

16. With a slicker, brush the hair on the front legs up and then down. Comb through the coat with the medium side of a comb. Lift the foot and shake the leg to allow the hair to fall naturally. Scissor the legs into cylindrical shapes. Use thinning shears to blend in any uneven line you may have between the shaved areas and the unshaved areas. Blend into the shoulder to create a straight line from shoulder to foot. Shape the foot so that it is round and compact, but don't expose the nails.

17. Scissor evenly the furnishings on the sides of the body, making them fuller over the ribs and chest. Trim the underline even; neaten and define the tuckup. Point the shears down and angle them under the dog, toward the feet on the opposite side. Tipping helps the coat stand up and out.

18. Brush the rear legs up and then down, comb, and shake free. With scissors, blend the hip area into the rear leg. The rear legs should show good angulation and should be trimmed evenly. Trim inside the thighs on the rear legs and from the groin down. Tip the rear hock to create a perpendicular line from hock to ground. Comb and remove stray hairs on the front portion of the legs. Round the legs and define the stifle. The lower portion of the rear leg should form a cylinder when viewed from any angle.

19. Comb the topknot forward, over the face. With scissors, pointing toward the nose, scissor the topknot to about 1 inch (2.5 cm) at the back of the skull. Gradually increase the length of hair as you go forward to the eyes. Hair length should blend with hair on the ears and into the forelock on the face.

20. To form a rectangular look with no puffiness on the cheeks, lift the ear and trim the cheeks with scissors.

21. Comb forward the Wheaten's "fall" (a fringe or shock of hair on the top of the head, falling forward). With scissors, pointing toward the nose, trim the hair beside the outside corner of the eye to make the eye visible but not fully exposed. Do not create a visor or eyebrow effect.

22. Comb the beard forward, and, to give a neat appearance, trim any straggly or extra long whiskers.

23. Lightly spray mink oil from above and allow it to mist over the coat. Brush through the coat with a pure bristle brush to add a beautiful gloss and aroma.

For a trim closer to the show trim, follow the preceding instructions, but do not use the #4 blade for any areas that are to be clipped. Do the entire dog with thinning shears or use a #10 blade with a #1 guard attached. If using thinning shears, remember that they are used for thinning and tipping. Thinning encourages the coat to lie flat. Tipping helps the coat to stand up and out. In creating your outline, leave at least ¾ inch (2 cm) to 1 inch (2.5 cm) of coat and blend the entire coat so that it appears natural and in proportion to the body. In creating a natural look, be sure to leave coat along the topline so that it is long enough to lie down. It should never stand up; rather, it must blend into the sides. Tip and thin hair on the flanks so as to blend into the shorter hair on the rear end.

Thin any excess hair at the base of the tail so that the topline blends smoothly into the tail. Be sure not to create a bare look; the hair on the rump should be at least ¾ inch (2 cm) to 1 inch (2.5 cm) long. The back of the tail should be scissored to remove any hairs that stand out like a flag. The underside should be flat and clean; the top and sides should be well covered and must blend into the body.

The front shoulders may be thinned so that the coat blends smoothly into the legs with gradual widening from the withers to a point one-third of the way down to the elbow. From the elbow, the coat should drop in a straight line to the foot.

If you elect to use a #10 blade with a #1 guard, follow instructions for clipping; however, after clipping with the #10 and #1, scissor all areas that have been clipped to neaten and even out the coat. Scissoring also helps to blend clipped areas into unclipped areas in order to achieve an overall natural look.

Staffordshire Bull Terrier

TOOLS AND EQUIPMENT

- Chamois cloth
- Cotton balls
- Eye drops (eye stain remover)
- Lanolin coat conditioner
- Medicated ear powder
- Nail clipper
- Scissors
- Sisal (natural bristle) brush

GROOMING PROCEDURE

1. Brush the entire coat with a sisal brush, using long deep strokes for a thorough massage.

2. Clean the ears using medicated ear powder.

3. Clean the eyes by wiping them with a cotton ball that has been moistened with eye drops. This will also help to remove stains around the eyes.

4. Cut the tips of the nails with a nail clipper, being careful not to cut the quick.

5. With scissors, snip the whiskers from the muzzle, under the chin, the sides of the face, and above the eyes. [Note: Clipping the whiskers is a decision to be left to the owner if the dog is not a show dog.]

6. Place a cotton ball in each ear (this prevents water from entering the ear canal), and bathe the dog. Cage dry him.

7. Put a few drops of lanolin coat conditioner into the palms of your hands, rub them together lightly, and massage into the coat.

8. Brush the coat with a sisal brush to distribute the conditioner, and then lightly rub over the coat with a chamois cloth to give it a nice sheen.

The Staffordshire Bull Terrier should be groomed every 10 to 12 weeks. The ears should be checked weekly and cleaned if necessary, and the nails should be checked monthly and cut if necessary.

GROOMING PROCEDURE

1. Brush the entire coat with a slicker brush. Comb through with a metal comb.

2. Clean the ears using medicated ear powder, and lightly pluck any stray hair from the insides.

3. Clean the eyes by wiping them with a cotton ball that has been moistened with eye drops. This will also help to remove stains around the eyes.

4. Cut the tips of the nails with a nail clipper, being careful not to cut the quick.

5. With a #10 blade, shave the head, starting at the center of the eyebrows and working back to the base of the skull. Then shave from the center again to the outer corners of the eyes. This line should be about ¾ inch (2 cm) above the inner corner of the eye and should taper into the outer corner, thus making a triangle. Next shave down from the outer corners of the eyes to within ¾ inch (2 cm) of the corner of the mouth; continue this line across, under the chin.

6. Shave both sides of the ears. From the back edges of the ears, shave down diagonally to a point at the base of the throat, thus forming a "V" shape.

7. Shave the anal area, being certain not to put the blade in direct contact with the skin (½ inch [1 cm] on either side).

8. Shave the abdomen from groin to navel and down the insides of the thighs.

9. With a #10, #8½, or #7 blade (according to the length of coat desired), start at the base of the skull and clip down the back to the base of the tail.

10. Clip the entire tail.

11. With a clipper, clip down the sides of the neck to the shoulders and down to the elbows.

12. Clip down the chest to the breastbone and slope the pattern down diagonally to the center front of the legs.

13. From the first clip down the back, clip down the sides of the abdomen to the flank and from the flank straight down to the hock joint.

14. Continue clipping the entire rear end. (From the side view, the pattern line should slope down diagonally from the breastbone, continue straight across the tops of the front legs, slope up across the abdomen, and slope down sharply to the hock joint, creating a large "V" on the rear leg.

15. Brush through the coat with a slicker brush to remove excess hair.

continued

Standard Schnauzer

TOOLS AND EQUIPMENT

- Cotton balls
- Eye drops (eye stain remover)
- Large nail clipper
- Metal comb (medium)
- Medicated ear powder
- Oster A-5 clipper/#7, #8½, #10 blades
- Scissors
- Slicker brush

16. Put a cotton ball in each ear to prevent water from entering the ear canal. Bathe the dog, and cage dry him.

17. Brush and comb through the coat.

18. Using the same blade on the Oster A-5 clipper as before, repeat the process for the pattern, blending the hair down on the top of the pattern with the blade.

19. Scissor around the edges of the ears.

20. Scissor a "V" in the center of the eyebrows for the separation.

21. Make a part down the center of the muzzle and comb downward. Trim the edges to taper into the outer corners of the eyes.

22. Comb the eyebrows forward. Align the base of your scissors with the nose and the tip of your scissors with the outer corner of the eye. Scissor the eyebrows from this angle, thus making a deep triangle (being careful not to cut any hair from the top of the muzzle).

23. Trim hair between the pads of the feet; while the dog is standing, scissor around the edges to give a round effect. (Doing this first will give you a guide for scissoring the legs.)

24. Scissor the front legs into straight tubular shapes.

25. Scissor evenly the bottom of the chest fringe.

26. Scissor the belly fringe, following the contour of the dog's body and tapering up from the elbows on the front legs to the flanks at the rear.

27. Scissor the rear legs, following the natural contours. The insides should be straight to the hock joint and taper up to the shave line.

28. Lightly comb through the legs, fringes, and face, removing all excess hair.

The Standard Schnauzer should be groomed every 6 or 8 weeks. The ears should be checked weekly and cleaned if necessary, and the nails should be checked and cut at the grooming session. It should be noted that the head, face, and throat should be shaved with the grain of the hair.

#5, #7, #8½

← #10

#10, #7, #8½
↓

GROOMING PROCEDURE

1. Nails should be cut by removing only the tips; avoid cutting the quick. If the nail bleeds, apply styptic powder to arrest the bleeding. Any rough nail edges may be smoothed with a file.

2. Clean the ears with a liquid cleaner. Apply cleaner to a cotton ball and wipe accumulated dirt and wax from all crevices in both ears.

3. With a #15 blade, remove hair between the pads on the bottom of the feet.

4. With a #10 blade, cut the belly hair. Clip with the direction of hair growth and work from groin to navel.

5. Brush out the dog to remove any matting and/or dead coat.

6. Bathe the dog in a shampoo of your choice and rinse him thoroughly. A conditioning rinse may be used to help cut down on static electricity and to make the coat lie smoothly.

7. Towel dry the dog. Finish drying with a blow dryer and by brushing the coat in its natural direction of growth. The coat should be encouraged to lie smoothly.

8. With blending shears, remove excess hair that grows between the toes on the top side of the foot. This gives the foot a tidy look.

9. With blending shears, remove any stray hairs from the face and muzzle.

10. With blending shears, remove excess hair from the tops of the ears and blend the hair in this area into the skull. Any stray hairs on top of the head should be removed as well. Remove extra hair from under the ear flap and in front of the ear opening; this encourages air circulation and makes the ear lie closer to the head.

11. Remove any excess hair from the back of the hocks.

12. Remove any stray hairs that may be giving the outline an uneven appearance.

TOOLS AND EQUIPMENT

- Blending shears
- Comb
- Cotton balls
- Ear cleaner
- Nail clipper (guillotine or scissor)
- Oster A-5 clipper /#10, #15 blades
- Shampoo
- Slicker brush
- Straight shears
- Styptic powder

Swedish Vallhund

TOOLS AND EQUIPMENT

- Cotton balls
- Eye drops (eye stain remover)
- Medicated ear powder
- Metal comb (medium)
- Metal rake
- Nail clipper
- Scissors
- Slicker brush

GROOMING PROCEDURE

1. Starting at the head, brush through the entire coat with a slicker brush.

2. With a metal rake, gently rake through the coat. During the nonshedding season, do not rake out the undercoat; simply untangle it with a metal rake. Comb through the coat to remove all loosened hair.

3. Clean the ears using medicated ear powder, and lightly pluck any stray hair from the insides.

4. Clean the eyes by wiping them with a cotton ball that has been moistened with eye drops. This will also help to remove stains around the eyes.

5. Cut the tips of the nails with a nail clipper, being careful not to cut the quick.

6. With scissors, clip the whiskers from the muzzle, under the chin, the sides of the face, and above the eyes. [Note: Clipping the whiskers is a decision to be left to the owner if the dog is not a show dog.]

7. Place a cotton ball in each ear (this prevents water from entering the ear canal), and bathe the dog. Cage dry him.

8. With scissors, snip the hair between the pads and toes on the feet to give a neat appearance.

9. Brush and comb through the entire coat.

The Swedish Vallhund should be groomed every 8 to 10 weeks. Regular brushing by the owner will help to keep the coat healthy and the undercoat free of tangles. The ears should be checked weekly and cleaned if necessary, and the nails should be checked and cut at the grooming session.

GROOMING PROCEDURE

1. Thoroughly brush the entire coat with a slicker brush, paying special attention to the neck, chest, tail, and thighs. Remove any mats from these areas with a mat-splitting comb and/or a metal rake.

2. Comb through the coat to remove all loosened hair.

3. Clean the ears using medicated ear powder, and lightly pluck stray hair from the insides, without removing any of the outer protective hair.

4. Clean the eyes by wiping them with a cotton ball that has been moistened with eye drops.

5. Cut the tips of the nails with a nail clipper, being careful not to cut the quick.

6. Using a damp cotton ball, clean the insides of the lips, removing any trapped food particles.

7. With scissors, snip the whiskers from the muzzle, under the chin, the sides of the face, and above the eyes. [Note: Clipping the whiskers is a decision to be left to the owner if the dog is not a show dog.]

8. Place a cotton ball in each ear (this prevents water from entering the ear canal), and bathe the dog. Cage or fluff dry.

9. With scissors, snip the hair between the pads and toes of the feet and around the edges. This gives the feet a neat appearance.

10. With scissors or thinning shears, trim straggly hair from around the ankles on the front feet and from the hocks to the feet on the hind legs.

11. Brush and comb through the coat.

TOOLS AND EQUIPMENT

- Cotton balls
- Eye drops (eye stain remover)
- Mat-splitting comb
- Medicated ear powder
- Metal comb (medium)
- Metal rake
- Nail clipper
- Scissors
- Slicker brush
- Thinning shears

Tibetan Terrier

TOOLS AND EQUIPMENT

- Cotton balls
- Eye drops (eye stain remover)
- Mat-splitting comb
- Metal comb (medium)
- Nail clipper
- Oster A-5 clipper/#10 blade
- Scissors
- Slicker brush

GROOMING PROCEDURE

1. Starting at the head, thoroughly brush the entire coat with a slicker brush. Remove any mats with a mat-splitting comb. Comb through the coat to remove all loosened hair. If the dog is excessively matted, start at the feet and brush the legs upward in sections. Do the same from the rear to the front of the body.

2. Clean the ears using medicated ear powder, and lightly pluck any stray hair from the insides.

3. Clean the eyes by wiping them with a cotton ball that has been moistened with eye drops. This will also help to remove stains around the eyes.

4. Cut the tips of the nails with a nail clipper, being careful not to cut the quick.

5. With a #10 blade, shave the anal area, being certain not to put the blade in direct contact with the skin (½ inch [1 cm] on either side).

6. Shave the abdomen from groin to navel and down the insides of the thighs.

7. Place a cotton ball in each ear (this prevents water from entering the ear canal), and bathe the dog. Cage dry him to remove excess water.

8. Place the dog on the grooming table and complete the drying with a blow dryer and a slicker brush.

9. Scissor the hair between the pads of the feet; while the dog is standing, lightly scissor around the edges of the feet to make a neat appearance.

GROOMING PROCEDURE

1. Nails should be cut by removing the tips only; avoid cutting the quick. If the nail bleeds, apply styptic powder to stop the bleeding. Any rough nail edges may be smoothed by filing.

2. Clean the ears with a liquid cleaner. Apply cleaner to a cotton ball and wipe accumulated dirt and wax from all crevices in both ears.

3. Card (use the stripping knife like a comb) out the coat to remove excess hair, if present.

4. Bathe the dog in a shampoo of your choice. Use a rubber brush to lather the dog and to help remove dead coat. Rinse the dog well. Apply an after-bath conditioning rinse or use a hot oil treatment if the dog has dandruff.

5. Towel dry the dog and place him in a cage with a dryer until he is completely dry.

6. Any seams (where two different growths of hair come together) may be blended. Excess hair on the back of the thigh may be removed, as well as untidy hair on the back edge of the front legs. The underneath side of the tail may be neatened up, too.

7. Whiskers and eyebrows may be removed if desired.

8. As a final touch, a small amount of spray conditioner or coat gloss should be lightly misted over the dog and buffed shiny with a clean cloth or hound brush.

The completed Vizsla should have a crisp outline and shiny coat. This grooming should be done every 10 to 12 weeks.

TOOLS AND EQUIPMENT

- Blending shears
- Cotton balls
- Ear cleaner
- Hound brush
- Nail clipper (guillotine or scissor)
- Rubber brush
- Shampoo (all-purpose or conditioning)
- Spray conditioner
- Straight shears
- Stripping knife
- Styptic powder

Weimaraner

TOOLS AND EQUIPMENT

- Blending shears
- Cotton balls
- Ear cleaner
- Hound brush
- Nail clipper (guillotine or scissor)
- Rubber brush
- Shampoo
- Spray conditioner
- Straight shears
- Stripping knife
- Styptic powder

GROOMING PROCEDURE

1. Nails should be cut by removing the tips only; avoid cutting the quick. If a nail bleeds, apply styptic powder to stop the bleeding. Any rough nail edges may be smoothed with a file.

2. Clean the ears with a liquid ear cleaner. Apply ear cleaner to a cotton ball and wipe accumulated wax and dirt from all crevices in both ears.

3. Card (use a stripping knife like a comb) out the coat to remove excess hair, if present.

4. Bathe the dog in a shampoo of your choice. Use a rubber brush to lather the dog and to help remove dead coat. Rinse the dog well. Apply an after-bath conditioning rinse or use a hot oil treatment if the dog has dandruff.

5. Towel dry the dog and place him in a cage with a dryer until he is completely dry.

6. Any seams (where two different directions of hair growth come together) may be blended. Excess hair on the back of the thighs may be removed, as well as untidy hair on the back of the front legs. The underneath side of the tail may be neatened up, too.

7. Whiskers and eyebrows may be removed if desired.

8. As a final touch, lightly apply a small amount of spray conditioner or coat gloss to the coat and buff with a clean cloth or a hound brush until shiny.

The completed Weimaraner should have a crisp outline and a shiny coat. This grooming should be done every 10 to 12 weeks.

GROOMING PROCEDURE

1. Brush through the coat with a slicker brush and then comb through to remove all loosened hair.

2. Clean the ears using medicated ear powder, and lightly pluck any stray hair from the insides.

3. Clean the eyes by wiping them with a cotton ball that has been moistened with eye drops.

4. Cut the tips of the nails with the nail clipper, being careful not to cut the quick.

5. With scissors, cut the whiskers from the muzzle, under the chin, the sides of the face, and above the eyes.

6. With a #10 blade, shave the anal area, being certain not to put the blade in direct contact with the skin (½ inch [1 cm] on either side).

7. Shave the abdomen from groin to navel and down the inside of the thighs.

8. Place a cotton ball in each ear to prevent water from entering the ear canal. Now bathe the dog and cage dry him.

9. Brush and comb through the coat.

10. Using thinning shears, trim any straggly hair from the head and sides of the face.

11. Using thinning shears, trim any straggly hair from the top of the back so that the coat lies flat.

12. Using scissors or thinning shears, trim straggly hair from the hock joints to the feet on the hind legs and from around the ankles on the front legs.

13. Using scissors, cut the hair between the pads and toes of the feet and around the edges for a neat effect.

14. Using scissors, trim evenly the leg fringes.

15. Comb through the entire coat to remove all loosened hair.

The Welsh Springer Spaniel should be groomed every 6 to 8 weeks. The ears should be checked weekly and cleaned if necessary, and the nails should be checked monthly and cut if necessary.

Welsh Springer Spaniel

TOOLS AND EQUIPMENT

- Cotton balls
- Eye drops (eye stain remover)
- Medicated ear powder
- Metal comb (medium)
- Nail clipper
- Oster A-5 clipper/#10 blade
- Scissors
- Slicker brush
- Thinning shears

Welsh Terrier

TOOLS AND EQUIPMENT

- Cotton balls
- Eye drops (eye stain remover)
- Medicated ear powder
- Metal comb (medium)
- Nail clipper
- Oster A-5 clipper/#5, #7, #8½, #10 blades
- Scissors
- Slicker brush
- Thinning shears

GROOMING PROCEDURE

1. Brush the entire coat and tail with a slicker brush. Comb through with a metal comb, paying attention to any tangles.

2. Clean the eyes by wiping them with a cotton ball that has been moistened with eye drops. This will also help to remove stains around the eyes.

3. Clean the ears using medicated ear powder, and lightly pluck any stray hair from the insides.

4. Cut the nails with a guillotine-type nail clipper. Nails should be cut monthly.

5. With a #10 blade, shave the head, starting at the center of the eyebrows and continuing back to the base of the skull. Then shave from the center again to the outer corners of the eyes. This line should be about ¾ inch (2 cm) above the inner corner of the eye, tapering into the outer corner to create a triangle. Next, shave down from the outer corners of the eyes to within ¾ inch (2 cm) from the corners of the mouth and continue this line across, under the chin.

6. Shave both sides of the ears; from the back edge of the ears, shave down diagonally to a point at the base of the throat, thus forming a "V" shape.

7. Shave the anal area, being certain not to put the blade in direct contact with the skin (½ inch [1 cm] on either side).

8. Shave the abdomen from groin to navel and down the insides of the thighs.

9. With the #8½, #7, or #5 blade (according to the length of coat desired), start at the base of the skull and clip down the back to the base of the tail.

10. Clip the top half of the tail and blend down either side of the fringe. Comb the fringe downward and scissor the lower edge, thus making a feather shape.

11. With a clipper, clip down the sides of the neck to the shoulder and down to the elbow.

12. Clip down the chest to the breastbone and slope the pattern down diagonally to the center front of the legs.

13. From the first clip down the back, clip down the sides of the abdomen, arching the pattern over the hips. (From the side, the pattern line should slope down diagonally from the breastbone, continue straight across the tops of the front legs, slope up across the abdomen, and arch up over the hips and down to a point in the rear.)

14. Brush through the coat with a slicker brush to remove any excess hair.

15. Place a cotton ball in each ear (this prevents water from entering the ear canal), and bathe the dog. Cage dry him.

16. Brush and comb through the coat.

17. Using the same blade on the Oster A-5 clipper as before, repeat the process for the pattern, blending the hair down from the top of the pattern with the blade.

18. Scissor around the edges of the ears.

19. Scissor a "V" in the center of the eyebrows.

20. Comb the hair on the face and eyebrows forward and downward, aligning the base of your scissors with the nose and pointing the tip of the scissors toward the outer corner of the eye. Scissor the eyebrows from this angle, thus making a deep triangle. Be careful not to cut any hair from the top of the muzzle.

21. Lightly scissor stray hairs from around the edge and sides of the beard. Use thinning shears to shape the beard, which should be long and barrel-shaped.

22. Use thinning shears to trim any stray hairs from the top of the muzzle.

23. Trim hair between the pads of the feet; while the dog is standing, scissor around the edges to give a round effect. Doing this first will give you a guide for scissoring the legs.

24. Scissor the front legs into straight tubular shapes.

25. Scissor evenly the bottom of the chest fringe.

26. Scissor the bottom of the belly fringe, following the contour of the dog's body and tapering up from the elbows on the front legs to the flanks at the rear.

#5, #7, #8½, #10

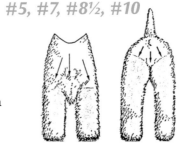

27. Scissor the rear legs, following the natural contours. (From the back view, the legs should be straight on the outsides. Inside, they should be straight, up to the thighs, and then arch up and into the shave line.)

28. Lightly comb through the legs, fringes, and face, removing all excess hair and trimming any stray hairs as necessary.

The Welsh Terrier should be groomed every 6 or 8 weeks. The ears should be checked weekly and cleaned if necessary, and the nails should be checked and cut at the grooming session. It should be noted that the head, face, and throat should be shaved with the grain of the hair.

#10 →

#5, #7, #8½
↓

West Highland White Terrier

TOOLS AND EQUIPMENT

- Alcohol
- Comb
- Cotton balls
- Mineral oil
- Nail clipper
- Oster A-5 clipper/#5, #7, #8½, #10 blades
- Scissors
- Slicker brush
- Styptic powder
- Thinning shears

GROOMING PROCEDURE

1. Trim the tips of the nails with a nail clipper. Have styptic powder handy in case the vein inside the nail bleeds. You might prefer to do this in the tub; dogs are less nervous there.

2. Brush through the coat with a slicker brush, removing all mats, tangles, dead hair, and other debris.

3. The ears can be cleaned with cotton and liquid ear cleaner; however, it is recommended that you use alcohol in place of the cleaner.

4. Using an Oster A-5 clipper and a #10 blade, clip within ½ inch (1 cm) on either side of the anus.

5. With the same blade, remove all hair from the groin area.

6. Using the same clipper with a #5, #7, or #8½ blade (depending on coat length preference), clip from the top of the neck down to the base of the tail.

7. From the top of the neck, clip down to the shoulders.

8. Using the shoulders as a guide line, clip down the body to the rump in the same fashion.

9. With the same blade, clip from the top of the neck down to the breastbone.

10. With a #10 blade, clip the top half of the ear.

11. With scissors, round off the top of the ears to give a neat appearance.

12. Using the same blade, clip from the base to the tip of the tail, leaving the hair on the opposite side.

13. Using thinning shears, trim the hair on the other side of the tail in the shape of half a Christmas tree (leave the base of the tail longer).

14. Trim the hair under the feet so that it is even with the foot pads.

15. Using scissors, trim the hair on the bottom of the feet to give a round appearance.

#5, #7, #8½

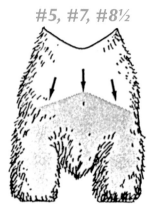

16. Use thinning shears on the Westie's head, making the front view of the face look round.

17. The eyebrows may be trimmed with thinning shears to create an awning shape from the side. There should only be one long eyebrow, which resembles a visor.

18. Carefully trim the hair from under the eyes.

19. Bathe the dog. Because the Westie is a white-haired dog, you may want to use whitening shampoo or shampoo for sensitive skin.

20. Cage or fluff dry.

21. Comb out the dog, and use thinning shears to trim away any fly-away hairs that are out of place.

The Westie should be groomed every 4 to 6 weeks.

← #5
#7
#8½

Whippet

TOOLS AND EQUIPMENT

- Chamois cloth
- Cotton balls
- Eye drops (eye stain remover)
- Lanolin coat conditioner
- Nail clipper
- Scissors
- Sisal (natural bristle) brush

GROOMING PROCEDURE

1. Brush the coat briskly with a sisal brush.

2. Clean the ears using medicated ear powder.

3. Clean the eyes by wiping them with a cotton ball that has been moistened with eye drops. This will also help to remove stains around the eyes.

4. Cut the tips of the nails with a nail clipper, being careful not to cut the quick.

5. Using scissors, clip the whiskers from the muzzle, under the chin, the sides of the face, and above the eyes. [Note: Clipping the whiskers is a decision to be left to the owner if the dog is not a show dog.]

6. Put a cotton ball in each ear to prevent water from entering the ear canal. Now you are ready to bathe the dog. Cage dry him.

7. Put a few drops of lanolin coat conditioner into the palms of your hands, rub them together, and gently massage into the coat.

8. Brush the coat with a sisal brush to distribute the conditioner. Then lightly rub over the coat with a chamois cloth to give it a nice sheen.

The Whippet should be bathed every 8 or 10 weeks. Regular brushing between baths by the owner helps maintain a healthy, shiny coat. The ears should be checked weekly and cleaned if necessary, and the nails should be checked monthly and cut if necessary.

GROOMING PROCEDURE

1. Nails should be cut by removing only the tips; avoid cutting the quick. If a nail bleeds, apply styptic powder to stop the bleeding. Any rough nail edges may be smoothed with a file.

2. Ears should be cleaned with a liquid cleaner. Apply the cleaner to a cotton ball and wipe accumulated wax and dirt from all crevices in both ears.

3. Brush through the coat with a slicker brush to remove all dead hair and mats.

4. Bathe the dog with a shampoo of your choice. Rinse well.

5. Towel dry the dog until damp. Finish drying him in a cage dryer until he is completely dry.

6. The Wirehaired Pointing Griffon is a relatively natural-looking dog; however, this does not mean that his appearance should not be neatened up. Any hair that sticks out and ruins the basic outline of the dog should be plucked out. Hair on the top of the head, on the cheeks, and on the ears should be a bit shorter than on the rest of the coat. There should be a subtle accentuation of the eyebrows and beard. Hair on the neck should be shortened to accentuate the length of the neck. The underside of the tail may be neatened up.

7. With straight scissors, cut the hair between the foot pads and along the outer edge of the foot. The top of the foot should be neatened up by removing the hair that grows between the toes and on the top of the foot.

The Wirehaired Pointing Griffon should appear in his natural state but should be neatened up periodically to prevent overgrowth of the hair. This breed should be groomed every 8 to 12 weeks.

Wirehaired Pointing Griffon

TOOLS AND EQUIPMENT

- Comb
- Cotton balls
- Ear cleaner
- Nail clipper (guillotine or scissor)
- Shampoo (all-purpose or texturizing)
- Slicker brush
- Straight scissors
- Styptic powder

Yorkshire Terrier

TOOLS AND EQUIPMENT

- Cotton balls
- Eye drops (eye stain remover)
- Matting comb
- Medicated ear powder
- Metal combs (medium/fine)
- Nail clipper
- Oster A-5 clipper/#10, #15 blades
- Rubber bands
- Scissors
- Slicker brush

GROOMING PROCEDURE

1. Brush the entire coat with a slicker brush. The coats vary on these dogs, from fine and silky to thick and cottonlike. The latter tends to mat easily; if this should happen, use a small matting comb to remove the mats. Finish all dogs (whether silky or cottony textured) by combing through the coat with a fine-toothed metal comb.

2. Clean the ears using medicated ear powder, and lightly pluck stray hair from the insides of the ears.

3. Cut the tips of the nails with a nail clipper, being careful not to cut the quick.

4. Clean the eyes by wiping them with a cotton ball that has been moistened with eye drops. If the eyes are excessively watery and sticky, snip stained hair from the corners with scissors.

5. Using a #15 blade, shave the tips of the ears (approximately ½ inch [1 cm]) inside and out. Scissor the hair around the shaved tips for a neat finish.

6. Using a #10 blade, shave the anal area being certain not to put the blade in direct contact with the skin (½ inch [1 cm] on either side).

7. Using a #10 blade, shave the abdomen from groin to navel and down the insides of the thighs.

8. Place a cotton ball in each ear (this prevents water from entering the ear canals), and bathe the dog. Fluff dry him.

9. With the medium metal comb, part the coat down the center of the back from the top of the head to the base of the tail.

10. Make a part on the head from the outer corner of each eye to the front corner of each ear, and across the head from ear to ear. Comb this hair evenly, slightly to the back, and secure it with a rubber band. Attach a bow. An alternative is to gather the hair, comb it evenly, and make a small braid. Secure the end with a rubber band and then the bow.

11. Scissor the hair between the foot pads. Comb the hair on the legs downward; while the dog is standing, scissor around the edges of the feet to give a round effect.

12. Scissor the hair underneath the tail and round the edges of the tail for a neat appearance.

13. Comb through the entire coat with a fine-toothed metal comb.

Some dog groomers use conditioning rinse and similar products on the Yorkie; however. I have found through experience that these products cause the coat to become more matted in the long run, and that a good protein-enriched shampoo is entirely adequate.

The long-coated Yorkshire Terrier should be groomed every 3 or 4 weeks. The ears should be checked weekly, and the nails should be checked at the grooming session.

An alternative for owners who prefer a short, cuddly look, is the Teddy Bear clip. (See the General Information section.)

About the Contributors

Denise Dobish

Denise Dobish has been breeding and showing Bichon Frises for the past thirteen years; prior to this she bred and groomed Miniature Schnauzers. Of the seven Bichons that she owns or co-owns, four (shown by her) are finished champions.

When Denise was showing her first Bichon to her championship, she would travel to Long Island to an excellent groomer by the name of George Temmel. He allowed her in the back of his shop and gave her pointers on how to show-groom Bichons. Denise also attended night school for courses on dog grooming, graduating with top honors.

Since that time, Denise has had her own dog grooming shop, which specializes in Bichons. She has also helped many of her customers learn the art of dog showing, and they have since attained championships on their dogs. Denise has always been available to anyone who calls her home seeking advice on the behavior or grooming of their dogs, or just the all-around well-being of their pets.

 • Contribution to this book: Bichon Frise.

Gay M. Ernst

Gay M. Ernst has been involved in grooming, breeding, and showing dogs since 1955. With the purchase of a show-quality Cocker Spaniel that year, and an apprenticeship to the proprietor of a grooming shop in Manhattan, she became totally immersed in the dog world.

In 1961 she married William Ernst, who became a top handler of show Cockers. Together they owned and operated the Dapper Dog Den in Manhattan from 1961 to 1969. Bill and Gay Ernst combined names to establish BeGay Cockers and bought a kennel in New Milford,Connecticut, which they owned and operated from 1966 to 1977.

The untimely death of Bill in 1977 brought about the closing of the kennel, and Gay moved to East Hampton, New York, with the couple"s three children and their Cocker Spaniels. In 1978 she established a grooming shop in nearby Bridgehampton and continued to breed Cockers under the BeGay prefix. To date, there are over 50 BeGay champion Cocker Spaniels, including many record-breaking dogs of unusual colors.

 • Contribution to this book: Cocker Spaniel, American.

Susan Gutman

Susan Gutman is the owner of Dog Patch, an all-breed grooming shop in Westfield, New Jersey. A graduate of the New York School of Dog Grooming, she has been working in the field of grooming since 1974. Her shop, which employs nine people, has offered its services to local fundraising organizations, such as the American Heart Association, for which she has sponsored a yearly groom-a-thon.

Susan has lectured to the Union County 4-H dog club and the seeing-eye club on routine home pet care and has opened her shop to local scout groups who are studying pet care in order to achieve their merit badges.

In 1986, Susan was the first guest on the Storer Cable Communications network's pet program, speaking on the topic of summer pet care.

- Contribution to this book: Afghan Hound, Basset Hound, Beagle, Bloodhound.

Sandy King

Sandy King has been in business as a dog groomer since 1965 and has taught dog grooming since 1970. Besides grooming, she has been active in other aspects of the dog fancy, namely, in the showing of Siberian Huskies, Doberman Pinschers, and German Shepherd Dogs. She has also been a writer of a dog column for the Easton Express for twelve years. Sandy is a member of the National Dog Groomers Association and is the Pennsylvania coordinator for the Pet Industry Joint Advisory Council.

- Contribution to this book: Alaskan Malamute, Australian Cattle Dog, Australian Terrier, Bearded Collie, Belgian Malinois, Belgian Sheepdog, Belgian Tervuren, Bernese Mountain Dog, Border Terrier, Boston Terrier, Bouvier des Flandres, Briard, Brittany Spaniel, Bull Terrier, Cardigan Welsh Corgi, Collie (Rough Coat), Collie (Smooth Coat), Dandie Dinmont Terrier, English Springer Spaniel, English Toy Spaniel, Fox Terrier (Smooth), Gordon Setter, Great Pyrenees, Greyhound, Harrier, Ibizan Hound, Irish Setter, Irish Terrier, Irish Wolfhound, Italian Greyhound, Japanese Toy Spaniel, Keeshond, Kerry Blue Terrier, Kuvasz, Lakeland Terrier, Manchester Terrier (Standard), Manchester Terrier (Toy), Mastiff, Miniature Pinscher, Newfoundland, Norfolk Terrier, Norwegian Elkhound, Pembroke Welsh Corgi, Portuguese Water Dog, Puli, Shetland Sheepdog, Soft-Coated Wheaten Terrier. General Information section.

Gloria Lewis

Gloria Lewis has been a breeder of champion Miniature Schnauzers for 25 years. She is a professional groomer and show handler of this breed, as well as coauthor (with Beverly Pisano) of *Miniature Schnauzers*, published by TFH Publications, Inc. Many of her show dogs are featured in Anna Katherine Nicholas's *The Book of the Miniature Schnauzer* (also published by TFH) and on several covers of the AKC *Gazette*.

- Contribution to this book: Miniature Schnauzer.

Susan Tapp

Susan Tapp has been involved with dogs for over 15 years, having obtained obedience titles and breed championships on many of them. She is a certified master groomer (C.M.G.) by the Professional Pet Groomers Certification, Inc. (P.P.G.C.) and has won several grooming contests to date. Susan was an instructor at a large, accredited grooming school for some time, and currently she gives private lessons. She is involved with local grooming associations and kennel clubs and is very active in showing her Irish Water Spaniels in obedience, breed, and grooming contests. With such a busy schedule, she still finds time to run her own grooming salon, Canine Castle.

- Contribution to this book: Affenpinscher, American Water Spaniel, Black and Tan Coonhound, Borzoi, Boxer, Brussels Griffon, Bulldog, Chesapeake Bay Retriever, Chihuahua (Smooth Coat), Chihuahua (Long Coat). Chinese Shar-Pei, Chow Chow, Clumber Spaniel, Cocker Spaniel (English), Curly-Coated Retriever, Dalmatian, Doberman Pinscher, English Setter, Field Spaniel, Flat-Coated Retriever, French Bulldog, German Shorthaired Pointer, German Wirehaired Pointer, Golden Retriever, Irish Water Spaniel, Labrador Retriever, Papillon, Pomeranian, Rottweiler, Sussex Spaniel, Vizsla, Weimaraner, Wirehaired Pointing Griffon.

Risa Platau

- Contribution to this book: Cairn Terrier, West Highland White Terrier.

Pat Wehrle

Pat Wehrle is a dog groomer and freelance artist. She has exhibited Pugs for five years and has owned them for seventeen. In 1983 Pat was Category Winner in the Pug Dog Club of Greater New York Photo Contest, taking the Grand Prize in 1984.

- Contribution to this book: Pug.

Chelsea Youngblood-Killeen

Chelsea Youngblood-Killeen started grooming a few years ago, back home in England. She and her family lived in a small town, Woodstock, on the outskirts of Oxford, and her parents owned two miniature Poodles. Chelsea was always interested in how these dogs were groomed, and one time when they were due to be clipped, she took her mother's dressmaking scissors and did a wonderful chop-up job on both of them! The initial shock to her parents was dismay, which gradually changed to humor, and eventually to wild laughter. However. they decided that if that was what she wanted to do, then she could practice on their dogs. This she did religiously, for weeks, until she could scissor both dogs into cute fluff balls, which she now did with the help of a metal comb and professional scissors purchased by her mother.

At that time, Anne, the wife of the local pet shop owner, decided to retire from grooming dogs and become a full-time mother and housewife. Geoff, her husband, then asked Chelsea if she would be interested in learning how to groom dogs. She was ecstatic and said she could start the next day! Armed with her comb, scissors, and an acquired brush, she rushed over bright and early. Geoff gave her a Poodle, a clipper, and blades and told her to groom the dog. It took about three hours from start to finish, and Chelsea had no problem with the scissoring, as she had practiced for so many weeks at home.

From then on it became easier with Geoff's and Anne's guidance, and improvement came with every dog she clipped. She stayed with the shop for about three years, learning a great deal about dogs and clips from numerous visits to the Crufts Dog Show.

Over the years Chelsea has groomed dogs in Germany, where she lived for a while and learned the Van Buren Poodle Clip. This consists of not shaving anything except the belly and rear areas, and scissoring the whole dog evenly (which reminded her of her formative years in grooming).

In the United States Chelsea first lived in South Carolina, working in a grooming shop where the owner owned and showed five Bichon Frises. The owner taught her how to groom Bichons for show and in accordance with what judges would be looking for.

Chelsea now resides and grooms dogs in New Jersey. When she looks back to the different countries and states she has worked in, she can see differences in styles and the various techniques that professional groomers use. Chelsea has always watched and listened and managed to pick up tips here and there; she has never forgotten from whom and where these so-called "secrets" were learned.

Chelsea's sincere thanks go to Phyllis (Columbia, South Carolina) for putting up with her and to the "Bichons;" to Caroline (Columbia, South Carolina) for the "secret" of scissoring the Poodle head; and to her close friend Lynnsie (Connecticut) for help and advice on the "pie face" and the Spaniel "V."

• Contribution to this book: Airedale Terrier, Akita, American Staffordshire Terrier, Anatolian Karabash Dog, Australian Kelpie, Basenji, Basset Fauve de Bretagne, Bedlington Terrier, Border Collie, Bullmastiff, Bull Terrier (Miniature), Cavalier King Charles Spaniel, Chinese Crested Dog, Dachshund (Long Coat), Dachshund (Smooth Coat), Dachshund (Wire Coat), English Toy Terrier (Black and Tan), Eskimo Dog, Estrela Mountain Dog, Finnish Spitz, Foxhound (American), Foxhound (English), Fox Terrier (Wire), German Shepherd Dog, German Spitz, Giant Schnauzer, Glen of Imaal Terrier, Great Dane, Hamiltonstovare, Hovawart, Irish Red and White Setter, Italian Spinone, Japanese Spitz, King Charles Spaniel, Komondor, Lancashire Heeler, Large Munsterlander, Leonberger, Lhasa Apso, Lowchen, Maltese, Maremma Sheepdog, Neapolitan Mastiff, Norwegian Buhund, Norwich Terrier, Old English Sheepdog, Otterhound, Pekingese, Petit Basset Griffon Vendeen, Pointer, Polish Lowland Sheepdog, Poodle (Dutch Clip, Kennel Clip, Lamb clip, Puppy Clip, Royal Dutch Clip, Summer Clip, Town and Country Clip), Poodle Heads and Faces (Clean Face, Moustache, French Moustache), Rhodesian Ridgeback, St. Bernard (Rough Coat), St. Bernard (Smooth Coat), Saluki, Samoyed, Schipperke, Scottish Deerhound, Scottish Terrier, Sealyham Terrier, Shih Tzu, Siberian Husky, Silky Terrier, Skye Terrier, Sioughi, Staffordshire Bull Terrier, Standard Schnauzer, Swedish Vallhund, Tibetan Mastiff, Tibetan Terrier, Welsh Springer Spaniel, Welsh Terrier, Whippet, Yorkshire Terrier, Mixed Breeds, Teddy Bear Clip.

About the Illustrator

Richard Davis

Richard Davis received his Masters Degree in Fine Arts from Mason Gross School of the Arts, New Brunswick, New Jersey, and his Bachelor of Fine Arts from Monmouth College, West Long Branch, New Jersey. He divides his time between painting, freelance illustrating, and being employed as an adjunct art instructor at Ocean County College, Toms River, New Jersey.

Richard's work has been widely exhibited throughout New Jersey, including group shows at The State Museum, Trenton. Outside New Jersey, he has participated in shows on Long Island and in New York City.

Richard has always been interested in nature and often incorporates wildlife, both domestic and exotic, in his work.

Photo Credits

Resources

Associations and Organizations

Breed Clubs

American Kennel Club (AKC)
5580 Centerview Drive
Raleigh, NC 27606
Telephone: (919) 233-9767
Fax: (919) 233-3627
E-mail: info@akc.org
www.akc.org

Canadian Kennel Club (CKC)
89 Skyway Avenue, Suite 100
Etobicoke, Ontario M9W 6R4
Canada
Telephone: (416) 675-5511
Fax: (416) 675-6506
E-mail: information@ckc.ca
www.ckc.ca

Federation Cynologique Internationale (FCI)
Secretariat General de la FCI
Place Albert 1er, 13
B – 6530 Thuin
Belgique
www.fci.be

The Kennel Club (KC)
1 Clarges Street
London
W1J 8AB
England
Telephone: 0870 606 6750
Fax: 0207 518 1058
www.the-kennel-club.org.uk

United Kennel Club (UKC)
100 E. Kilgore Road
Kalamazoo, MI 49002-5584
Telephone: (269) 343-9020
Fax: (269) 343-7037
E-mail: pbickell@ukcdogs.com
www.ukcdogs.com

Grooming Associations

International Professional Groomers, Inc (IPG)
Hayley Keyes, President
123 Manley Ave.
Greensboro, NC 27407
Telephone: (336) 340-7915
www.ipgcmg.org

International Society of Canine Cosmetologists (ISCC)
2702 Covington Drive
Garland, TX 7540
www.petsylist.com

National Dog Groomers Association of America (NDGAA)
P.O. Box 101
Clark, PA 16113
Telephone: (724) 962-2711
www.nationaldoggroomers.com

Pet Sitters

National Association of Professional Pet Sitters
15000 Commerce Parkway, Suite C
Mt. Laurel, NJ 08054
Telephone: (856) 439-0324
Fax: (856) 439-0525
E-mail: napps@ahint.com
www.petsitters.org

Pet Sitters International
201 East King Street
King, NC 27021-9161
Telephone: (336) 983-9222
Fax: (336) 983-5266
E-mail: info@petsit.com
www.petsit.com

Rescue Organizations and Animal Welfare Groups

American Humane Association (AHA)
63 Inverness Drive East
Englewood, CO 80112
Telephone: (303) 792-9900
Fax: (303) 792-5333
www.americanhumane.org

American Society for the Prevention of Cruelty to Animals (ASPCA)
424 E. 92nd Street
New York, NY 10128-6804
Telephone: (212) 876-7700
www.aspca.org

Royal Society for the Prevention of Cruelty to Animals (RSPCA)
Telephone: 0870 3335 999
Fax: 0870 7530 284
www.rspca.org.uk

The Humane Society of the United States (HSUS)
2100 L Street, NW
Washington, DC 20037
Telephone: (202) 452-1100
www.hsus.org

Sports

Canine Freestyle Federation, Inc.
E-mail: secretary@canine-freestyle.org
www.canine-freestyle.org
International Agility Link
E-mail: yunde@powerup.au
www.agilityclick.com/~ial

North American Dog Agility Council
11522 South Hwy 3
Cataldo, ID 83810
www.nadac.com

North American Flyball Association
1400 West Devon Avenue, #512
Chicago, IL 6066
Telephone: (800) 318-6312
www.flyball.org

United States Dog Agility Association
P.O. Box 850955
Richardson, TX 75085-0955
Telephone: (972) 487-2200
www.usdaa.com

World Canine Freestyle Organization
P.O. Box 350122
Brooklyn, NY 11235-2525
Telephone: (718) 332-8336
www.worldcaninefreestyle.org

Therapy

Delta Society
875 124th Ave NE, Suite 101
Bellevue, WA 98005
Telephone: (425) 226-7357
Fax: (425) 235-1076
E-mail: info@deltasociety.org
www.deltasociety.org

Therapy Dogs Incorporated
PO Box 5868
Cheyenne, WY 82003
Telephone: (877) 843-7364
E-mail: therdog@sisna.com
www.therapydogs.com

Therapy Dogs International (TDI)
88 Bartley Road
Flanders, NJ 07836
Telephone: (973) 252-9800
Fax: (973) 252-7171
E-mail: tdi@gti.net
www.tdi-dog.org

Training

Animal Behavior Society (ABS)
www.animalbehavior.org
Association of Pet Dog Trainers (APDT)
150 Executive Center Drive, Box 35
Greenville, SC 29615
Telephone: (800) PET-DOGS
Fax: (864) 331-0767
E-mail: information@apdt.com
www.apdt.com

National Association of Dog Obedience Instructors (NADOI)
PMB 369
729 Grapevine Hwy.
Hurst, TX 76054-2085
www.nadoi.org

Veterinary and Health Resources

Academy of Veterinary Homeopathy (AVH)
P.O. Box 9280
Wilmington, DE 19809
Telephone: (866) 652-1590
Fax: (866) 652-1590
E-mail: office@TheAVH.org
www.theavh.org

American Academy of Veterinary Acupuncture (AAVA)
100 Roscommon Drive, Suite 320
Middletown, CT 06457
Telephone: (860) 635-6300
Fax: (860) 635-6400
E-mail: office@aava.org
www.aava.org

American Animal Hospital Association (AAHA)
P.O. Box 150899
Denver, CO 80215-0899
Telephone: (303) 986-2800
Fax: (303) 986-1700
E-mail: info@aahanet.org
www.aahanet.org/index.cfm

American College of Veterinary Internal Medicine (ACVIM)
1997 Wadsworth Blvd., Suite A
Lakewood, CO 80214-5293
Telephone: (800) 245-9081
Fax: (303) 231-0880
E-mail: ACVIM@ACVIM.org
www.acvim.org

American College of Veterinary Ophthalmologists (ACVO)
P.O. Box 1311
Meridian, ID 83860
Telephone: (208) 466-7624
Fax: (208) 466-7693
E-mail: office@acvo.com
www.acvo.com

American Holistic Veterinary Medical Association (AHVMA)
2218 Old Emmorton Road
Bel Air, MD 21015
Telephone: (410) 569-0795
Fax: (410) 569-2346
E-mail: office@ahvma.org
www.ahvma.org

American Veterinary Medical Association (AVMA)
1931 North Meacham Road, Suite 100
Schaumburg, IL 60173
Telephone: (847) 925-8070
Fax: (847) 925-1329
E-mail: avmainfo@avma.org
www.avma.org

ASPCA Animal Poison Control Center
1717 South Philo Road, Suite 36
Urbana, IL 61802
Telephone: (888) 426-4435
www.aspca.org

British Veterinary Association (BVA)
7 Mansfield Street
London
W1G 9NQ
England
Telephone: 020 7636 6541
Fax: 020 7436 2970
E-mail: bvahq@bva.co.uk
www.bva.co.uk

Canine Eye Registration Foundation (CERF)
VMDB/CERF
1248 Lynn Hall
625 Harrison St.
Purdue University
West Lafayette, IN 47907-2026
Telephone: (765) 494-8179
E-mail: CERF@vmbd.org
www.vmdb.org

Orthopedic Foundation for Animals (OFA)
2300 NE Nifong Blvd.
Columbus, MO 65201-3856
Telephone: (573) 442-0418
Fax: (573) 875-5073
Email: ofa@offa.org
www.offa.org

Websites

Pet Groomers
PetGroomers.com

Nylabone
www.nylabone.com

TFH Publications, Inc.
www.tfh.com

Publications

Books

Adamson, Eve, and Sandy Roth. *Animal Planet: Complete Guide to Grooming.* New Jersey: TFH Publications, Inc., 2010.

Anderson, Teoti. *Puppy Care & Training.* New Jersey: TFH Publications, Inc., 2007.

Anderson, Teoti. *The Super Simple Guide to Housetraining.* New Jersey: TFH Publications, Inc., 2004.

Boneham, Sheila Webster, Ph.D. *The Multiple-Dog Family.* New Jersey: TFH Publications, Inc., 2009.

Boneham, Sheila Webster, Ph.D. *Training Your Dog for Life.* New Jersey: TFH Publications, Inc., 2008.

Dainty, Suellen. *50 Games to Play With Your Dog.* New Jersey: TFH Publications, Inc., 2007.

DeGioia, Phyllis. *The Mixed Breed Dog.* New Jersey: TFH Publications, Inc., 2007.

DeVito, Russell-Revesz, Fornino. *World Atlas of Dog Breeds, 6th Ed.* New Jersey: TFH Publications, Inc., 2009.

Gagne, Tammy. *Designer Dogs.* New Jersey: TFH Publications, Inc., 2008.

Gagne, Tammy. *The Happy Adopted Dog.* New Jersey: TFH Publications, Inc., 2009.

Gagne, Tammy. *Living Green With Your Dog.* New Jersey: TFH Publications, Inc., 2009.

King, Trish. *Parenting Your Dog: Complete Care and Training for Every Life Stage.* New Jersey: TFH Publications, Inc., 2010.

Knueven, Doug, DVM. *The Holistic Health Guide for Dogs.* New Jersey: TFH Publications, Inc., 2008.

Morgan, Diane. *Feeding Your Dog for Life: The Real Facts About Proper Nutrition.* California: Doral Publishing, 2002.

Morgan, Diane. *The Living Well Guide for Senior Dogs.* New Jersey: TFH Publications, Inc., 2007.

Morgan, Diane. *The Simple Guide to Choosing a Dog.* New Jersey: TFH Publications, Inc., 2003.

Young, Peter. *Groom Your Dog Like a Professional.* New Jersey: TFH Publications, Inc., 2009.

Magazines

AKC Family Dog
American Kennel Club
260 Madison Avenue
New York, NY 10016
Telephone: (800) 490-5675
E-mail: familydog@akc.org
www.akc.org/pubs/familydog

AKC Gazette
American Kennel Club
260 Madison Avenue
New York, NY 10016
Telephone: (800) 533-7323
E-mail: gazette@akc.org
www.akc.org/pubs/gazette

Dog & Kennel
Pet Publishing, Inc.
7-L Dundas Circle
Greensboro, NC 27407
Telephone: (336) 292-4272
Fax: (336) 292-4272
E-mail: info@petpublishing.com
www.dogandkennel.com

Dog Fancy
Subscription Department
P.O. Box 53264
Boulder, CO 80322-3264
Telephone: (800) 365-4421
E-mail: barkback@dogfancy.com
www.dogfancy.com

Dogs Monthly
Ascot House
High Street, Ascot,
Berkshire SL5 7JG
United Kingdom
Telephone: 0870 730 8433
Fax: 0870 730 8431
E-mail: admin@rtc-associates.freeserve.co.uk
www.corsini.co.uk/dogsmonthly

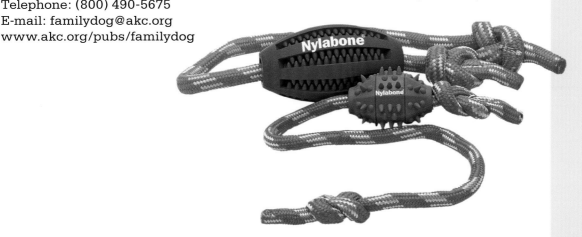

Index

All-Breed Dog Grooming

NATURAL with added VITAMINS
Nutri Dent
Promotes Optimal Dental Health!

Visit
nylabone.com
Join Club NYLA
for coupons &
product
information

360° Design
NYLABONE™
Cleaning Action!

Dogs Love 'em! ™

AVAILABLE IN MULTIPLE SIZES AND FLAVORS.

Nylabone®

Trusted For Over 40 Years

MADE IN THE USA

Our Mission with Nutri Dent® is to promote optimal dental health for dogs through a trusted, natural, delicious chew that provides effective cleaning action...GUARANTEE to make your dog go wild with anticipation and happiness!!!

Nylabone Products • P.O. Box 427, Neptune, NJ 07754-0427 • 1-800-631-2188 • Fax: 732-988-5466
www.nylabone.com • info@nylabone.com • For more information contact your sales representative or contact us at sales@tfh.com

A27